Deconstructing the Cherokee Nation

UNIVERSITY PRESS OF FLORIDA

Florida A&M University, Tallahassee
Florida Atlantic University, Boca Raton
Florida Gulf Coast University, Ft. Myers
Florida International University, Miami
Florida State University, Tallahassee
New College of Florida, Sarasota
University of Central Florida, Orlando
University of Florida, Gainesville
University of North Florida, Jacksonville
University of South Florida, Tampa
University of West Florida, Pensacola

Deconstructing the Cherokee Nation

Town, Region, and Nation among Eighteenth-Century Cherokees

▷◁

Tyler Boulware

University Press of Florida
Gainesville · Tallahassee · Tampa · Boca Raton
Pensacola · Orlando · Miami · Jacksonville · Ft. Myers · Sarasota

Copyright 2011 by Tyler Boulware
Printed in the United States of America. This book is printed on Glatfelter Natures
Book, a paper certified under the standards of the Forestry Stewardship Council (FSC).
It is a recycled stock that contains 30 percent post-consumer waste and is acid-free.
All rights reserved

16 15 14 13 12 11   6 5 4 3 2 1

The publication of this book is made possible in part by a grant from the Arts and
Sciences Endowment Development Fund of the Eberly College of Arts and Sciences at
West Virginia University.

Library of Congress Cataloging-in-Publication Data
Boulware, Tyler.
Deconstructing the Cherokee nation : town, region, and nation among eighteenth-
century Cherokees / Tyler Boulware.
p. cm.
Includes bibliographical references and index.
ISBN 978-0-8130-3580-2 (alk. paper)
1. Cherokee Indians—History—18th century. 2. Cherokee Indians—Ethnic identity.
3. Group identity—Social aspects—United States—History—18th century. I. Title.
E99.C5B744 2011
970.004'97—dc22
2010040991

The University Press of Florida is the scholarly publishing agency for the State University System of Florida, comprising Florida A&M University, Florida Atlantic University,
Florida Gulf Coast University, Florida International University, Florida State University,
New College of Florida, University of Central Florida, University of Florida, University
of North Florida, University of South Florida, and University of West Florida.

University Press of Florida
15 Northwest 15th Street
Gainesville, FL 32611-2079
http://www.upf.com

For John and Julie

Contents

	List of Illustrations	ix
	Acknowledgments	xi
	Introduction	1
1.	Town, Region, and Nation	10
2.	"the antient Friendship and Union": The Anglo-Cherokee Alliance	32
3.	"in constant hostility with the Muskohge": The Cherokee-Creek War	57
4.	"the disaffected people of Great Tellico": The Struggle for Empire in a Cherokee Town	75
5.	"in a discontented mood": The Crisis in Virginia	94
6.	"every Town wept for some": The Anglo-Cherokee War	110
7.	"now all our Talks are about Lands": Unstable Borderlands	130
8.	"half war half peace": The American Revolution in Cherokee Country	152
	Epilogue. Toward the Cherokee Nation	178
	Notes	183
	Bibliography	217
	Index	227

Illustrations

MAP 1. Cherokee Regions before 1776   20

MAP 2. Cherokee Country, 1730   35

MAP 3. Thomas Kitchin, *A New Map of the Cherokee Nation*, c.1760   36

MAP 4. Cherokee Country during the Seven Years' War   73

MAP 5. Newly Settled Towns during the American Revolution   154

MAP 6. Cherokee Regions before 1776 and c.1795   177

TABLE 1. Reported Invasions of Cherokee Country, 1776–1794   163

Acknowledgments

My appreciation runs deep for the many forms of assistance I have received over the years. Jessica Kross first sparked my interest in early American history and changed the direction of my future research. I am fortunate to have been under her tutelage. I also thank Alice Kasakoff, Dan Littlefield, Dean Kinzley, Kathryn Edwards, Larry Glickman, Pat Maney, Lacy Ford, Mark Smith, Ken Clements, and Robert Weir for their instruction and support.

Since arriving at West Virginia University, my colleagues and students have greatly assisted me in the early stages of my career. Ken and Liz Fones-Wolf welcomed us to Morgantown and have since proved invaluable friends and mentors. Bob Blobaum has likewise provided guidance and friendship, usually on the golf course, where such advice is most regarded. Ken, Matt Vester, and Brian Luskey generously donated their time to review portions of this work. Isaac Emrick deserves special mention for turning crude hand-drawn maps into their current form.

Colleagues at other institutions have further enriched my research. I thank Christina Snyder for critiquing an initial draft of this manuscript. Ted Gragson helped me to better understand Cherokee country through maps. Elaine Forman Crane lent her support at a crucial time in my career. Josh Piker has been an invaluable mentor for many years, which has greatly aided my professional development. Meredith Morris-Babb is a first-rate editor, and the staff at UPF has been very helpful in seeing this project through. Manuscript readers Andrew Frank and Steven Hahn deserve ample credit for challenging me to improve the book's style, structure, and argument.

This book also would not have been possible without generous financial support: The Jacob Price Fellowship awarded by the William L. Clements Library funded research at the University of Michigan. The Phillips Fund

Fellowship granted by the American Philosophical Society allowed for research in Philadelphia. The Huntington Library's Fletcher Jones Foundation Fellowship provided generous support for research and writing in San Marino, California. The Archie K. Davis Fellowship from the North Caroliniana Society enabled me to utilize the collections at Western Carolina University's Hunter Library. West Virginia University and the Eberly College of Arts and Sciences provided funding through the Faculty Senate Research Grant and the Riggle Fellowship in the Humanities. This project was also completed with financial assistance from the West Virginia Humanities Council, a state program of the National Endowment for the Humanities. I sincerely thank all the many individuals at these institutions, who are too numerous to list here, for their hospitality, expertise, and guidance.

Several of these chapters draw upon and rework previously published pieces. Portions of the introduction and chapter 1 appeared in "Native American and National Identity in Early North America," from *History Compass* (August 2006), 927–32 and in "The Effect of the Seven Years' War on the Cherokee Nation," from *Early American Studies: An Interdisciplinary Journal* (Fall 2007), 395–426, the latter of which also included material from chapters 5 and 6. Chapter 3 reworks my essay, "'Bound to live and die in defence of their country': Conflict and Community in Cherokee Country," first published in *Journal of Early American Wars and Armed Conflicts* (November 2005), 2–21.

Beyond doubt the greatest encouragement for my research has come from family members. My mother and father have given too much of their wealth, love, and guidance over the years to recount here. This book is for them. My brother Hunt, also a professor of early American history, has helped me to become a better teacher and scholar. Our discussions about history, teaching, and research have been most rewarding, something to which brother Bret can attest. Dan and Eola read portions of this manuscript, and I additionally thank all my extended family for their support. Last but not least, my wife, Jenny, challenged me the most. When asked to proof my writing, her usual response was "How long is it?" In all seriousness, she has meant more to my well-being and professional development than she could possibly know. She and our children, Bennett, Jessup, and Mazie, keep me grounded in the important things in life.

Introduction

The story must have shocked its Cherokee listeners. Apparently a Cherokee war party from the Overhill town of Chilhowee killed and scalped four villagers from Cowee. Sent initially to attack their Shawnee enemies, the Chilhowee warriors started north toward the Ohio country but quickly changed course for Cowee, a large town in the Middle Cherokee region. Rather than enter the village in a friendly manner, the Chilhowee warriors remained concealed near the path, where they murdered the four Cowee people. The war party then hurried home with their trophies and a grand tale of how they defeated the Shawnees in battle. The Chilhowee people accordingly gathered in the townhouse for the scalp dance, whereupon they celebrated what was thought to be a great victory over their Shawnee enemies.

The false warriors of Chilhowee, however, had made a crucial mistake: they had returned with a gun belonging to one of the victims. Coincidentally, a Cowee visitor named Gûlsadihï' attended the scalp dance and recognized the weapon. He said nothing and returned home to ascertain how these Overhill Cherokees had acquired the gun. It did not take long for Gûlsadihï' to solve the mystery. He immediately told the leading headman of Cowee that the murders "had been done, not by a hostile tribe, but by the false men of Chilhowee." The headman replied it could not be possible, that it "seemed too much to believe," but he at last became convinced by Gûlsadihï', upon which "all Cowee was eager for revenge."

Ten of the bravest Cowee warriors under the leadership of Gûlsadihï' traveled to Chilhowee days later. They secretly killed a woman beyond the village and hid outside the townhouse as the Chilhowee people held a second scalp dance to honor their warriors. In the middle of the ceremony, Gûlsadihï' rushed into the townhouse, bragged of killing the Chilhowee woman, and accused those townspeople of deception. He announced,

"'Cowee will have a ball play with you!'—and everyone knew this was a challenge to battle." The Cowee warriors then returned to their own village to organize a stronger war party, which included men from the neighboring Middle Towns. Their plan to exact revenge on Chilhowee was thwarted, however. Fearing reprisals for what their warriors had done, the Chilhowee people fled.[1]

Although an intriguing account, it is unlikely that the above incident actually happened in the manner described. Rather, the oral tradition known as "The False Warriors of Chilhowee" was more likely a means to instruct its audience about appropriate Cherokee behavior—perhaps the most important being the gravity of killing another Cherokee, even if from another town and region. Indeed, one of the bonds that held Cherokees together during the eighteenth century centered on kinship connections, which extended to clan members throughout the southern Appalachian Mountains. These connections were further reinforced by the law of clan revenge, whereby the nearest relations of a slain clan member were obligated to mollify the spirits of the deceased, either through direct retaliation or acceptance of proper compensation from the offending party. In "The False Warriors of Chilhowee," Cowee warriors attempted to avenge the death of four clan members and townspeople by directing an attack against the offending town of Chilhowee. While no intertown or clan-based warfare resulted, the threat of retaliation and the subsequent displacement of the Chilhowee people were strong reminders of the consequences of killing a fellow Cherokee.[2]

The myth reveals additional secrets about the Cherokees and their understandings of community. It casts doubt on the perception that the Cherokees were a homogeneous sociopolitical group united by kinship, and instead highlights the deep-rooted town and regional fractures that complicated Cherokee collective identity. The Chilhowee warriors were from the Overhill Towns, while Cowee was in the Middle Settlements. This difference was not simply a matter of geography, although geography and settlement patterns played an essential role in shaping Cherokee localism and regionalism. It was also a matter of kinship connections and political associations. The closest friends and nearest family members typically lived in the same town or the same region. When the Cowee people sought revenge against Chilhowee, it was no surprise they looked to clan members and neighbors within the Middle region to assist them.

The intraregional response of the Middle Cherokees likewise speaks to the centrality of politics to Cherokee definitions of community. Power often rested in the local village unit, and Cherokee peoples nearly always identified themselves—and were identified by others—on the basis of town affiliation. But there also existed a regional dimension to political identity. Local headmen and their constituents sustained the most vigorous political dialogue with townspeople of the same region, and distinguished village leaders often exerted intraregional influence by speaking for one or more neighboring towns. Town and region were therefore key components of community which, in addition to kinship, formed the triad of Cherokee identity and collectivity during the eighteenth century.

These multilayered identities and associations provide the starting point for this book, since understanding Cherokee sociopolitical organization is central to understanding Cherokee history. One cannot fully comprehend Cherokee economic, diplomatic, and military behavior if inadequate attention is given to the ways in which Cherokee peoples organized society. Until recently, the writing of eighteenth-century Cherokee history within the context of identity and collectivity was a relatively uncomplicated affair. When the historian John P. Brown asked during the Great Depression, "Who were the Cherokees?" the answer at that time and for many years afterward appeared straightforward. The Cherokees were the Ani-Yun-wiya, or "the Real People," of the southern Appalachian Mountains. Although culturally similar to other southeastern Indians, the Cherokees could be distinguished by their Iroquoian language, which stood in sharp contrast to the Muscogean, Siouan, and Algonquian tongues of their indigenous neighbors. Membership in one of the seven clans further differentiated Cherokees from other peoples, as did political affiliation with the local village unit and, to a lesser extent, the national council. "Nation," in fact, is one of the most frequently used models through which scholars address the issue of collectivity among early Cherokees. This is not surprising, since nation as a theoretical construct has been applied to a variety of peoples and societies, and Native Americans during the colonial era are no exception.[3]

It is through such conceptualizations, however, that we encounter great difficulties when trying to answer Brown's query. Recent scholarship demonstrates the dangers of unequivocally applying the nation concept to Native Americans. Foremost is the tendency to exaggerate the homogeneity of indigenous peoples. The Cherokees, for example, were a markedly divided people during much of the eighteenth century. Although loosely bound by ties of kinship, cultural commonality, and ancestral origin, well-entrenched town and regional loyalties often presented a considerable challenge to Cherokee unity. Scholars have long recognized the fractured nature of Cherokee society and focused much of their attention on gender roles, generational gaps, and political factionalism. Paradoxically, while many studies identify towns and regions in the opening pages as geographic reference points and a source of discord, they then proceed to discuss the Cherokees as a singular entity. Thus, despite the many influential works on the early Cherokees, there are areas of Cherokee culture and history in need of further development. One of these is the importance of town and region to Cherokee identity, group allegiance, and sense of community.[4]

This is not to say the village world of the Cherokees is untrodden territory. Colin Calloway and Tom Hatley have each written on a specific Cherokee town (Chota and Keowee, respectively). Such efforts reflect a growing awareness of the town's importance to the social, political, economic, and spiritual life of Native American peoples. Josh Piker, in *Okfuskee: A Creek Indian Town in Colonial America*, offers one of the most thorough accounts of "the local level of Native life" by showing how Creek peoples were "profoundly influenced by events and processes that centered on their towns and villages." Nonetheless, most writers of Cherokee history do not explore town or regional identities and interactions, and no book-length monograph provides an in-depth treatment of such issues. This is not a minor concern. While town and region were but two ways in which Cherokees ultimately structured group identity, they were arguably the most recognizable markers by which Cherokees distinguished themselves during the colonial era. Local allegiances based on town and regional affiliation, in fact, not only dictated how Cherokees identified themselves and others but also shaped the ways in which Cherokees interacted with outsiders.[5]

Clan membership proved equally significant to Cherokee identity, especially in terms of defining the Cherokees as a distinct ethnopolitical community. Yet we know little about eighteenth-century Cherokee clans from the documentary record. "Clans are difficult to discern," writes Theda Perdue, "because most European observers were unaware of or uninterested in them." While certainly true, we should also recognize that Cherokees themselves seemed very uninterested in asserting their clan identities to Europeans. Town membership and regional affiliation instead became the reference points by which Cherokees projected their identities and understandings of community to colonial newcomers.[6]

Despite this lack of evidence, or perhaps because of it, anthropologists and ethnohistorians have turned to nontraditional sources, especially those from a later period, to describe clan and kinship for eighteenth-century indigenous peoples. The result is an imperfect consensus, which asserts that kinship superseded all other factors in determining how Cherokees and other Native Americans defined community. Perdue, for example, devotes an entire chapter in *Cherokee Women* to "Defining Community," wherein she concludes, "Only kinship seems to have bound Cherokees together in the early eighteenth century.... Cherokees distinguished themselves from others not by skin color or political allegiance but by their membership in a Cherokee clan." To be sure, kinship transcended town and regional boundaries, and clan membership differentiated Cherokees from other peoples and among themselves. The point here, however, is that political allegiance was at the heart of how Cherokees distinguished themselves from outsiders during the colonial era. More often than not, this political allegiance rested with the town and region.[7]

My aim is not to dismiss the significance of kinship, but to elevate town and region to an equal footing with clan membership in how we understand eighteenth-century Cherokee sociopolitical organization. Charles Hudson certainly had it right when he wrote more than thirty years ago, "One can scarcely overemphasize the importance of kinship in the social life of the Southeastern Indians." The preeminent southeastern Indian anthropologist followed this assertion with an important qualifier: "Kinship was not all there was to their social life: there was the added dimension of politics and law." War, trade, and diplomacy were both familial and community affairs, making the two nearly inseparable. Membership in a clan as well as a town-oriented community, in other words, coherently overlapped, shaping both daily interactions and larger diplomatic concerns with outsiders. Accordingly, a greater sensitivity to these multilayered identities—town, region, and nation—can provide richer insights into Cherokee history during the eighteenth century.[8]

This study therefore begins with an ethnohistorical discourse on the meaning of town, region, and nation to the early Cherokees. Chapter 1 engages recent anthropological and historical understandings of indigenous peoples to explore the ways in which diverse Cherokees were divided by an intense localism and regionalism. Region in particular is a principal organizing theme of Cherokee history that has received only cursory acknowledgment. Throughout the colonial era, the Lower, Middle, Valley, and Overhill Cherokees encountered varying geopolitical circumstances, situated as they were on the different borderlands of Cherokee country, and safeguarded their own interests by pursuing diplomatic, military, and economic agendas that could often be at variance. Yet nation was not an irrelevant concept for the Cherokees. Kinship, cultural commonality, and political interconnectedness provided the Cherokees with a sense of peoplehood that transcended localized identities.

This conceptual discussion then turns to historical narrative. The chapters that follow detail how Cherokee borderland experiences challenged town, regional, and national associations. Involvement in trade, imperial contestation, and border conflict especially reveal the cultural persistence of localism and regionalism throughout the eighteenth century. The Anglo-Cherokee alliance, for example, was foremost a trading alliance. The growth of the deerskin trade in the colonial South tied the Cherokees to the British, particularly to South Carolina and its capital at Charlestown.[9] Throughout these commercial exchanges, village leaders jealously guarded local and regional access to goods, which forced profit-seeking Carolinians to work within Cherokee community structures. But the deerskin trade also provided a degree of commonality for Cherokee peoples. Recognizing their reliance on Carolina for goods, aspiring headmen understood that access to power often rested on access to trade. Cherokee leaders increasingly spoke for more than their own town when it came to the trade, which widened political communication between Cherokee peoples.

Like the deerskin trade, the Cherokee-Creek War (1715-55) forced the British to more clearly understand and engage Cherokee localism and regionalism. The Cherokees remained disunited throughout most of the war, as each region exhibited varying degrees of involvement in both war and peace. At midcentury, however, a new phase of the conflict emerged. Large-scale Creek attacks against the Lower Cherokees pressed those townspeople to abandon their homes and seek shelter in other regions. The resulting refugee crisis conveyed the realities of war to other towns and regions, thereby bringing other Cherokees more directly into the conflict. Many Cherokees responded by welcoming Iroquois and other "Northward" Indians as allies against the Creeks, but this marriage of convenience complicated Cherokee relations with Carolina, the Creeks, and other southeastern Indians. Fear of war on all sides of their unstable borderlands eventually prompted Cherokees from every region to distance themselves from the Northward Indians and establish peace with the Creeks. The result was a shift in the burdens of war to the Overhill people who lay more exposed to hostile Indians from the north. The need to safeguard their own towns and secure a reliable trade forced Overhill headmen to widen their search for allies, which included the French in Louisiana.

The pursuit of new trading alliances sharpened during the Seven Years' War. The renewal of imperial warfare galvanized Cherokee diplomatic maneuverings, particularly within the Overhill Towns, which emerged as the dominant regional power after midcentury. In 1756 villagers from Great Tellico undertook a divisive diplomatic mission to the French at Fort Toulouse and New Orleans. Prompted by other Overhill headmen, the leaders of the Tellico affair sought to challenge the Carolina monopoly by establishing multiple outlets for trade and alliances. The incident, however, unleashed a political firestorm throughout Cherokee country. Mindful of their need for the British and the political backing of Cherokees in other towns and regions, Overhill headmen outwardly rejected the Tellico faction. They were joined by Cherokees from the Lower, Middle, and Valley Towns who reaffirmed the Anglo-Cherokee alliance by sending hundreds of warriors to support the British war effort.

It was at this juncture that the alliance faltered. Initially the most dependable British ally with hundreds of warriors at their assistance, the Cherokees emerged by 1759 as their bitterest enemy. Trade disputes, disagreements over gift-giving, land encroachments, and murders led to a limited border war between the Cherokees and Virginians. Local and regional tensions surfaced repeatedly throughout the crisis, but the British failed to exploit these divisions. Instead, the isolated conflict gave way to a general war as Cherokees from every region attacked Carolina and her sister colonies. The British responded with two invasions of Cherokee country in 1760 and 1761. These expeditions brought destruction to the Lower, Middle, and Out Towns as soldiers scorched homes, council houses, and agricultural fields. The Anglo-Cherokee War marked a new epoch in Cherokee history, as mountain villagers witnessed a level of dislocation and cross-regional resistance rarely found in earlier conflicts with neighboring indigenous peoples.

This legacy was most immediately felt during the interwar years. Between the end of the Seven Years' War and the onset of the American Revolution, the Cherokees sought a return to normal hunting, farming, and trading cycles that had been disrupted by war. But efforts to normalize trade relations with Carolina and Virginia proved exceedingly difficult as the deerskin trade dwindled. Despite the tenuous nature of the trade, Cherokees remained steadfast in the British interest, even as natives throughout Indian country rebelled against the English. Pontiac's Uprising did not extend to the southern Appalachians, largely because of Britain's singular power, the fresh memories of the Anglo-Cherokee War, and the Cherokees' long-standing hostility with northern and western Indians. To the contrary, the interwar years witnessed a period of debilitating warfare between the Cherokees and a diverse array of Indians from Iroquoia, the Ohio country, and Great Lakes. Compounding this turmoil was the rapid encroachment of British settlers onto Cherokee hunting territory. Land increasingly became an issue for all Cherokees, a crisis that worsened as American colonists revolted against Britain.

The American Revolution brought the most radical changes to Cherokee country. Unlike the fighting of an earlier generation, the militia campaigns of the Revolution successfully targeted every mountain region. Cherokees responded with the combined tactics of limited resistance and wholesale retreat, but the inability to find sanctuary in the more remote villages prompted some Cherokees to seek refuge in unfamiliar territory. Dragging Canoe, an Overhill warrior at the center of resistance, conducted hundreds of Cherokees from every region away from their ancestral lands to resettle on the borders of Creek country. This removal of a large number of Cherokees—now called Chickamaugas—presented a potential challenge to the preservation of a distinct ethnopolitical community. Yet these dissidents tenaciously held on to their identity as Cherokees. Rather than the beginnings of a new tribe, the Chickamaugas represented the formation of a new and distinct Cherokee region. They ultimately became known as the Chickamauga Cherokees who established the Five Lower Towns near present-day Chattanooga, Tennessee.

The withered remains of older Cherokee regions continued amid the revolutionary turmoil, but the two dominant regions to emerge from the ashes of the American Revolution were the Upper and Lower Towns. The Lower Cherokees, or Chickamaugas, continued their fight against the United States until 1794, whereas the Upper Towns became an accommodationist stronghold. Although frontier settlers were well aware of these divisions, American militiamen targeted both hostile and neutral towns in their punitive expeditions. All told, more than sixty Cherokee towns in every region had been destroyed at least once by the time the fighting ended.

The revolutionary era demonstrated both the entrenched nature of Cherokee localism and regionalism and the ascension of a broader national identity. This movement toward a more distinct and diffuse Cherokee national consciousness was not an evolutionary process. It ebbed and flowed, depending on circumstances. At times, local allegiances clashed with what could be considered the common good for all Cherokees, thereby challenging identification with the broader community. At other times, the need for mutual support in the face of hostile non-Cherokee populations overrode local concerns. As cross-cultural exchanges became more volatile over the course of the century, Cherokees were forced to confront powerful adversaries, which demanded a more centralized political response. Accordingly, this work concludes by examining how border warfare and threats to ancestral lands widened Cherokee conceptualizations of community. The result, I argue, was that while town and region remained important markers of collective identity, a broader ethnic, or national, awareness crystallized in response to these dramatic events, which laid the foundation for the emergence of an institutionally based Cherokee Nation by the early nineteenth century.

1

Town, Region, and Nation

For many native peoples throughout North America, the town was the central feature of social and political life, perhaps even more so for the Cherokees and other southeastern Indians. Cherokee village life, as Tom Hatley reminds us, was "intensely local," which made town identities especially entrenched. When a Virginia officer neared Cherokee country in 1761, for instance, a party of Overhill hunters approached the peace envoy and asked "to what town we belonged." Likewise, after twelve Cherokees arrived in Charlestown without official invite, the governor first enquired, "What town are they of?" The above questions signify that Cherokees and their neighbors foremost identified one another according to locality. The documentary record is explicit on this point. Even a brief perusal of William L. McDowell Jr.'s frequently cited *Documents Relating to Indian Affairs* reveals that Cherokees throughout the colonial period adamantly emphasized town affiliation. Although most eighteenth-century documents that relate to, or speak for, Native Americans were written by outsiders, they nevertheless testify to the centrality of local identities among Cherokees and other indigenous peoples. What is especially revealing is that Cherokees without exception attested or signed documents by projecting their town affiliation, not their clan. This contrasts sharply with many northern Indians, particularly Algonquian peoples, who identified themselves according to clan and lineage. Perhaps this is attributable to the seasonal mobility and multiethnic composition of many northern villages, but the difference is nonetheless striking.[1]

Such differences may also stem from more ancient roots. The town's relevance to Cherokee peoples dates well before the arrival of the British. For much of the Mississippian Period (c. 800–1600), hierarchical chiefdoms organized around ceremonial town centers dominated the southeastern landscape, which also featured smaller, more dispersed settlements. Although the Mississippian Southeast experienced vast changes by the end of the era, Spanish explorers in the mid-sixteenth century nonetheless encountered both paramount chiefdoms and lesser towns. Records left from the de Soto (1540–42) and Pardo (1566–67) expeditions in particular reveal remarkable continuity between Cherokee peoples from the sixteenth through the eighteenth centuries. Foremost is the importance of the town to Cherokee ancestors. The Spanish not only recognized town units as key to societal structure; they also recorded town names that would remain relatively constant for 200 years (despite differences in Spanish, English, Muscogean, and Iroquoian languages). Tocae (Toqua), Xeneca (Seneca), Quetua (Kituhwa), Nequase (Nequassee), Estate (Estatoe), and Tacoru (Tugaloo) are just a few of the many towns identified by Hernando de Soto and Juan Pardo. Other continuities in village life are evident from these accounts: cross-town military action, strategies of village retreat before a superior force, fortified towns, the presence of earthen mounds, headmen leading at the consent of their people, the desire for European goods, indigenous hospitality, and rituals of gift exchange. While we do not get much sense of Cherokee regionalism from the Spanish entradas, it is clear that attachment to one's town was a significant part of daily life.[2]

This connectedness lasted well into the eighteenth century and was to a large degree political. The often-used phrase "all politics is local" certainly applies to the eighteenth-century Cherokees, as the town was the principal governmental unit they recognized. The trader James Adair observed, "Every town is independent of another." An Indian agent agreed the town "in Matters merely relating to itself has no manner of Dependence on the rest of the Nation." All adult villagers could participate in the decision-making process, and authority rested in the hands of leading men whose power derived ultimately with the townspeople. These leading men, or headmen, were usually elders who had risen through the ranks as warriors or councilors (also known as "beloved men"). This is initially evident in the many forms of correspondence between the British and Cherokees, in which the former made certain to address both "the Warriours & beloved men."[3]

Although notable warriors and beloved men shared political power, they performed distinct roles within the town's political structure. Beloved men governed the internal affairs of the village, while warriors handled the business of war. The Indian agent John Stuart observed that a beloved man was councilor and judge "in all matters relating to internal Police [policy] of his town." Another eyewitness found the beloved man was "little else than a Civil Magistrate." The Beloved Man of Chota, more readily known to the British as Old Hop, stressed the civil nature of his position to a British officer: it "did not belong to him as a beloved man to talk about war, his office was to govern His Young men and to Endeavour to Procure them Necessaries, in a peaceable manner." These distinctive political roles were also emphasized by warriors. As "we only are Warriors," admitted the famed Attakullakulla, "we have no great Knowledge in many Things where the Good of our Nation lyes, nor can we express ourselves or argue upon such Things, therefore must refer you to the good wise old Man [Old Hop], who knows such Affairs better than we."[4]

Too much can be made, however, of the war and peace dichotomy. The anthropologist Fred Gearing in his highly speculative work, *Priests and Warriors*, viewed "the council and war organizations as two selective systems," whereby Cherokee men served in either the "white" (peace) or "red" (war) leadership role. Some historians agree that Cherokees operated under a dual political system of peace and war chiefs. To be sure, distinctions were evident and head warriors and civil leaders did perform separate functions, but they were not mutually exclusive. Another anthropologist, Raymond Fogelson, is more convincing when he writes that white and red organizations of authority were not as clearly demarcated as Gearing suggests. He rightly argues that contrasts between the two have been overdrawn and the demarcation is "less neat."[5]

The evidence bears this out. The adventurer Alexander Cuming found that every town had a beloved man, but in some instances "it so happens that he is at the same Time a Head Warrior." The Beloved Man of Oconee, for instance, was also the "Mankiller of that Place." King Crow of the Lower Cherokees likewise managed domestic policies and led war parties. Skiagusta of Keowee, one of the most recognized leaders in the Lower Cherokee Towns who served in both a military and civil capacity, proclaimed, "I am an old Man, and have been a Warriour, and am a Warriour still." The overlapping roles of beloved men and head warriors were especially evident in their political and diplomatic affairs. Villagers appointed warriors and beloved men to speak on their behalf, and both types of leaders attempted to secure trading networks. In much the same way that Old Hop sought to procure "Necessaries" for his people, Attakullakulla, a leader respected for his war exploits and diplomatic achievements, exclaimed, "I have done all that I can for a Trade."[6]

The warrior/beloved man dichotomy is also complicated by a third element of Cherokee male leadership: the "conjurors." These conjurors, as the British often styled them, held great sway in Cherokee society largely because religion was a central feature of village life. They were especially influential during village ceremonies and other community rituals, which were often politically charged. Priests therefore carried great weight in village political activities. Cuming found that conjurors were "consulted in every Affair of Importance, and seem to have the Direction of every Thing." A British officer stationed at Fort Prince George during the tense winter of 1759–60 likewise recognized the influence of the Keowee priest over his townspeople. After warriors fired into the fort and killed a sentry, the officer directed cannon shot toward the Keowee townhouse and "particularly the old Conjurorers House."[7]

As in the case of warriors, priests could also become headmen, performing religious, military, and civil functions. The "Little Congeror of Keowee," "All Bones of Cheowee," and "the Conjuror of Hiwassee" represented their towns as headmen when dealing with the British. The Small Pox Conjuror of Settico, also known as "the Warriour of Setticoe," led war parties, managed the internal affairs of his town, and performed religious rites. Near the onset of the Anglo-Cherokee War, for example, he was reportedly "conjuring every Day" to encourage his young warriors to attack the British. Indeed, priestly influence in war proved equal to their religious and political powers. Conjurors often traveled with Cherokee war parties, where they were "called to predict the fortune of the campaign; and it is not uncommon for them to stop all operations."[8]

There is also the question of how Cherokee priests, head warriors, and beloved men led their people. In other words, how did they maintain their authority as headmen? The short answer is that village leaders exercised authority only by the will of their people. The Emperor of Tellico, according to one governor of South Carolina, held his position at "the Desires and Wishes of a willing People." King Crow of the Lower Towns was similarly understood to be "more under the Comands of his Subjects then they are under him." Even Old Hop admitted he "could say nothing till his Head Men and Warriors came in from Hunting." These examples demonstrate the limited authority invested in village leaders. John Stuart found that no headman held coercive power, but they were "tolerably well obeyed."[9]

Headmen were obeyed only if villagers approved of their leadership. Townspeople appointed certain leaders to give and receive talks and "Returned thanks" when they favored a speech. Their disapproval, on the other hand, could be shown in a variety of ways. Villagers might refuse to hear a headman's speech or fail to "mind his Talk" once given. They could invoke targeted laughter as a means of social control, as experienced by one village leader when "all the rest of the head men at the Meeting Laughed at him wch is their way when any of their head men do any thing without the Consent of their King and the head men of the other Towns." Villagers could also shame their leaders with jests, barbs, and even threats. Headmen seemed always mindful of these restraints. In a meeting with South Carolina governor James Glen in Charlestown, Skiagusta of Keowee at one point directed "his Speech to his own People," saying, "Some of them . . . said If I talk Anything out of the Way [they will] put me to Rights." When Skiagusta therefore voiced anything not previously discussed by those he represented, he made certain to publicly declare, "This is a Thought of my own and not the Advice of my People."[10]

The advice of his people derived from informal discussions but more so from public meetings held within the council house. This centrally located structure was the focal point of a community's political and religious activities. Townhouses were frequently built atop prominent mounds that first emerged among Cherokee ancestors during the Mississippian Period. Adair observed every town had this "mountain house," within which the beloved men and head warriors met to discuss important business. The Indian agent Edmond Atkin likewise found elder headmen spent their time "almost intirely in the Town Round Houses, where the Youth and others daily report; relating to them the History of their Nation, discoursing of Occurrences, and delivering precepts and Instructions for their Conduct and Welfare." The townhouse was not limited to village leaders. These structures were often large enough to hold the entire village population, as demonstrated by archaeological reconstructions of the Chota council house, which could seat up to five hundred people. Public councils were held inside the townhouse wherein villagers voiced their political views. They were also the focal point of frequent ritual activity, as dances, feasts, and other ceremonies occurred within or adjacent to this central structure. The townhouse was of such importance to Cherokee sociopolitical organization, according to one source, that they allowed "no settlements to be called towns, except where they have a [town]house for their own public consultations."[11]

The townhouse and mound also held importance for Cherokee agriculture. One visitor to Cherokee country described how a town elder climbed onto the mound every morning "at the Time of the Work in the Field" and called "the People with a loud voice together." Adair likewise recorded that a beloved man "goes aloft, and whoops to them with shrill calls" to begin planting. Even the "war-chieftains" were engaged in this work, since "Distinction is upon this occasion laid aside." Although agriculture was the domain of women, there were certain tasks, such as planting crops, in which all able villagers were expected to participate. Such activities reinforced local relationships as townspeople worked toward common goals vital to their survival. To be sure, individual households privately controlled designated lands. Cherokees had "a sort of Distinct property," noted Stuart, by which town leaders measured portions of land for each household. This was done according to their numbers, and "each Family depends upon the produce of the Land alloted it." But private control should not obscure the fact that agricultural fields were communally owned. Townspeople accordingly assisted one another in cultivating and planting lands belonging to that town. One eyewitness observed, for instance, that "tho' every Family has its own Field, yet they begin fellowshiply on one End, & continue so one after the other till they have finished all."[12]

Such observations reflect the social realities of clan loyalties among Cherokee peoples. While kinship connections extended throughout Cherokee country, clan members of the same town had more intimate connections with each other than with clan members from many miles away. Town-based communities also meant that Cherokees from different clans within a town sustained daily interactions and intimacies with each other more so than with their own clan members from distant villages. Townspeople of different clans, as noted above, "fellowshiply" planted their agricultural fields together. Likewise, when they built new houses, "the whole town . . . assist[s] one another." Ceremonies in particular brought all members of the community together. The Green Corn

Ceremony, regarded as the most important Cherokee ritual, was a multifaceted, town-centered religious and political gathering. It occurred over a span of three to five days in summer, with most activities taking place either in the townhouse or town square. A major part of the festivities included the performance of various dances, such as the Green Corn Dance and Friendship Dance. According to the anthropologist Frank Speck, the Friendship Dance served as a "symbol of Amity" among men and women of the village. Speck interpreted the dramatizations more precisely as a representation of hospitality, progressive friendship, and familiarity through association.[13]

Another summer ritual, which ranked just below the Green Corn Ceremony in importance, was the ball play. This was a decidedly community-based activity, for it compounded tendencies among Cherokees to differentiate peoples according to local criteria. The ball game was organized not along clan lines but by town affiliation, since matches typically pitted one town against another. They were violent and intense, as were the ball play rituals. During the course of a dance, for instance, a specially chosen singer yelled in the direction of the rival settlement. Townspeople hoped their opponents, who were engaged in their own ceremonies, would hear the shouts and become terrified and lose all heart for the game. Other prayers asked for much worse. The anthropologist James Mooney found that one conjuror desired his town's adversaries to be "driven through the four gaps into the gloomy shadows of the Darkening Land, where they will perish forever from remembrance." During another recital in this atmosphere of "highly charged emotion," women of the village called for rival players to be "put under the earth." Such statements appear more symbolic than real, but the ball game and its rituals nevertheless reinforced local relationships and fostered allegiance to the most basic social and political unit of Cherokee daily life—the town. Although clan identities and relationships were central to the Green Corn and ball play rituals, a balanced view of these ceremonies should remind us that clan loyalties did not always reign supreme. As Charles Hudson writes, "Clans were not so much social groups as *categories* of people who believed themselves to be of one 'blood.'" In contrast to what we find for Cherokee townspeople, "Clans rarely if ever assembled together as a group."[14]

Frequent interactions and connections with close family members and neighbors proved analogous to relationships with the land. Knowledge of the landscape was another important element of Cherokee localism. Familiarity with a particular environment, Hatley writes, was in many cases the product of "generations of experiment, of individual fields, microclimates, and soils, and knowledge crucial to farming success." This engendered "an affection for individual places," which was evinced by the repeated resettlement of Keowee in the aftermath of disruptive warfare. Cherokees also demonstrated local attachment throughout the era of displacement as they transplanted old town names to new environments in northern Georgia, Alabama, and eventually Oklahoma. This local knowledge extended beyond the fields, too. Hudson notes that southeastern Indian place-names often derived from topographical features, such as nearby flora, fauna, and events connected to a particular locale. These place-names infused Cherokee mythology and typically revealed a strong spiritual component. As Mooney observed, "Each spirit of good or evil has its distinct and appropriate place of residence."[15]

The oral tradition known as "The Great Leech Of Tlanusi'yï," for example, centered on a "spot where Valley river joins Hiwassee" in present-day Murphy, North Carolina, which the Cherokees called "Tlanusi'yï," or the "leech place." The story tells of a deep hole in Valley River wherein lived a massive leech, "full as large as a house." The leech often made the water "boil and foam" and surge into the air in "a great column of white spray . . . like a waterspout." Inattentive Cherokees who passed this location were in danger of being swept downriver. More than a few Cherokees had been killed in this manner, "and their friends would find the body afterwards lying upon the bank with the ears and nose eaten off." This dangerous spot discouraged Cherokees from going to that part of the river, but those who "laughed at the whole story" and disregarded the great leech were "never seen again." Other legends recorded by Mooney, such as "The Spirit Defenders of Nïkwäsï," "A Legend of Pilot Knob," and "Kâldetsi'yûñyï: Where the Bones Are," connected Cherokees both physically and spiritually to a specific location in their mountain homeland.[16]

The significance of the town to Cherokee definitions of community cannot be overstated. Thanks to a growing body of literature devoted to the study of Native American communities, we know more about the village world of Cherokees and other indigenous peoples than could have been imagined even twenty years ago. Much less, however, has been written about Cherokee regionalism. It is not from a lack of awareness either.

Nearly every scholar of Cherokee history acknowledges the regional structure of Cherokee country. John Reid, for instance, emphasized more than three decades ago that "few nations [were] so separated by regionalism as the Cherokees." Reid is among a short list of authors who attempt to incorporate this regional dimension into their scholarship. To the contrary, most scholars perfunctorily identify settlement groupings and then fail to explore their deeper significance to Cherokee identity, community boundaries, and cross-cultural interactions.[17]

Perhaps one reason for this shortcoming is the difficulty involved in categorizing Cherokee regionalism. Eighteenth-century sources project much confusion and contradiction in their regional classifications of Cherokee country. In the early years of Anglo-Cherokee contact, South Carolina traders typically recognized only the Lower and Upper Cherokees, but when jealousies arose over presents allotted by Charlestown, it soon became apparent that a Middle region existed as well. Some Carolinians remained confused after Cherokees asserted even more multifaceted regional identities; for example, when Colonel George Chicken visited the Cherokees in 1725, he lumped the Middle, Valley, and Overhill Towns into the "Upper Settlements." Chicken's journal the following year recorded even greater imprecision, as when he delivered his talk to "the upper and Lower King of the Cherokee Nation and also with the Headmen of the lower Towns and upper Middle Settlements & lower Towns & lower Middle Settlements at Nacoochee." Another Indian agent thirty years later distinguished only between "the lower Settlements or Nation, on this side of the Mountains," and "the upper nation or Settlements on the other side of the Mountains." Speaking for his indigenous trading clients, James Adair similarly observed that Cherokees made "two divisions of their country, which they term *Ayrate*, and *Ottare*, signifying 'low,' and 'mountainous.'" The Ayrate villages were on "the head branches of the beautiful Savanah river," whereas the Ottare towns were along the banks of the Little Tennessee River. Other contemporary accounts from traders, agents, headmen, and townspeople complicated this narrow view of Cherokee regionalism by recognizing at one time or another the existence of the Lower, Middle, Valley, Out, and Overhill Settlements.[18]

Eighteenth-century observers were not the only ones at odds over Cherokee settlement locations. No scholarly consensus has since emerged in regard to Cherokee regionalism; some authors contend there were three regions, while others argue there were four or possibly five. Such contradictions make it difficult—but not impossible—to effectively categorize Cherokee regions. One key is to not treat Cherokee regions ahistorically or statically. The historian Michael Zuckerman cautions against this tendency in his critique of colonial American historians and regionalization in British North America. Zuckerman criticizes the way his colleagues "have taken regions as timeless and even teleological categories rather than as constellations and constructions that themselves have histories. . . . They have scarcely thought to conceptualize them as dynamic social categories that form and fade with time." Although pertaining to such categories as "The South," "New England," and "Middle Colonies," Zuckerman's analysis provides needed insights into the study of Cherokee regionalism.[19]

Cherokee regions should foremost be seen as dynamic structures that did "form and fade with time." Cherokee localism and regionalism in 1750, for instance, looked very different than that which existed in 1800. At midcentury, four powerful Cherokee settlement groupings commanded the attention of both Europeans and Indians in the southeastern borderlands. A half-century later, Cherokee country had been thoroughly reshaped with the loss of millions of acres and the widespread displacement of entire towns and regions. The Lower Towns in particular were no longer a regional power in northwestern South Carolina, as the refugees of those villages relocated to town sites scattered across northern Georgia, Alabama, and eastern Tennessee. The former Lower Towns did reorganize to become a regional influence in these new locations, but they were in many ways a new entity, as will be discussed in the book's final chapters.

This chapter, however, concerns the mid-eighteenth century, and it is there to which we must return. By 1750, four regions—the Lower, Middle, Valley, and Overhill Settlements—had been consistently recognized by both Euroamericans and Cherokees, with the Out Towns perhaps best characterized as an ephemeral quasi-region. Their locations are well known. The Lower and Middle Towns were mostly situated on the upper reaches of the Savannah and Little Tennessee Rivers, respectively. The Valley Settlements lay directly to the west of the Middle Towns along the Valley and Hiwassee Rivers, and the Overhills were primarily along the lower reaches of the Little Tennessee and Tellico Rivers. The Out Towns, which achieved temporary prominence during the Seven Years' War, existed to

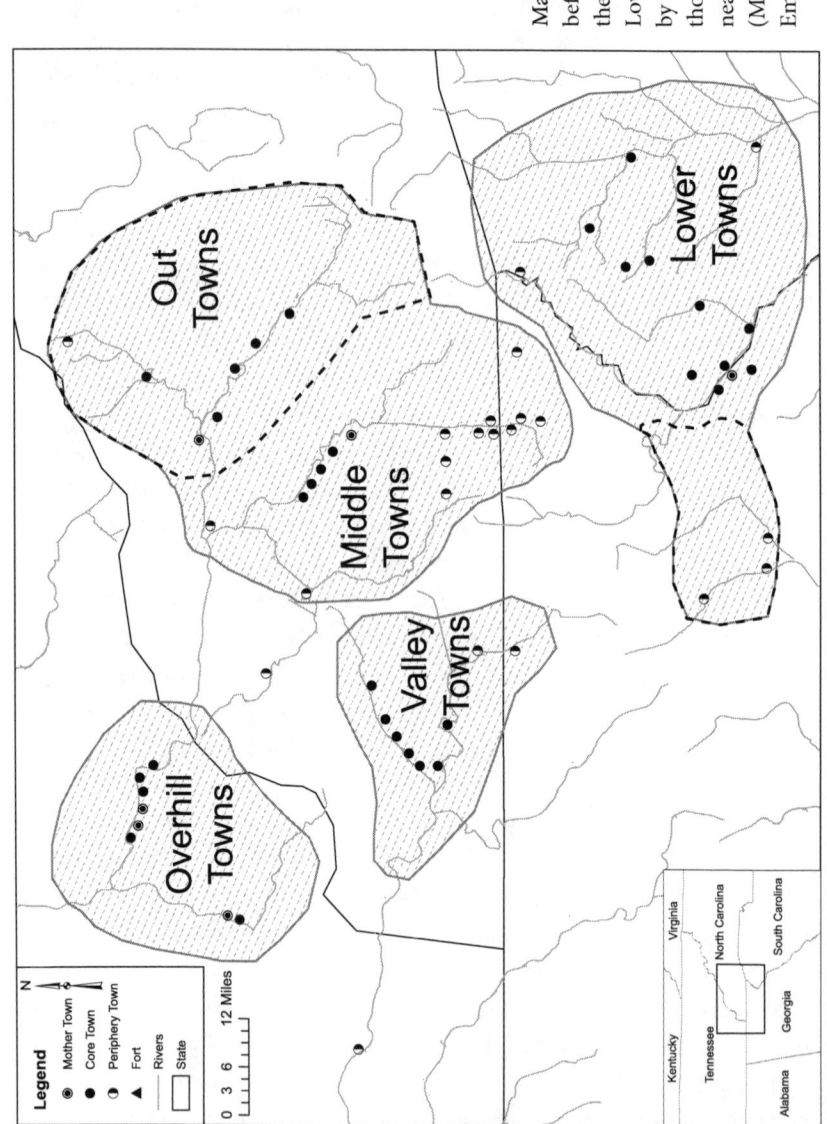

Map 1. Cherokee Regions before 1776. The area in the western part of the Lower Towns (surrounded by dotted line) contains those peripheral towns nearest to Creek country. (Map designed by Isaac Emrick.)

the north and east of the Middle Towns along the Tuckasegee River (see map 1).

While these brief descriptions might seem as if Cherokee regions were in proximity to one another, in fact the opposite is true. The southern Appalachians, more commonly known as the Cherokee Mountains during the colonial era, contained some of the roughest topography in eastern North America. With numerous peaks ranging above 6,000 feet—the highest east of the Mississippi River—the Cherokee Mountains were difficult to traverse, as the naturalist William Bartram found when he slowly navigated trails "incommoded with shattered fragments of the mountains, and in other places with boggy sinks, occasioned by oozy springs and rills stagnate sinking in miceous earth." Edmond Atkin encountered mountain passages "so narrow, that two Horses can scarce go abreast." Another well-traveled observer depicted the land dividing the Out and Middle Settlements as "the strongest country I ever saw," its mountainous pathways being "much worse than the passage of the Alps." A contemporary agreed that "the Difficulty of the Passes" from the Lower to Middle Settlements "can hardly be imagined," adding that even "these are not to be compared" to the more arduous routes to the Overhill Towns. Indeed, the journey from the Lower to Overhill Towns was no trifling affair. One eyewitness reckoned Keowee to be nearly two hundred miles from Tenasee and three hundred miles from Charlestown, "but by Reason of the Mountains, Tannassy is reckoned as far distant as Charles Town."[20]

As the distance between Keowee and Tenasee demonstrates, the Cherokees were predisposed to "live greatly dispersed," as John Stuart noted, because of their "extremely Mountaineous" country. The steep ridges, narrow valleys, and intermittent level ground of the southern Appalachians promoted scattered regional settlements that "lay straggled on a large extent of ground, many miles from one another." While Cherokee regions were disconnected by distance and topography, town proximity within regions varied. Mid-eighteenth-century maps depict a relatively compact Overhill cluster but more diffuse town locations in the Lower region. The Valley Towns were also grouped closely, for as Charlestown merchant Christopher Gadsden explained, they "lay all in one open valley, from the first to the last not exceeding 12 miles." Though variations existed, the trend was toward more compact towns clustering within a settlement area, especially outside the Lower Towns.[21]

This peculiar geography influenced settlement patterns, but it also bore directly on regional cultural distinctiveness. Atkin recorded in 1755, for instance, that "upper and lower Cherokees differ from each other, as much almost as two different nations." Cherokee regionalism was more nuanced than Atkin allowed, but his point is well taken. There were noticeable differences among Cherokees, and these differences were not a recent phenomenon. The anthropologist Roy S. Dickens Jr. argues that regional variations had long been in the making by midcentury. He finds that three distinct subregional developments of Mississippian culture began to emerge in the southern Appalachians 1,000 years ago. Although cross-regional and interethnic exchanges encouraged a greater degree of cultural commonality over time, Dickens nevertheless concludes regionalism had been firmly established by the contact period. Differences in ceramics and other material culture were paralleled by linguistic disparities that additionally reflected and reinforced local and regional identities.[22]

Language, like culture, remained a centerpiece of ethnic identity and provided a degree of commonality for Cherokee peoples, but internal linguistic differences also served as important markers of distinction among their own population. These differences to some extent followed along regional lines. The primary dialects in Cherokee country were the "Eastern," or Lower Town, the "Middle," also designated as Kituhwa, and the "Western," which the Overhill and Valley people used. Added to this Iroquoian-based language were numerous other dialects brought by individuals and refugee groups who were incorporated into Cherokee communities over the course of the eighteenth century. Inclusion of Natchez, Shawnee, and Creek peoples, for instance, complicated the ethnic structure of Cherokee society and intensified sectionalism. The Lower Towns, in proximity to the Creeks of northern Georgia and Alabama, witnessed frequent intermixing with their Muscogean neighbors. A headman of the Lower Towns called the Yamasee Creeks "his ancent peapall," and some Lower Cherokees continued to speak the Yamasee language well after those peoples removed to the environs of St. Augustine following their war with Carolina in 1715. With such varieties of speech, it was not uncommon that a Cherokee from one region might not readily understand the dialect of another. During official correspondence with the British, Cherokees from different regions preferred linguists who were knowledgeable in their particular dialect. One Hiwassee headman, for example, requested the governor's talk be sent to the Lower and Valley Towns separately, and "Mr. Beamer to be Interpreter for them, and Mr. Bunning for us." Thus, just as their Iroquoian language distinguished Cherokees from their Algonquian, Siouan, and Muscogean neighbors, dialectic variations among Cherokee speakers likewise differentiated local and regional populations throughout their mountain homeland.[23]

Regionalism was entrenched among Cherokee peoples for other reasons, such as the limited extent of town mobility. When not uprooted by the refugee crises of late eighteenth-century warfare, core towns remained relatively constant in terms of location. Resource exhaustion appears to have had little effect on village relocation. According to the anthropologists Ted Gragson and Paul Bolstad, local resources (excluding deer) easily met Cherokee demands within a short proximity to each town. Larger core towns accordingly occupied the same (or nearby) space over time, thereby enhancing the regional cohesion and identity of the different Cherokee settlements.[24]

Equally important was the political dimension of Cherokee regionalism. Although town politics guided life on a daily basis, the Cherokees and their neighbors understood regions to be politically distinct entities. Regional headmen, councils, and "beloved" towns were three means by which political associations extended beyond the village and reinforced regional cohesion. Distinguished headmen were key agents in widening political connections. John Stuart found notable warriors held titles, such as the Raven, Slavecatcher, Mankiller, and Skiagusta, that afforded "a certain degree of Respect & Influence, which with the Number of his Followers and Adherents increase in proportion to the Eloquence & other Abilities of the Bearer." For this reason, respected warriors and beloved men gained large followings beyond their own villages. Wawhatchee of Keowee was one of many such individuals. Sometimes called the "Head Warrior of all the Southern Towns," he was known to have "the whole Management" of Keowee and the other Lower Towns. The Raven of Hiwassee was another regional leader who claimed to "have six more Towns under my Command" in the Valley Settlements. His aliases therefore included "the Raven of the Valley" and "King of the Valley." The authority bestowed upon Wawhatchee and the Raven was not absolute, of course, as other warriors, beloved men, and conjurors both complemented and challenged their leadership, but they fittingly represent the capacity of certain headmen to become regional leaders.[25]

Such influence could become national in scope, but Wawhatchee, the Raven, and other prominent headmen typically wielded the most authority within their own region. The British recognized these regional limitations in their frequent dealings with the Cherokees. Following the Anglo-Cherokee War, Gadsden found the ability of Tistoe of Keowee and the Old Warrior of Estatoe to make peace "lay entirely amongst the Lower Settlement Indians." The Charlestown merchant added that other peace representatives had even less authority, noting that those who "were dubbed headmen . . . might have some influence in his or their own particular town, but not one of any general weight in their settlements [region], much less THROUGHOUT the nation." Gadsden's observations reflect the reality of Cherokee political structures, as regional leaders often proved adamant in asserting distinct identities and allegiances. Middle Town headmen in the fall of 1759, for example, affirmed their desire to treat separately with Governor Lyttelton of South Carolina, expressing "an Aversion to be joined with those of the Upper and Lower Towns (who they say are bad) lest they should not be distinguished, but treated as one People." When such entreaties failed and Lyttelton detained headmen from every region within the confines of Fort Prince George, Overhill leaders worked to free five Overhill hostages, declaring "that they take no concern for the Rest who may remain there." The above are just a few of the many examples of sectional politics that will be explored throughout this book, but they expediently illustrate the entrenched nature of Cherokee regionalism.[26]

Regionally based political associations were also reinforced by the existence of beloved, or "mother," towns within each settlement grouping. Commonly identified mother towns included Tugaloo (Lower), Chota (Overhill), Nequassee (Middle), and Kituhwa (Out). It was not unusual, however, for more than one beloved town to be acknowledged within a particular region, and disagreements resulted as to which town was the accepted regional center. The Overhill towns of Great Tellico, Tenasee, and Chota, for instance, at one time or another claimed beloved town status. While such confusion stemmed in part from imperfect observations, it also reminds us, in the words of Zuckermann, that regions and towns were "dynamic social categories." Like regions, beloved towns rose and fell depending on political leadership, demographic changes, and geopolitical circumstances.[27]

Though a certain degree of fluidity characterized the loci of Cherokee political power, the preeminence of beloved towns should not be undervalued. Beloved towns held a special place within Cherokee society. They were considered regional "capitals," or council seats, which provided focal points for intraregional political activity. Alexander Cuming believed "Mother Towns" governed the "whole Cherokee Nation," as "each of these Towns chuse a King to preside over them and their Dependants." Cuming's view represents an oversimplified understanding of Cherokee leadership arrangements, but it nevertheless testifies to the political significance of beloved towns. Principal headmen often resided in these towns, from which they dispatched runners carrying official messages to neighboring villages. Beloved towns also provided the setting for separate regional councils. These councils typically met to discuss matters of general consequence. Although representatives from other towns regularly attended, these councils were organized and led by headmen from the same region.[28]

The language used to describe beloved towns reveals deeper connections within regions. Beloved towns, as Cuming noted, were also referred to as "Mother Towns," and "their Dependants"—meaning towns of the same region—were often called "Brother Towns" by the Cherokees. A headman from Noyowee informed Carolina officials that he also represented Tomatly "and several brother-towns" in the Valley. During a similar occasion, Oconastota assured a British officer that all his "Brother Towns" in the Overhill Settlements were inclined toward peace. Even their most hostile "Brother Town of Settiquoh," another headman added, made a present of tobacco "to smoak it, in Token of Friendship." This use of kinship terminology defined relationships between towns, for kinship likewise determined how individual Cherokees behaved toward one another. Brother towns conveyed a status of relative equality, especially in terms of power relations, as well as a sense of familial connection. And as a matrilineal society, whereby Cherokees traced kinship through women, mother towns possessed even greater standing over their "Dependant" towns, since gender and generation demarcated nearly all distinctions within Cherokee clans.[29]

A beloved town could achieve its prominent position not only from political influence or sizable population but also from its ancestral significance. The historian David Corkran suggests mother towns were "so called because they may have been the original towns of their groupings." As the first settlement established by Cherokee migrants in the area, a mother town eventually became too large for its own townhouse and local resources. Through a process called "fissioning," members of the original town broke away to form a new village on nearby lands. This fissioning repeated until the population stabilized and resulted in town clusters that provided the foundation for Cherokee regionalism. Throughout these changes, the mother town continued as a recognized regional center. When George Chicken met Lower Town leaders in 1725, headmen wanted the meeting to take place at Tugaloo, it "being the most Antient Town in these parts."[30]

The town of Kituhwa along the Tuckasegee River sheds additional light on the ancestral significance of mother towns. Kituhwa is generally accepted as the original nucleus not only of the Out Towns but for all Cherokee peoples. One of the terms Cherokees call themselves is Ani-Kituhwagi, or "people of Kituhwa." Once the core Cherokee settlement that sent "colonizers" throughout the Blue Ridge Mountains and beyond, Kituhwa had been relegated to minor political and demographic importance by the mid-eighteenth century. Although located on the fringes of Cherokee country, both geographically and politically, Kituhwa nevertheless maintained its distinction as the "Council Fire Place of all the Nation." Cherokee oral tradition relates how Kituhwa, as a beloved town, served as a sacred regional and national center during the Green Corn Dance. Prior to the dance, all fires throughout the settlements were extinguished. Villagers then renewed their fires during the ceremony by drawing upon "the honored or sacred fire" at Kituwha.[31]

Rituals such as the Green Corn Ceremony contained elements decidedly local in nature, as previously discussed, but they also widened relationships between Cherokee peoples, as evinced by neighboring towns drawing upon the sacred fire at Kituhwa. The Green Corn Ceremony therefore proved essential to intertown associations. Chicken noted in 1725 that several headmen from Tugaloo "as well as other towns" arrived for "the Great dance." A British officer in later years found that Settico and Tellico townspeople jointly participated in the Green Corn Dance. In another instance, Tistoe of Keowee requested a steer from the English to "entertain the other towns" at the upcoming ceremony. To further solidify the bonds between towns, Green Corn Dances were reportedly held "every year in a different town, and when they have been held in all towns, they begin again with the first."[32]

It is unclear if the above observation meant towns within a region or throughout the nation, although the former appears more likely since these gatherings often brought Cherokees together from adjacent towns. But the Green Corn Ceremony could also be an interregional affair, especially when it turned more overtly political. When Creek warriors threatened Cherokees during Chicken's visit, Little Tellico in the Valley welcomed "at the Corn dance Several of the head men over the hills and also the Major part of the head men of the other Towns in the Upper Settlements" to coordinate defensive measures. A report in 1759 indicated war would commence between the Cherokees and British once Middle Town warriors visited the Lower Settlements "under pretence of seeing the green Corn Dance." A headman from the Out Towns attempted to forestall these attacks. Round O of Stecoe arrived at the Lower Towns during the ceremony and threatened to "kill all the Creek Indians that was In their Towns & Bring a Suthard Warr as well as a Norward."[33]

The multifaceted nature of Cherokee ceremonies demonstrates that local, regional, and national associations were not mutually exclusive. Instead, the interplay of local and broader identities was ever-present during Cherokee interactions with outsiders as well as those that took place among themselves. Understanding the Cherokees as a nation, or "People," is therefore important to understanding their political developments during the eighteenth century. The Cherokee nation as a political entity was less structured and institutionalized at midcentury than it would be fifty years later, but informal mechanisms were in place which linked Cherokees from different towns and regions politically. Beloved towns, for instance, could become so hegemonic that their influence became national in scope. Chota in the Overhill country was one such town whose political authority extended beyond its own region, prompting one trader to identify it as "the Mother Town of that Nation." Middle Cherokee warriors used similar language when describing Chota as "the beloved Town that all the other Towns in the Nation regards." Ostenaco, an Overhill headman, agreed that Chota was "the head of all the Nation." The British similarly viewed Chota as "the metropolis of the country," a view which stemmed in part from their attempts to centralize relations with the Cherokees.[34]

Essential to its role as the Cherokee "capital" was Chota's designation as the site of national councils, wherein headmen from all towns and regions were expected to participate in policy-making decisions. These meetings typically involved matters of great import that affected all Cherokees. John Stuart specified that "Great & National concerns, such as Embassies from other Nations, or to Determine upon Peace & War; are discussed in a general meeting of Deputies from all the Towns in the Nation." When Creek messengers appeared in Chota during the summer of 1757, a leading Overhill headman sent runners "to all the Towns, even as far as Keowee to Summons people of all the Nation to be present at that Talk." Although Cherokees from other towns and regions frequently challenged Chota's preeminence, such as refusing to attend national councils, the beloved Overhill town nevertheless became a cross-regional epicenter of political power during the eighteenth century.[35]

The rise of Chota and other towns whose influence transcended local politics resulted largely from the ability of leading headmen to garner interregional support. Not only did notable warriors and beloved men become town and regional leaders, but the more prominent headmen could also attract a national following. Attakullakulla (Little Carpenter), Ostenaco (Judd's Friend), Oconastota (Great Warrior of Chota), Kittagusta (Prince of Chota), Willinawaw, and Old Hop formed the core of Overhill leadership who ensured Chota's ascendancy in cross-cultural negotiations after midcentury. Attakullakulla, in particular, proved to be a tireless cross-regional diplomat who seemingly spent as much time in Keowee as he did in Chota during the Seven Years' War. It was largely through such influential leaders that a more clearly defined Cherokee political community began to take shape on a national level.[36]

Political connections and kinship networks encouraged Cherokees to envision themselves as part of a broader community. Clan membership was a central component of Cherokee ethnic identity long before institutionalized political mechanisms conjoined Cherokees into a nation-state. As Perdue notes, those who belonged to one of the seven clans were considered Cherokee, regardless of differences in language, residence, or race. These seven primary clans—imperfectly translated in English to mean Wolf, Blue, Twister, Bird, Paint, Deer, and Wild Potato—differentiated Cherokees from other Indians. They also dictated to a large extent how Cherokees interacted and associated with one another. Being part of a particular clan brought with it obligations owed foremost to members of that kinship group. James Adair found among southeastern Indians in general that each clan formed "a little community within the nation" whereby "they are commonly negligent of any other tribe [clan] but their own." If a Cherokee knew another to be of the same clan, for instance, then that person was regarded as having familial privileges. A Cherokee traveler to another town would, according to Adair, "enquire for a house of their own tribe; and if there be any, they go to it, and are kindly received, though they never saw the persons before—they eat, drink, and regale themselves, with as much freedom, as at their own tables."[37]

Although central to categorizing people within Cherokee country, clan identities did not generate the same friction as did town and regional affiliation. One reason for this is that clan relations extended beyond the individual town, thereby forging a broader sense of community among all Cherokees, as Adair's observations testify. Since members of all seven clans could be found in nearly every Cherokee village, kinship in a sense united the towns both ancestrally and politically. Clan responsibilities, especially within a legal context, proved a primary means by which town and regional boundaries were transcended. John Reid has written much about the "law of clan revenge" and the ways kinship obligations "conjoined the Cherokees into one nation and one people." The law of clan revenge, in its simplest form, meant that Cherokee clan relations were responsible for avenging or satisfying a homicide, either through revenge killing or the acceptance of some form of compensation.[38]

Clan membership and the law of revenge broadened Cherokee understandings of community, but other cultural foundations reinforced a distinct sense of peoplehood. The Cherokees' Iroquoian language, while different dialectically between regions, nevertheless magnified differences between themselves and their indigenous neighbors. Charles Hudson finds that the geographical distribution of Iroquoian languages in the Southeast was so restricted, it could not be found to any significant extent outside the Blue Ridge Mountains. The moniker "Cherokee," in fact, might be a derivative of "Chalaque," a Creek (Muscogean) word meaning "people of a different speech." The description is fitting, since few peoples south of the Ohio River were Iroquoian speakers. The Creeks, Choctaws, and Chickasaws spoke variations of Muscogean, while the Catawbas were Siouan, and the Shawnees spoke Algonquian. The brand of Iroquoian used by the Cherokees also differed in grammar and lexicon from other Eastern Woodlands Iroquoian speakers, such as the Six Nations. These differences are especially significant because anthropologists, sociologists, and other scholars agree that language is a cornerstone of ethnic identity.[39]

A sense of place, embedded in a particular geography and communal ownership of land, also transcended town and regional boundaries. The southern mountains were key to this shared identity. A well-known origin story told by all Cherokees detailed how the earth once was "flat and very soft and wet." It was during this time that the Great Buzzard "flew all over the earth" to locate dry ground for the animals, but when he reached the Cherokee country he grew tired and his wings began to strike the ground. Wherever his wings "struck the earth there was a valley, and where they turned up again there was a mountain. When the animals above saw this, they were afraid that the whole world would be mountains, so they called him back, but the Cherokee country remains full of mountains to this day."[40]

This common mountain identity inundated the diplomatic discourse between the Cherokees and the British throughout the eighteenth century. In 1730 the first Cherokees visited England and informed King George II, "We are come hither from a mountainous place." Nearly fifteen years later, Governor Glen assured Cherokee headmen that any peace agreement would be "fixed and immoveable, like your native Mountains." Outsiders additionally referred to the southern Appalachians as the Cherokee Mountains, while others styled the Cherokees as the "Mountaneers," "Muntins," and "the Mountings." Association with the southern mountains was so entrenched by 1755 that Cherokees denied they migrated "from any other country, but affirm that their ancestors came out of the ground where they now live."[41]

A shared identity had its limits, however. Throughout this chapter, I demonstrate how town and region differentiated Cherokees even as a broader national identity loosely conjoined the Ani-Yun-wiya, or "the Real People," into a distinct ethnopolitical community. When we therefore ask, "Who were the Cherokees?" as did John P. Brown more than seventy years ago, we should recognize a cultural commonality as well as a multiplicity of social and geopolitical disparities that often challenged identification with, and allegiance to, the larger ethnic community. A deeper understanding of the multilayered structures of community likewise applies to indigenous peoples beyond the Cherokees. As the historian Richard

White explains, "There have been few peoples as culturally, politically, and socially complicated as Indians. They demand histories worthy of their dense and tangled lives." These histories should more fully appreciate that the concept of identity, as Raymond Fogelson stresses, "is neither singular nor monolithic but has many dimensions." Such is the case for Native Americans who incorporated a wide array of social and political identities into their own understanding of themselves and their colonial neighbors. We must therefore not approach indigenous sociopolitical organization on an either/or basis, but instead explore the multilayered nature of this collectivity to further unravel the "dense and tangled lives" of Native Americans in early North America. Toward that end, this book delves into the complex world of Cherokee political behavior at the town, regional, and national levels, particularly during the second half of the eighteenth century.[42]

2

"the antient Friendship and Union"

The Anglo-Cherokee Alliance

The year 1670 marked a seminal moment in Cherokee history. Far from the Cherokees' mountain homeland, British colonists planted the seeds of a new epicenter of regional power near the confluence of the Ashley and Cooper Rivers. Charlestown would eventually become the fourth largest city in British North America and the hub of a vast trading network that connected the Atlantic world to the southern hinterlands. The Cherokees at first found little reason to take notice of English maneuverings in the lowcountry. The struggling frontier colony seemed like a distant backwater to the more populous and powerful Cherokees. But Charlestown's manipulation of the Indian slave trade quickly transformed Carolina into the dominant European presence in the colonial Southeast. By 1715, the Cherokees had become fully immersed in the British trade and the wars this trade spawned between indigenous peoples.[1]

The Yamasee War (1715–17) in particular ushered in a new epoch for Cherokee peoples, for it gave rise to both the Anglo-Cherokee alliance and a forty-year war with the Creeks. The alliance in large part centered upon trade. Cherokees harvested large numbers of deerskins in exchange for British manufactured goods, a mutually dependent relationship that became more dependency-based for the Cherokees as the eighteenth century progressed. As early as 1725, a Tenasee headman related they had "been brought up after another Manner than their forefathers," since "they could not live without the English." A Valley headman one generation later assured traders he "loves to see the white People for what is it we can make of ourselves[?]" Immediately following the Seven Years' War, John Stuart agreed that a "Modern Indian cannot subsist without Europeans" due to "their incapacity of subsisting without European Commodities."[2]

Such unambiguous allusions to dependency do not mean scholars are in agreement about the effects of European trade on indigenous cultures. Some scholars envision a rapid transition from native-centered material culture to near total reliance on new tools and weapons. Others see signs of cultural continuity as Indians adapted European technology to complement and maintain indigenous customs. For this study, the issue of dependency is not as important as consumer demand. By the mid-eighteenth century, Cherokee participation in the deerskin trade had become so extensive that villagers from every region eagerly sought inclusion into a wider transatlantic exchange of goods. Whether the Cherokees were truly dependent on European goods thus matters less than their insatiable demand for these goods.[3]

This intense desire and competition for manufactured goods impelled Cherokee leaders to safeguard local and regional access to trade. The English grew increasingly aware of these sociopolitical divisions as a decentralized trading system adapted to the realities of Cherokee community structures. The Anglo-Cherokee trade thus emerged as a town-centered locus of exchange that at times aggravated deep-rooted local and regional tensions. Yet the deerskin trade also provided a degree of commonality among Cherokee peoples. The Cherokees were almost exclusively tied to the British trade based largely out of Charlestown. This reliance on Carolina generated concern as well as frequent efforts to secure other sources of trade, but the remoteness of the Cherokee Mountains meant that Carolina remained the most dependable outlet. Cherokee leaders consequently strengthened their ties to the colony. Through this widening of commercial exchanges with their allies, aspiring headmen learned they could not speak for their own towns only when it came to the trade. The result was a broadening of political communication between Cherokee peoples as headmen embraced regional and national interests to maintain and elevate their authority.

The interplay of multiple identities and allegiances also played out in another immediate consequence of the 1715 Indian uprising, the Cherokee-Creek War (1715–55). Like the deerskin trade, the war forced the British to more clearly understand and engage Cherokee localism and regionalism. South Carolina's agents in Cherokee country, particularly George Chicken, John Herbert, and Alexander Cuming, encountered stiff resistance in their attempts to utilize Cherokees against hostile Creeks. Headmen rejected calls for interregional action against their Muscogean neighbors. Village leaders likewise refused to attend national councils, particularly if convened in a different region, which frustrated Carolina's efforts to centralize relations with the Cherokees. At the same time, however, an increased British economic and diplomatic presence worked against these parochial interests. Intertown and interregional communication intensified among Cherokee peoples as they engaged their new allies. The Treaty of 1730, which tied Cherokees from every village to the British and their trade, correspondingly bound the Cherokees more closely to one another (see maps 2 and 3).

The benefits of this new alliance were not uniformly enjoyed, however. Certain towns and regions held advantages over others during these early years of contact. The Lower Towns especially took advantage of their geographic proximity to Carolina by negotiating trade agreements with representatives from Charlestown. Notable headmen such as the Conjuror of Tugaloo and King Crow of Keowee emerged as key figures in the diplomatic discourse connecting the two peoples, thereby elevating the regional and national importance of their two towns. Other Cherokees responded by manipulating Carolina's fears and ambitions to bring trade and influence to their settlements. The Overhill Towns, for example, initially remained on the periphery of Carolina-Cherokee relations. But colonial competition in the deerskin trade, a stronger French presence in the Southeast, and deteriorating relations with the Creeks forced Carolinians to listen more intently when Overhill leaders projected their own regional identity and power. This political and diplomatic maneuvering by village leaders accordingly played a decisive role in reshaping not only Anglo-Cherokee relations but also the regional dynamic within Cherokee country.

The British became steadily attuned to Cherokee sociopolitical divisions following the Yamasee War. Originating out of Carolina's malevolent role in the Indian slave trade, "the General Indian War in 1715," as many colonists remembered the conflict, witnessed a massive uprising of southeastern Indians against the young colony. Led by the Yamasees and supported by numerous Indians throughout the region, the conflict dramatically altered the geopolitical landscape of the colonial Southeast by displacing most natives from the immediate environs of the Carolina lowcountry. The British thereafter reoriented their Indian affairs toward more

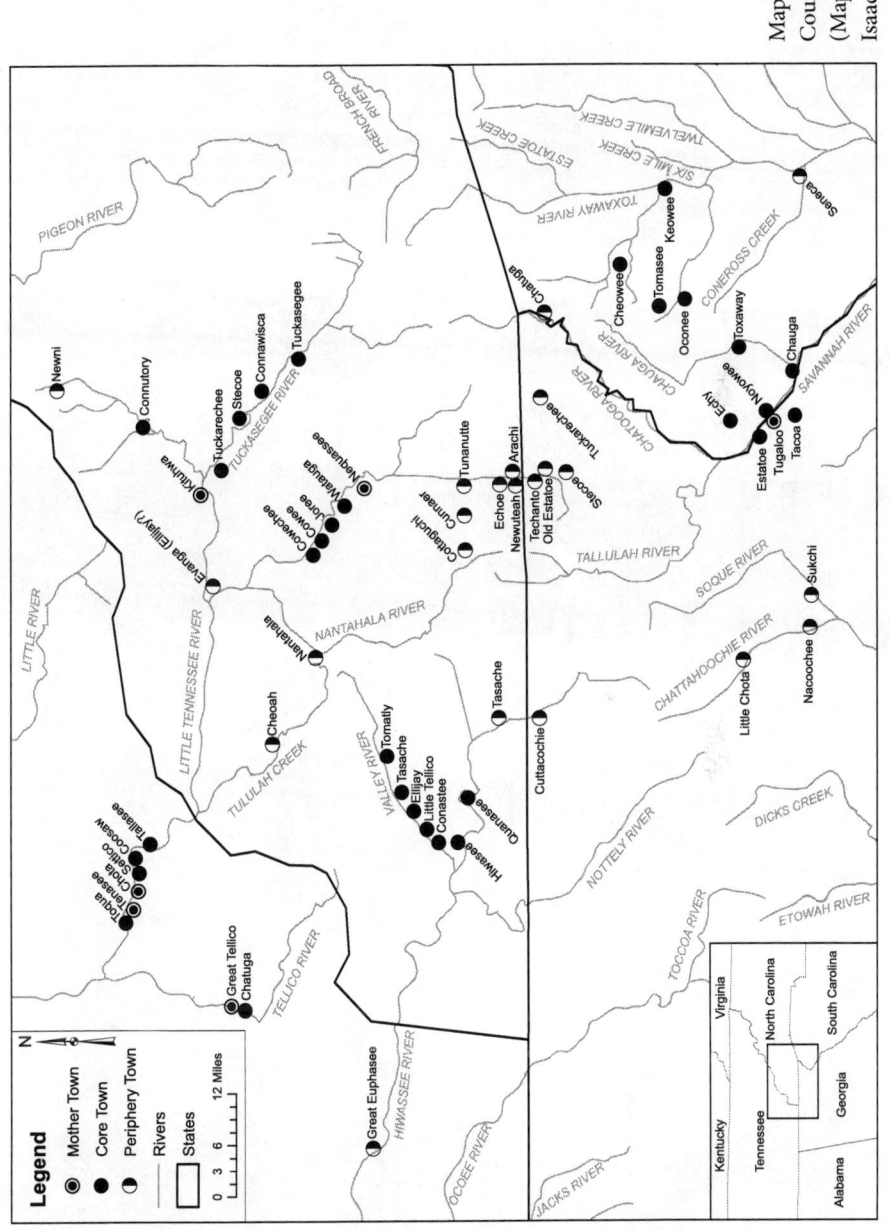

Map 2. Cherokee Country, 1730. (Map designed by Isaac Emrick.)

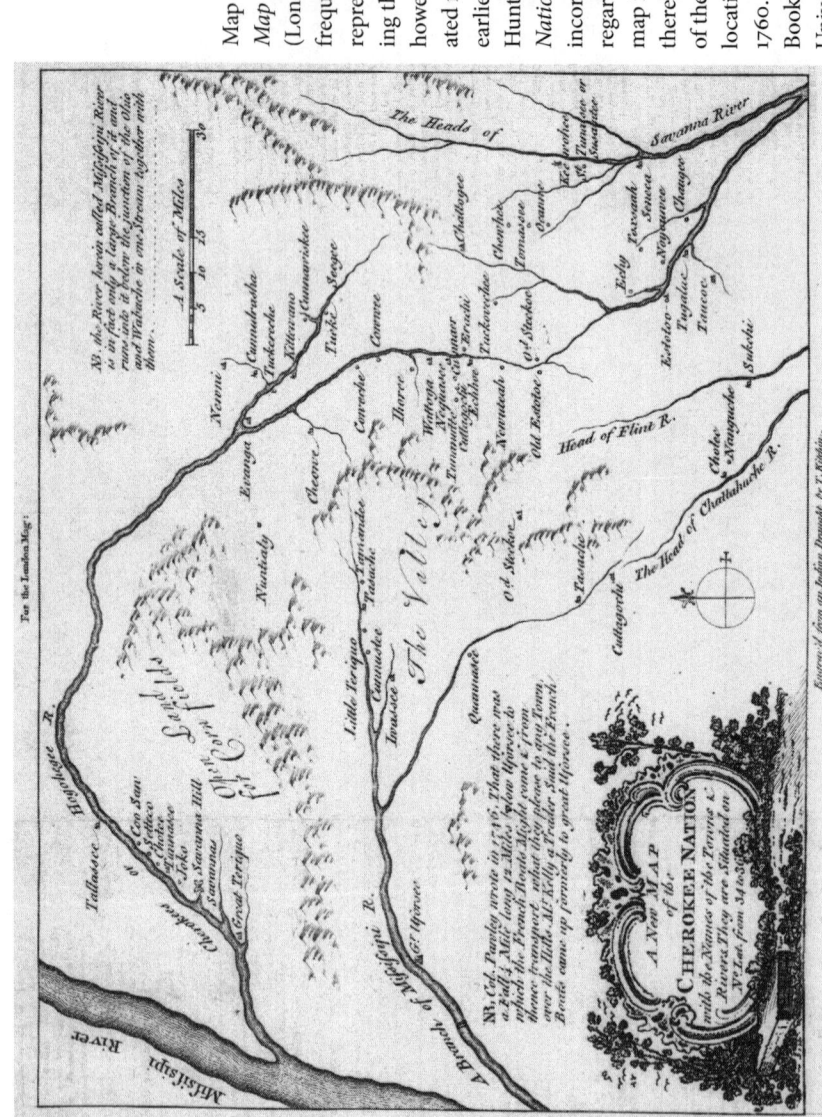

Map 3. Thomas Kitchin, *A New Map of the Cherokee Nation* (London, c.1760). Scholars have frequently employed this map to represent Cherokee country during the Seven Years' War. Kitchin, however, seems to have appropriated most of his information from earlier maps, particularly George Hunter's *Map of the Cherokee Nation—1730*. Although Kitchin incorporated new information regarding the Overhill Towns, his map is nearly identical to Hunter's, thereby giving a false impression of the precise number, names, and locations of Cherokee towns in 1760. (Courtesy of Hargrett Rare Book and Manuscript Library, University of Georgia Libraries.)

numerous and powerful polities in the hinterlands, such as the Creeks and Cherokees. Of particular relevance to these newly consequential relationships were economic exchanges. As suppliers of deerskins and, more importantly, consumers of manufactured goods, Cherokees were able to effectively manipulate the British trade. This was initially evident during the factory system, which characterized the early Anglo-Cherokee trade. In 1716 Carolina established a public monopoly for the Indian trade. This act restricted trade with Indians to factories, or trading posts, primarily located in the colony's interior, such as at Savannah Town and the Congarees. Carolinians expected Cherokees to transport deerskins and British goods to and from these factories. Since horses were not yet widely adopted and trading paths often exposed burdeners to enemy Indians, many Cherokees found the system far from satisfactory.[4]

The Lower Cherokees, however, were not as openly opposed to the system as were townspeople from other regions. The Lower Towns were nearest to Charlestown and thus had a decided advantage in the early stages of the trade. The Conjuror, a prominent Tugaloo headman also known as Charity Hagey, had already established strong ties to Carolina by 1716. John Reid describes him as "the first important Cherokee headman the British encountered," and this early connection to Carolina came with benefits. The Conjuror agreed in July to employ villagers from his towns as burdeners, whereby they would "fetch" goods from Savannah Town. He also ensured that his people would bring their skins to that factory without any promise of packhorses or payment. The Tugaloo headman additionally directed eighty villagers to assist Carolina "in erecting the Buildings" for the new factory at the Congarees. Why would the Conjuror and Lower Towns people agree to provide such generous assistance? They did so to avoid dangerous trading paths near the Cherokee-Creek borderlands, but they also wanted to gain special access to the British trade. The Conjuror received gifts and increased status, as did those townspeople under his direction.[5]

The favorable geopolitical position of Tugaloo and the Lower Towns vis-à-vis Carolina placed other Cherokee regions at a disadvantage. These trading inequities translated into increased regional tensions within Cherokee country. One consequence was that Cherokees from different regions rarely coordinated for their better security. It did not help either when Lower Cherokees appropriated Overhill goods as they passed through their towns, nor did tensions ease when burdeners returned home but failed to "give Notice to the adjacent Towns" of their arrival. Jealousies also arose over the distribution of presents. During the early stages of the trade, Carolinians were unaware of the exact nature of Cherokee regionalism. Traders and officials typically identified only the Upper and Lower Cherokees in their discourse, with the former label encompassing the Middle, Valley, and/or Overhill Towns. Cherokee headmen responded by asserting distinct regional identities, especially when gifts were at stake. When the commissioners of the Indian trade approved a present of 150 guns to the Lower Cherokees, they informed the governor that "the Upper [Cherokees] were promised and expected the same Quantity." Shortly thereafter, a Middle Town headman named Caesar announced that his people also "expect[ed] the Presents of Guns." The commissioners acquiesced, determining to give the Middle Cherokees "as much as to the upper-most People."[6]

When Caesar requested equal favors for the Middle Settlements, a tense intertown and interregional struggle ensued over a change in Carolina's trading policy. Officials in Charlestown, largely as a result of Cherokee pressure, considered establishing factories within Cherokee country itself. Although the commissioners initially demanded that all trade be conducted at Savannah Town and the Congarees, the Cherokees resisted, expressing their "utter dislike in coming down to the Garrisons, to deal." The more prominent headmen solicited Carolina's agent among the Cherokees to place traders and factories within their towns. The problem that emerged, however, was not the commissioners' resistance to the proposal, but Cherokee dissension over where these assistant factors and their posts should be established.[7]

These disagreements partly stemmed from local influences over the public trade. Charlestown allowed agent Theophilus Hastings significant leeway in selecting locations for his assistants, advising him "to place [them] at such Parts of the Nation, as you shall think most proper and beneficial to the Publick." Hastings at first proposed they be employed at Great Tellico (Overhill), Quanasee (Valley), Little Chota (Lower), Tugaloo (Lower), "and one to the Northward of that Place." Recognizing the benefits a trader could bring, Caesar advocated that the last factor reside at his town of Watauga in the Middle Settlements. Hastings approved, which prompted headmen of other towns and regions, such as at Cowee and Tenasee, to request that their towns "be settled with a Factor at each." The commissioners decided those two towns would not get a trader until the first five were established. This decision led to an ugly incident wherein warriors "had beaten Cesar very much" and threatened to kill him. Although the particulars of the disagreement are unknown, we do know that Watauga ultimately did not get a factory; it was placed instead at Cowee and Tenasee.[8]

The Cherokees continued to assert town and regional interests throughout the early stages of the Anglo-Cherokee trade. By refusing to burden packs, embezzling goods, threatening to trade with the Virginians or French, making formal complaints about equal treatment, and a host of other ways, Cherokees educated the British about the decentralized political structure these newcomers tidily labeled "the Cherokee Nation." It was primarily through the early Indian trade that Carolinians learned the realities of Cherokee localism and regionalism.[9]

Another offshoot of the Yamasee War, in addition to increased trade contacts between Carolinians and Cherokees, was the Cherokee-Creek War. The fallout between Cherokees and Creeks in 1715 did not represent a sharp break with the past. Their ancestors had a long history of unstable relations dating back many centuries. Archaeological evidence and place-name analysis indicate that between the sixteenth and eighteenth centuries, Cherokee peoples expanded beyond the mountains into Muscogean-speaking (Creek) areas. The Cherokee towns of Settico, Chilhowee, and Toskegee, for instance, are believed to be Iroquoian corruptions of Muscogean words. The result, according to Charles Hudson, is that "the linguistic frontier in eastern Tennessee shifted in favor of the Cherokees in early historical times, after the period of initial Spanish exploration." This contentious borderland persisted so that newly arrived English observers, such as Henry Woodward, noted in 1674 that Creeks and Cherokees were "at continual warrs." Relations were not eased by the onset of the Yamasee War, and the two peoples were primed for an explosive outbreak.[10]

The spark came at Tugaloo. Carolinians desperately searched for allies as the Indian crisis worsened, thus prompting officials in Charlestown to send a delegation to Cherokee country. Headmen from the Upper Towns had earlier promised to support Carolina against the Creeks, who they believed had instigated the Yamasees to attack the colony and who had also recently killed British traders within their villages. Lower Town headmen, however, appeared unwilling to fight the Yamasees or the Creeks. As the Carolina delegation visited the Overhill Towns, Creek headmen arrived at Tugaloo in the Lower Settlements to discuss the crisis. But Overhill warriors spoiled their talks. Intending to push Lower Cherokees to war against their Creek neighbors, Overhill Cherokees attacked and killed the Creek delegation in what later became known as the "Tugaloo Incident." This act of war not only upended diplomatic protocol of providing safe harbor to visiting delegations; it also forced the Creeks to retaliate, ultimately leading to the Cherokee-Creek War. John Reid attributes great importance to this incident in terms of cross-regional unity: "The killing of their ambassadors was such an insult that the entire Creek nation . . . was certain to demand blood. The Cherokees seldom faced so united a foe, and were themselves forced to unite." The Cherokees "would enter only one other war so united," he continues, "the war against South Carolina in 1759."[11]

Reid's appreciation of Cherokee unity during the Anglo-Cherokee War is well noted, as will be addressed later, but his claim of a unified Cherokee response during this prior conflict is less convincing, especially during its early phases. The war often remained a limited regional conflict as Overhill, Middle, Valley, and Lower Cherokees rarely pursued a common course of action against the Creeks. The decidedly non-national scope of the Cherokee-Creek War was particularly apparent when South Carolina sent Colonels George Chicken and John Herbert as agents among the Cherokees in the mid-1720s. Chicken visited Cherokee country in 1725 and again the following year, leaving detailed accounts of his diplomatic mission. Chicken had been authorized to discuss matters relating to trade, the Anglo-Cherokee alliance, and the Creeks. He arrived in the Lower Towns in midsummer and then traveled to other regions, including the distant Overhill Towns, to relate his intention of convening "a General Meeting of the head Men of the whole Nation" at Ellijay in the Valley Settlements.[12] Chicken, through previous dealings with the Cherokees during the Yamasee War, knew well the importance of personally visiting the different towns. Recognizing the local and regional structures of Cherokee leadership, he made certain to meet the "King of the lower people" as well as the "King of the Upper people" in their respective townhouses.[13]

The "King of the lower people" was a headman from Keowee, an indication of power shifts within the Lower Towns from "Togelo parts" to the Keowee River settlements. The Tugaloo River towns, which at that time included Chauga, Toxaway, Echy, Noyowee, Old Estatoe, Tacoa, and Tugaloo, had initially commanded Carolina's attention and favor. The

Conjuror of Tugaloo emerged as the leading spokesman for the region and a key middleman in the early Anglo-Cherokee trade. Carolina's principal factor established his residence at Tugaloo, and the town's proximity to the Lower Creeks ensured it remained a diplomatic center for Creeks, Cherokees, and Carolinians. But the Conjuror died in 1719. Tugaloo thereafter suffered not only from a leadership void but also from its location near the hotly contested Creek borderlands. (It did not help either that the massacre of Creek headmen occurred in the Tugaloo townhouse.) Creek warriors attacked Tugaloo and its adjacent towns and waylaid the trading paths that connected these Cherokees to Carolina.[14]

While not immune to Creeks raiders, Keowee and its neighbors proved the beneficiaries of these post-Yamasee developments. King Crow of Keowee supplanted the deceased Conjuror as the leading spokesman for the Lower Cherokees. Chicken understood he had the management of twenty-one towns, which included those villages along the Keowee, Tugaloo, Chatooga, and Chattahoochee River watersheds. Keowee subsequently became the focal point of Carolina's trading and diplomatic activities in the Lower Towns—a shift in intraregional power that would continue well into the eighteenth century. To be sure, Tugaloo and its adjacent towns remained important to Anglo-Cherokee relations, but Carolinians increasingly looked upon Keowee as "the first Town of the Cherrokees," both geographically and diplomatically.[15]

The Lower Towns were only one region, however. Cherokees in other areas protected their own interests, which could often be at odds. Chicken continually struggled against these regional political tensions during his travels throughout Cherokee country. The first signs of resistance began in Ellijay, the intended site of the upcoming interregional council. Chicken earlier informed Ellijay and other Middle and Valley leaders that he expected them to "go over the Hills" to attend his talks with the Overhill people at Tenasee. On the morning of their departure, Ellijay headmen notified Chicken "that they were desirous to hear the talk in their own Town and that they had no Mind to go over the Hills." The colonel responded in "a Sharp Manner," which prompted Middle and Valley leaders to reluctantly send three representatives "out of Each Town" to Tenasee.[16]

Following the Overhill conference, Chicken returned to Ellijay in preparation for the general meeting. He once again grew frustrated upon hearing that "the head men of the whole Nation were not mett at Elejoy according to their promise." Although the "King and head men of all the Upper People" arrived on schedule, Lower Town leaders failed to appear. Chicken learned the Lower Cherokee delegation had gathered some miles away at Nacoochee and "they Expected to have the talk there." The colonel immediately dispatched a messenger to remind the headmen of their previous agreement to hear the talk "at no other place then Elejoy." After missing the appointed day of the conference, the delegation finally showed, blaming a miscommunication about time as the reason for their delay. Still, not all Lower Cherokee leaders attended the meeting. Chicken noted that most headmen throughout the nation were present, but "a few of the Lower Towns" had boycotted the council. These ten towns later hosted Chicken at a Green Corn Dance at Keowee, where they listened to him deliver the governor's message.[17]

Chicken struggled to assemble the "whole Nation" at Ellijay, in part because the substance of his talks, especially those regarding the Creeks, fueled much disagreement within and between the different regions. When he arrived in Cherokee country in 1725, there were few signs that the Cherokee-Creek War was in remission. Chicken's journal frequently referenced borderland hostilities between Cherokee and Creek peoples. This ostensible common Creek enemy prompted Carolina's agent to encourage Cherokees from different towns and regions to unite their forces, but his proposals won few adherents among village leaders.

Chicken particularly wanted Cherokees to undertake joint offensive operations. Beginning with the most exposed Lower Towns along Tugaloo River, he "Sumoned all the head men of Togelo parts" to a meeting in mid-September. Chicken pressed these villagers to abandon their defensive tactics, which typically included taking refuge within their "well ffortifyed" towns and sending limited scouting parties to discover the enemy. The colonel advised them to instead "raise an Army" consisting of "Ten Men out of Each Town," which could meet the enemy "before they come Nigh your Towns." King Crow agreed to discuss the matter with headmen from adjacent towns, after which they promised to increase their scouting efforts. Chicken seemed little pleased with the Lower Cherokees' determination to defend their towns through scouting and fortification rather than by organizing an intraregional army as he suggested. King Crow responded that he appreciated Chicken's advice, but his people would "go to Warr when they pleased . . . and that they were not like White Men."

They "will have their own way of Warring," he continued, and "it would be good if the English would let them alone and see what they will do of themselv's." King Crow's resistance reflected cross-cultural disagreement over proper methods of warfare, but it also indicated an unwillingness among Lower Cherokees to attack the Lower Creeks, especially through participation in a multi-town fighting force.[18]

Chicken then attempted to effect the same measures among Overhill, Valley, and Middle Cherokees. He employed one of Carolina's most capable Overhill traders, Eleazar Wiggan, "to Encourage the people in your parts to goe out in a body" against the Creeks. Chicken specifically called upon the warriors of "their Inland Towns" to raise an army "to Defend their Frontier Towns." Equally presumptuous, he asked Wiggan to persuade this Upper Cherokee army "to Joyn these Lower people who I don't doubt but will be very ready to Joyn them." The Upper Cherokees seemed willing to comply. At the Green Corn Dance in early October, headmen from the Overhill, Middle, and Valley Towns met at Little Tellico to discuss the proposal. They agreed to "joyn a body of these lower [Cherokee] people" to attack the Upper and Lower Creeks at Okfuskee and Cussita towns. They also formulated a plan to let the Creeks "come to their Towns, but not undiscovered" and "give them a Smash in their Towns First and then to gather all their Strength and follow them" as the Creeks retreated with their wounded men. Unlike past strategies of warfare and ones that differed significantly with the Lower Cherokees, Upper Cherokee headmen vowed to not "lett them goe away and not follow them as they have always done." Once again, Lower Cherokees stymied Chicken's efforts to unite villagers from different towns and regions. Although King Crow "was very glad" Chicken traveled "amongst them to do good for the whole Nation," he nevertheless emphatically told Carolina's agent "that the Upper people might take their own Method [of war] as they would theirs."[19]

Chicken pressed Cherokees to war against the Creeks, even as South Carolina sought to stabilize relations with its Muscogean neighbors and to mediate a peace between the Cherokees and Creeks. Toward this end, Tobias Fitch served as Chicken's counterpart among the Creeks in 1725. He had been instructed to determine whether both the Upper and Lower Creeks desired to end hostilities against the Cherokees and, if so, to promote a general peace between the two peoples. Concluding a general peace, however, proved problematic for several reasons. First, sporadic raiding continued throughout the peace process. Younger warriors in particular complicated the efforts of conciliatory headmen as they revenged lost clan members and sought war titles. Difficulties also arose from perceptions of power, since neither Cherokees, Creeks, nor South Carolinians wanted to pursue peace from a position of weakness. Creek leaders spurned Carolina's mediation, for instance, arguing that peace talks could resume only after the "Blow that we think to give" the Cherokees. Likewise, when Cherokee headmen refused to send tokens of peace to the Lower Creeks, Fitch reminded them that such tokens were customarily sent "from a people Submitting to those they send to, which the Cherokees are not Submitting unto you." Fitch accordingly reiterated South Carolina's offer to negotiate peace so that "neither of you Submit to each other." But Lower Creeks failed to acknowledge Carolina's request at that time, prompting officials in Charlestown to play the same game. The Council proposed to "not further concern themselves" with peace until Creek leaders thought fit to apply to the government for that purpose.[20]

Two additional factors took precedence in hindering a general peace between the Cherokees and Creeks in the mid-1720s: the Tugaloo Incident and the Chickasaws. Bitter memories of the massacre at Tugaloo had not lessened ten years later. Most of that delegation had represented the Lower Creeks who accordingly proved the most unreceptive to reconciliation. Coweta headmen informed Fitch they "will hear nothing of a Peace . . . we have not forgot them Men yet that was killed there in Cold blood when the White People was there and that remains in our Minds and shall do as long as one of us is alive." Fitch countered this single-mindedness by noting that both Cherokees and South Carolinians were involved in the massacre. "If you insist upon Satisfaction for what was done at Tugolu," Fitch replied, "you must have it from us as well as the Cherrokees for we set the Cherrokees to do that and helped to do it our selves." Fitch hit upon a second stumbling block to peace that stemmed from the Tugaloo Incident. South Carolinians had allied themselves with the Cherokees who were longtime enemies of the Creeks. Lower Creeks thus blamed Cherokees and Carolinians for the deaths of notable village leaders at Tugaloo.[21]

They also blamed the Cherokee-Chickasaw alliance for the continuation of hostilities. Echoing arguments that would later apply to "Northward" Indians, Creek leaders refused to entertain peace proposals while Cherokees received assistance from Chickasaw warriors who also killed and enslaved their people. Chigilli of Coweta believed Creeks and Cherokees would always be at war "as long as the Chickesaw are harboured amongst them." If the Cherokees "will destroy the Chickasaws in their Towns," the Lower Creek headman added, "I shall readily consent to a peace." Fitch thought the request unreasonable, informing Chigilli it appeared unlikely that Cherokees would harm an ally "who have assisted them in their War against you."[22]

Neither Fitch nor his superiors could force the hand of Cherokees in regard to the Chickasaws. Nevertheless, the Chickasaws posed a severe obstacle to both Carolinian and Cherokee efforts to stabilize relations with the Creeks, especially the Upper Creeks. The possibility of a regionally based peace with the Upper Creeks only appeared likely as Lower Creeks rejected third-party mediation and continued hostilities against Carolinians and Cherokees. As efforts toward a general peace dissipated between 1725 and 1727, South Carolina attempted to isolate the Lower Creeks while simultaneously maintaining friendly relations with the Upper Creeks. To do so, they needed Cherokees from every region on board—a task commissioned to Colonel John Herbert.[23]

Herbert traveled among the Cherokees during the winter of 1727-28. At a meeting at Nequassee in the Middle Towns, Carolina's agent pressed their allies "to look no more on the Lower Creeks as friends to you or the English." The "Upper Creeks were still our friends," he added, and "it was the lower Creeks only that were the Rogues." Herbert repeated this message at Tasache in the Valley Settlements, obtaining assurances from those headmen and warriors they would "all go in a body [to war] & leave their Weomen to hoe their Corn." The Overhill people likewise accepted Herbert's talk at a meeting in the Great Tellico townhouse. The Long Warrior of Tenasee vowed to "never look on the Lower Creeks to be friends any more," while a headman from Tellico promised "to Warr against the lower Creeks." Herbert consequently reported to officials in Charlestown that his trip had been a success, for Cherokees from all regions had "as bad a Notion of the Lower Creeks as can be expected."[24]

Cherokee leaders received Herbert's talk because Lower Creeks continually rebuffed peace overtures. The Upper Creeks, on the other hand, were more receptive. Challenging the inflexible position of the Lower Creeks, and more particularly the town of Coweta, Upper Creek headmen appeared "resolved to make a Separate Peace." A headman from Okfuskee went even further, claiming "if the Lower [Creek] people would not make a peace that they would remove & settle some where near the Cherokee Towns." Although the Okfuskee people did not relocate, they and other Upper Creeks promised to end hostilities, but on one condition: the Chickasaws could not be included in any treaty. They weren't, and Herbert later observed during his visit to the Overhill Towns that "the upper Creeks are in firm alliance with them & us."[25]

Overhill leaders were the most active in easing tensions with the Upper Creeks, a trend that continued throughout the forty-year conflict with limited success. Village headmen at times pursued peace independently. Reports indicated in 1726, for example, that Overhill headmen had gone "last year to make a Peace with the Creeks of themselves." This was initially unwelcome news because Carolina seemed adamant about dictating the affairs of war and peace for their indigenous neighbors. They must not make a peace "without our Leave," read the Council's instructions to Chicken, for "we will take [it] upon us to bring it about." In an equally audacious manner, when Overhill headmen entertained peace overtures from Nottoway Indians, the Council bluntly declared, "We will not suffer them to make any peace with foreign Nations without our Consent and upon our Terms for that we know what is best for them."[26]

Such attitudes speak to the ways in which the external pressures of European diplomacy shaped internal Cherokee political structures. While British officials attempted to impose their authority on Cherokees, in fact they could not dictate to their allies; they could only persuade, much like leading men within the Cherokee villages. Colonial governors, for instance, bestowed commissions upon influential headmen. These commissions served to bolster the position of village leaders, for as the historian John Oliphant rightfully observes, "A claim of particular influence with the Europeans was a big step towards prestige and power at home." But the British did not create leaders. Instead, Cherokees chose their own headmen and allowed them to remain in power by way of consensus. The British would then confirm these leaders with commissions. Governor Glen acknowledged that a Tellico headman held power at the behest of his followers, yet he made certain the headman's authority was "confirmed to you by the Commission which I shall give you."[27]

In dismissing Cherokee agency, some scholars have made too much of British influences on Cherokee political structures. These authors stress the centralizing tendencies of Anglo-Cherokee interactions. Indeed, looking backward from the early nineteenth century, when Cherokees constructed a more western oriented nation-state, it is easy to see their political history as an evolutionary shift "toward a greater centralization of power." But scurrying to the end of what we know eventuated does not accurately recount eighteenth-century Cherokee politics and those generations of Cherokees whose political experiences and allegiances rested not with tribal sovereignty but instead at the local and regional levels. Nowhere is this more evident than in the fanciful journey of a Scottish adventurer, Sir Alexander Cuming.[28]

Cuming traveled to Cherokee country in 1730. As an unofficial agent working in the British interest, Cuming summoned Cherokee leaders from every region to meet at Nequassee. Pushing them further than Colonel Chicken, who earlier "expected their answers to be generall and in one Voice," Cuming insisted that representatives "bring full Power" to elect an "emperor" of the Cherokee nation. The chosen leader was Moytoy of Tellico. According to Cuming, he became "Emperor over the whole" and was given "unlimited Power . . . by the unanimous Consent of the whole People." Attempting to centralize Cherokee politics in relation to the British, Cuming declared that head warriors and other village leaders thereafter "should answer for the Conduct of their People to Moytoy," else "they might become no People, if they violated their Promise and Obedience." As Cherokee political history after 1730 demonstrates, however, the Emperor of Tellico never became the "Emblem of universal Sovereignty over the whole Cherrokee Nation" that Cuming desired. Instead, local headmen and regional leaders maintained their autonomy by resisting English efforts to create centralized leadership.[29]

Yet, in giving the Cherokees deserved agency in these processes, caution must be used so as not to downplay the significant transformative effect of British diplomacy on Cherokee political developments. The British, too, had a hand in the political maneuvering that took place within Cherokee villages. Already notable headmen and warriors "of their own Choosing" became even more influential once "Approved of by the English." Of course, those headmen most sympathetic to the British held advantages in the pursuit of political power. King Crow, for instance, held one of the highest positions in the Lower Cherokee body politic, but George Chicken dismissed his ability to lead. He instead favored Old Breakerface as the "properest person for a King for these parts." Chicken identified him as one of "the Most Noted Men in the Nation," in large part because he was "a good man to the English." In another example,

John Herbert's discourse with Choatehee of Tellico revealed how English approval—or the lack thereof—could affect the headman's standing with the government and thus his standing at home. When Choatehee's talk pleased Herbert, Carolina's agent told him this "would distinguish him as a good friend to the English," and he "should give the English Govr: an account of it." But once the Tellico headman's sincerity became suspect, Herbert casually threatened, "If you are not willing to mind the English Govr's: talk I can't help it, but can only acquaint him of it when I go down." Choatehee subsequently changed course to secure Herbert's approval once again.[30]

Early diplomatic ties to the British marked a watershed in Cherokee political history for other reasons, namely the intensification of interregional communication and connectedness. The loosely formed Cherokee nation of the early eighteenth century became more identifiable through increased interactions with South Carolina, which facilitated increased interactions among their own people. The diplomatic proceedings of Chicken, Herbert, Cuming, and others testify to the cross-regional political activity generated by British agents and the government they represented. What made the English vastly different from other borderland participants was the extent to which Cherokees from every town and region were forced to engage their new neighbor. Cuming's visit in 1730 played a critical role in this engagement, not because Cuming crowned the Emperor of Tellico at Nequassee, but because he accompanied a diplomatic envoy of Cherokee leaders to England that same year. These seven headmen, which included Attakullakulla, signed a treaty that made the Anglo-Cherokee alliance official and bound all Cherokees to the British and vice versa. We must not take this agreement lightly, though it is easy to do so. The history of Indian-white relations in North America is one of treaties and the total disregard of these treaties—often by peoples on both sides—but the Treaty of 1730 was considered sacred and legally binding by both the Cherokees and British. It was at its most basic level the foundation of their "antient Friendship and Union," which was begun at first contact, secured during the Yamasee War, and codified by the Treaty of 1730. And as Tom Hatley notes, it served as "the basis of relations between the tribe and colony" for more than thirty years.[31]

This treaty for the British was in many ways a continuation of Cuming's attempts at centralization that had occurred at Nequassee. Negotiators in London understood those seven headmen spoke with "the Words of all your People," for they had been deputed by the Emperor of Tellico "with the Consent and Approbation of the whole Nation of the Cherokee Indians at a General Meeting at Nikossen [Nequassee]." No doubt this understanding derived from the exaggerated accounts of Cuming while in Cherokee country, which notified the Board of Trade that Cherokee headmen had, on bended knee, declared their obedience to King George II. The British later interpreted this to mean that Cherokees had "paid their Homage to his Majesty as *Subjects*, and not as *Allies*, to the Crown of Great Britain." By declaring themselves "Subjects of Great Britain," which occurred "without either fraud or force," the Cherokees allegedly "made a formal Surrender of their Territories" to the king.[32]

Such accounts seem hardly believable, at least as they were fashioned by Cuming and his adherents. The Cherokees appear instead to have ritualized their alliance with Britain through ceremonial gestures. As Anglo-Cherokee relations thereafter would show, Cherokees interpreted the Treaty of 1730 as a trading alliance, not as a willing surrender of their lands to "His Majesty." The first of these "Articles of Friendship and Commerce" required "the English in Carolina, to Trade with the Indians, and to furnish them with all manner of Goods that they want." The fourth article additionally stipulated that Cherokees would "not suffer their People to trade with the white Men of any other Nation but the English." Herein lies the crux of the Anglo-Cherokee alliance and the rationale for the expectations that both peoples held for themselves and each other. The British, especially those in South Carolina, wanted to monopolize the deerskin trade at the expense of the French and Spanish (and to a lesser extent, their colonial competitors in Virginia and Georgia). Village leaders expected Carolina in turn to keep them fully supplied. Fulfilling these two all-important treaty obligations, however, proved remarkably difficult for both Cherokees and Carolinians.[33]

The demise of the factory system was one indication of problems yet to come. Failing to meet projected profits or the demands of their indigenous trading clients, Carolina's factory system gradually came to an end, replaced instead with an increasingly privatized and decentralized Indian trade. British traders and packhorsemen subsequently poured into Cherokee country in such numbers that Charlestown experienced great difficulty in attempting to enforce even minimal regulation of the trade. The result was the private sector largely directed its own course without significant governmental interference. This decentralized trading milieu allowed Cherokees to further manipulate the British trade in favor of local and regional interests.[34]

Edmond Atkin, who later became superintendent of Indian Affairs in the Southern District, wrote at length about this decentralized trade that coalesced during the second quarter of the eighteenth century. One of his biggest complaints was the lack of uniform regulation and enforcement, as each colony directed its own trade with the Indians. The "Conduct of our Colonies hath been as various as their different Interests," he noted, "which have been the Foundation of as many distinct local and partial Considerations." Though describing the British colonies, his observations readily apply to Cherokee country, which similarly exhibited its own brand of "local and partial Considerations." Atkin found that Cherokee visits to Charlestown had increasingly "become less National, and more Partial, and from Particular Towns only." One consequence of both British decentralization and Cherokee localism was that traders residing among their Indian clients wielded an extraordinary amount of influence.[35]

James Beamer, for example, had traded in the Lower Towns for almost twenty-five years by midcentury. Primarily based at Estatoe, eyewitnesses noted he was "so connected with that Place that the Savages are quite at his Command." When William Byrd of Virginia attempted to recruit Estatoe warriors to Virginia during the Seven Years' War, he praised Beamer for his assistance, for had the trader "been inclined he could have prevented me from raising a single man out of his town." This town-based trading relationship established by Beamer and the Estatoe people at times irritated other Lower Cherokees. Tistoe of Keowee complained to officials that his town had no trader except Beamer, "and that is like Borrowing, for when the Skins are gone he is gone." Equally disconcerting to Tistoe was the poor quality of goods Beamer carried to Keowee, they being "only the refuse of what his [Estatoe] People want."[36]

Cornelius Daugherty was another trader with long-established connections not only to his town of Quanasee but to all the Valley Cherokees. "I may say without Vanity," he wrote to Governor Glen, "that I have no small Sway and Influence over the Emperor and Tassittee, and all the head Men of these Parts." In another instance, he claimed "all the Towns in the Valley belong to him"—an assumption that did not sit well with his rivals, nor with some Valley headmen who desired additional traders to meet their people's growing demand for British goods. Daugherty's claims may have been self-serving; nevertheless, both he and Beamer exemplify the tendency for trader influences to remain strongest in the town and region wherein they lived. One of the few governmental regulations generally followed was the assigning of specific towns to individual traders. The more established traders therefore became intimately connected to both the people and place with which they were most familiar. Most traders married or partnered with Cherokee women who were often related to leading men. Traders and headmen themselves formed close personal and economic ties, which led to mutually beneficial (and binding) relationships. Traders could recommend headmen and warriors to the governor as well as channel goods and gifts to their favorites. Headmen, on the other hand, protected traders from angry townspeople or hostile enemies, while also offering protection from creditors and the authorities in Charlestown. When Carolina demanded the detainment of Samuel Jarron at Toqua, an Overhill headman refused because he regarded Jarron "as one of our Brothers. He has lived among us several Years; he has had some of our Women, and has got Children by them. He is our Relation, and shan't be taken up."[37]

As alluded to by the Overhill headman, Cherokee kinship structures reinforced local and regional patterns of trade. Village leaders first looked after their own people when attempting to secure a trade because, to a certain degree, the more immediate family members lived within the same town. This is particularly true in the case of the household. One visitor to Cherokee country observed how a notable headman had created "a numerous family of children and grand-children,—they all together form a little village." Another eyewitness noted that the village at Wachowee had "twelve houses and families, all related to one another." Cherokee towns therefore consisted of multigenerational, matrilineal households that could be large. Headmen, as husbands, were part of these households, so when headmen sought goods for their towns, they also looked to supply their households. But too much preferential treatment to one's household or clan could undermine a leader's standing in the community. Since Cherokees from all seven clans usually lived within each town, headmen were expected to behave as if they had no clan affiliation. Minding the welfare of the entire town was evident in the redistribution of trade goods. John Stuart found village leaders "often the poorest and worst provided of any in the community," as they placed a town-based community ethos above the individual, household, or clan.[38]

Familial ties also had an intertown dimension, as marriage complicated any singular town loyalty for headmen. Husbands were not of the same clan as their wives, because the incest taboo prevented men from marrying within their own clan. Once married, men moved into the household of their wives, which might be in a town different from their place of birth. Husbands subsequently developed loyalties to both towns—a point made by Raymond Fogelson in his study of the Cherokee ball play. Fogelson finds that married men showed "allegiance both to their town of origin and to the town in which they reside." If a match has been organized between a player's two towns, for instance, "he usually does not play ball against his town of origin." Furthermore, if a married man maintained close connections to his town of origin, he could play for his old town against another town but not against the town in which he currently lived. This also held true for conjurors of the ball play rituals, since "No instances have been encountered in which a conjurer worked against his town of origin or town of residence."[39]

These same principles applied to leadership. The town affiliation of a headman could derive from his birthplace or newly acquired residence (or both), thereby creating dual political loyalties and associations. Saluy, for example, noted that two towns belonged to him, Tugaloo and Estatoe. Tugaloo was his birthplace, while Estatoe was his town of residence. The "Raven of Toogoloo, formerly of Nookasee," the "Warriour of Toogelo & Chagey," and "Ulustee of Keowee" who lived at Tomatly were other headmen with political connections between towns. These connections most likely stemmed from marriage, though the records do not specify such. Regardless, the larger point is that both towns held significance for married headmen, and this factored into the pursuit of trade goods from their English allies.[40]

Kinship connections within the village and beyond encouraged the Anglo-Cherokee trade to become more regional and national in scope. Though headmen strived to protect local access to trade, the necessity of acquiring goods for neighboring villagers increasingly became apparent to ambitious leaders. The Raven of Toxaway learned this lesson the hard way. Upon receiving a large supply of presents from Governor Glen, the Raven "never gave the Kewohee People any Thing . . . for which Reason they will not hear any Thing from him." Other Lower Town headmen sided with the Keowee people and would "not hear your Excellency's Talk from the Raven." They instead voiced their desire to visit the governor in Charlestown to personally make known their intention to "not allow the

Raven of Tacksaway to be Head Man but of his own Town [only]." In this instance, Governor Glen approved of the Raven as a person of expansive authority, but Keowee and other Lower Cherokee leaders resisted British efforts to elevate an objectionable headman as a regional leader.[41]

Aspiring headmen who failed to acquire goods for other towns and regions took note. The deerskin trade subsequently encouraged greater interaction between Cherokees from different towns and regions, as village leaders aimed to ensure a steady supply of European goods throughout their mountain homeland. Overhill headmen reminded the British of this policy, declaring that "they looked out for a supply for their whole Nation." Superintendent Atkin similarly maintained that acquiring goods was a "National Interest" for all Indians. "The policy of Indians is Simple and Plain," he wrote. "Tis confined to the Securing their personal Safety, a Supply of their Wants, and fair Usage." Thus, when parochial interests threatened their trading activities, Cherokees from all towns and regions vigorously responded. Nowhere was this more evident than in the Panic of 1751.[42]

In 1751 a series of incidents, compounded by the spread of rumors, tested the Anglo-Cherokee trading alliance. At the Out Town of Stecoe, Cherokees plundered the store of British trader Bernard Hughs. Lower Town warriors from Keowee attacked and killed an Englishman at the Oconees in northern Georgia, while warriors from another Lower Town, Estanauly, shot and wounded a trader named Murphy. The Overhill Town of Tenasee forgot its place and sent Governor Glen an insolent talk that seemed "to despise the Power of this Government." The Panic of 1751, as it has been termed by the historian Gregory Evans Dowd, elicited a strong reaction from James Glen.[43]

Governor Glen threatened the Cherokees with "certain Ruin and Destruction" if they failed to offer proper satisfaction. Yet Glen also intimated he had no intention of punishing "the Innocent for the Guilty." His initial response was therefore fully grounded in an awareness of, and appreciation for, Cherokee localism and regionalism. Glen recognized the offenses had been given by "some few particular Persons, and of two or three Towns," and he assured Cherokee leaders that those "who behaved well have Nothing to fear." The governor accordingly made selective threats against the most culpable towns, specifically the Out towns of Stecoe, Kituhwa, and Conontoroy (Connutory) and the Lower towns of Estanauly and Keowee. He simultaneously wrote to Carolina's "good

Friends" in other towns within the same region to pressure their misguided neighbors. Glen asked Tomasee leaders, for instance, to interpret his talk to both Estanauly and Keowee to effect a speedy delivery of the guilty individuals. To the Out Towns, he requested that Tuckasegee headmen "condemn the Conduct of your three neighboring Towns, Kettewa, Stickhoy, and Conotory."[44]

Glen was especially active in maintaining correspondence with the Raven of Hiwassee, one of the most influential Valley headmen who carried great weight among townspeople from other regions. Utilizing a longtime trader as a go-between, Glen stressed the "friendly and affectionate Manner" for which he had always held the Raven. He commended the Valley leader for preventing "your own Towns from being infected with the Madness of others." Glen, however, remained firm in his efforts to exact justice, advising the Raven it was "for the Good of the whole Cherokee Nation to punish those few who have misbehaved." Perhaps overestimating the significance of regional divisiveness, Glen expected the Raven and his Valley people "to join us if at any Time we should be under a Necessity of sending Forces . . . to punish any other Towns who have behaved ill and as Enemies."[45]

However improbable it might seem for Cherokees from one region to join against those of another, Glen's communications appropriately underscore the importance of town and regional political structures. Cherokee responses to the crisis reinforced Glen's belief that only certain individuals and towns were involved in the recent troubles, as village leaders quickly distanced themselves from the incidents. Overhill headmen later told Glen, "When there was much Disturbance in other Parts of the Nation they were quiet here," as they "had little or no Hand in the Mischief." A Lower Town leader likewise related he lived "a great Way from the Towns where those Things happened and from whence those bad Talks came." The Raven of Hiwassee in particular denounced the actions of "those rogue Towns" and sent messengers to tell the Out Towns that "their Doggs, and their Hoggs, and themselves run mad." Using more than strong words to chastise the offenders, the Raven looked to the power of trade as a deterrent. The Valley headman advised Glen "that those [Out] Towns who done this Mischief should have no Traders amongst them." If trade with the Out people was temporarily suspended, counseled the Raven, then those villagers would more readily "acknowledge their Faults" after having "weary Leggs to walk to Traders in other Towns to buy what they want."[46]

Officials in Charlestown liked what they heard from the Raven and pressed Governor Glen to enact a trade embargo, not against the guilty towns, as the Raven suggested, but against all Cherokees. Glen initially resisted, arguing that their behavior had "not merited any such Treatment as entirely to stop the Trade from the whole Nation." It was true some towns in the Lower and Out Settlements had "not been so much our Friends as could be wished," but "what have the other two or three and forty Towns done. It can never be surmissed that the overhill Towns and the valley Towns have ever misbehaved." Glen reminded the Committee on Indian Affairs that his policy of exploiting town and regional differences had worked before in a similar situation. On that occasion, a packhorseman had been killed, and villagers refused to hand over the murderer. Glen subsequently pressured Cherokee leaders from neighboring towns to act, which led to "a general Meeting of the Head Men . . . who came to a Resolution to reduce that Town to Ashes, and to put all in it to Death, unless they give Satisfaction to the English, which was immediately done."[47]

Glen nevertheless acquiesced to political pressure and ordered all traders to leave Cherokee country until "they come to a better Way of thinking." Yet the governor did not abandon his policy of working within the Cherokee political framework, for he believed an embargo would prevent disturbances from becoming general by encouraging blameless Cherokees to act against hostile towns. Instead, the embargo heightened tensions between Carolina and the Cherokees as a dwindling supply of goods negatively impacted all townspeople. Headmen throughout Cherokee country pleaded for the reestablishment of trade. They frequently referenced previous agreements, particularly the Treaty of 1730, in which the British promised to keep the Cherokees well supplied. Since Carolina failed to uphold its end of the alliance, Cherokees intensified their efforts to establish trading partnerships with Georgia, Virginia, and the French. The Panic of 1751 therefore held long-term consequences for the Anglo-Cherokee alliance, as the pursuit of trading outlets drew mountain villagers into the heart of the impending imperial crisis, as will be discussed in chapters 4 and 5.[48]

The more immediate concern, however, lay in resolving the conflict with Carolina. A cross-regional delegation accordingly visited Charlestown to smooth relations. Promises were made on both sides to make amends, but, as it turned out, satisfaction was not forthcoming. Cherokee leaders did not fully reimburse traders or deliver the guilty individuals for punishment. A steady trade was also slow in returning to the Cherokee towns. It seemed in the best interests of both parties to let recent troubles pass without pressing the issue. Why such an uneventful end to the crisis? For one, many of the most alarming reports were later unsubstantiated. Carolinians also worried about the growing French presence in the Southeast and held a similar uneasiness about their commercial competitors in Georgia and Virginia. The Cherokees had their own problems, namely, rapidly destabilizing relations with the Creeks, and thus maintaining solid relations with Carolina was of the utmost importance.[49]

The entrenched nature of Cherokee localism and regionalism became steadily apparent to Carolinians through their economic and diplomatic exchanges with the Ani-Yun-wiya. Villagers and their headmen manipulated both the deerskin trade and borderland unrest to promote local interests, which could complement or challenge the interests of Cherokees in other towns and regions. The British recognized these divisions even as they attempted to centralize relations with their indigenous neighbors. Though largely stymied in these efforts throughout the first half of the eighteenth century, the British nevertheless profoundly shaped Cherokee politics. Political communication and connections intensified among villagers as the Anglo-Cherokee trading alliance touched nearly every corner of their mountain homeland.

The British also influenced shifts in town and regional power. The Lower Towns people in particular emerged as key go-betweens connecting Cherokees and Carolinians. Tugaloo and then Keowee benefited most directly from this association, but these benefits came with costs. The burgeoning Anglo-Cherokee friendship corresponded with a meltdown in Cherokee-Creek relations, the consequences of which proved most detrimental to the Lower Towns. As the Creek War escalated, Cherokees in other regions more forcefully projected their own agendas as they looked to secure trading and diplomatic privileges from the British. This local and regional competition additionally undercut Lower Cherokee influence, thereby laying the groundwork for the emergence of the Overhill Towns as the key rival for regional power within Cherokee country after midcentury.

3

"in constant hostility with the Muskohge"

The Cherokee-Creek War

The Cherokee-Creek War, which lasted roughly from 1715 to 1755, was the longest and most destructive conflict between Cherokees and other indigenous peoples during the eighteenth century. The war's early phases revealed customary disunity among Cherokees from different towns and regions, since villagers rarely had a common enemy when it came to intertribal warfare. Edmond Atkin testified to this regional dimension of Cherokee warfare when he observed that Upper and Lower Cherokees "seldom take part in each others Wars." The "upper Cherokees do not always take part with the lower," he added, especially when fighting their Muscogean neighbors. Lower Cherokees often fought against Lower Creeks, while villagers from other regions typically warred against the Upper Creeks (when uninterrupted by a temporary peace). The same held true for Cherokees and other native peoples. James Adair found that Lower Cherokees were "in constant hostility with the Muskohge," whereas the "upper towns . . . were always engaged in hot war with the more northern Indians."[1]

As the statements by Atkin and Adair suggest, different borderland experiences shaped the dynamics of Cherokee warfare. Cherokees engaged multitudes of Indians from near and far who all brought varying agendas to their mountain homeland. Imperial and colonial powers exerted additional pressure, which further complicated Cherokee relations with their indigenous neighbors. As a result, the Cherokee-Creek War was much more than a conflict between two southeastern Indian peoples. Issues of war and peace between the Cherokees and Creeks were particularly influenced by the northern Indians, "Settlement Indians," and South Carolina.

Peace with northern Indians, for example, typically meant war with the Creeks, who accused the Cherokees of recruiting Iroquois, Shawnee, and other "Northward" warriors to take Muscogean captives and scalps. Peace with the Creeks and Catawbas, in turn, invited raiders from the north to attack their own villages. Such varying geopolitical considerations pulled Cherokees in different directions, thereby ensuring that intertribal warfare remained a town and regional, rather than national, prerogative.

The latter stages of the Cherokee-Creek War challenged these long-held conventions. The war changed course near midcentury, as the Lower Creeks shifted from sporadic raids to full-scale attacks against the Lower Cherokee Settlements. Most of the Lower Towns temporarily disbanded, creating a refugee crisis that drew villagers from other towns and regions more directly into the war. What had generally been a regionally based conflict now emerged as a larger struggle between Cherokee and Creek peoples. By 1753 the debilitating effects of war on all Cherokees, whether through dislocation, bereavement, or interference with economic livelihoods, encouraged Cherokees from every region first to attack their Muscogean neighbors and then to seek and confirm a general peace with the Creeks. War and peace accordingly became more interregional affairs than in prior conflicts, a trend that would continue throughout the Seven Years' War. The Cherokee-Creek War, in short, and similar to the Anglo-Cherokee trading alliance, exposed the complicated structure of Cherokee sociopolitical organization. Both at times exacerbated local and regional tensions within Cherokee country, but they also revealed a remarkable tendency among Cherokees to transcend parochial interests during crises.

The war proved consequential in other ways; namely, the reshaping of regional power within Cherokee country. The beleaguered Lower Towns entered a state of flux as Creek attacks unsettled their villages. Into the void stepped the Overhill people. They protected the refugees and sent warriors against the Creeks, while also utilizing long established connections to Northward Indians to gain allies against their Muscogean enemies. As a result, the war turned in favor of the Cherokees, which allowed the Lower people to resettle some of their former towns. The Overhill Cherokees and their leaders therefore played an ever-expanding role in the affairs of those Cherokees living beyond their own villages. Ultimately, the war ensured the ascendancy of the Overhill Settlements and the beloved town of Chota.

The post-Yamasee phase of the long-standing Cherokee-Muscogee wars changed markedly near midcentury. The conflict escalated when Lower Creeks launched an intense campaign against the Lower Cherokee Towns in the Tugaloo River area, which later spread to include those settlements along the Keowee River and its tributaries. These attacks were not limited to small-scale raids as was typical in woodland warfare. In November 1750, a Creek trader informed officials that 400 Lower Creeks "went against the Cherokees and killed between 30 and 40 and brought in seven alive which they burned." Other accounts related that Creek warriors aimed to entirely "cut off" the Lower Towns; meaning that they intended to "Burn their Towns and kill every one, Men and Women they met with." Such threats proved genuine. The Creeks "burnt to the Ground two Towns" in December and "kill'd most of the Inhabitants upon the Spot, and carried the rest into Slavery." The situation grew increasingly desperate, and many feared their annihilation. James Beamer witnessed "the greatest Confusion with the Indians in these Lower Towns" than he had ever known in his twenty-eight years among the Cherokees. The trader added that the attacks "caused every one of the lower Towns to break up," except Estatoe and part of Toxaway. Keowee also remained, but most of the Keowee people relocated to Toxaway "and joined what few was left there." The dislocation became so widespread in the spring of 1752 that two Keowee and Estatoe headmen dejectedly informed Governor Glen that the Lower Towns people "wander all over the Nation."[2]

As the two headmen related, the severity of the attacks—and rumors of impending attacks—forced many Lower Cherokees to flee their homes and seek refuge in other regions. Displaced Lower Cherokees "removed further up into the Nation," away from the contentious borderlands they shared with the Lower Creeks. Some sought refuge in the Middle Towns, where their stories of Creek atrocities found an eager audience. A Joree headman, speaking for nine towns "besides a great many which is driven amongst us by the Enemy," delivered a talk to the governor describing "the Creeks who are like Dogs." The Out Towns additionally offered indirect support, as Beamer felt confident he could persuade villagers from that region to relocate southward "and fill up the vacant Towns that is diserted."[3]

The majority of the Lower Town refugees, however, fled to the Overhill Settlements. The Overhill region was at the time less exposed to Creek raiders, but perhaps the most compelling reason for this choice of relocation was access to trade. The Panic of 1751 had subsided but little, and the South Carolina embargo resulted in a scarcity of goods throughout Cherokee country. The Overhill people challenged the embargo and Carolina's trading monopoly by dealing with Virginia, which provided a strong incentive to the refugees. Lower Towns people proved eager to obtain supplies, and "The Northward Traders" were just as eager to have more clients. Some Lower Cherokees even petitioned the Virginia government to settle near that colony. They did so, at a place called Aurora, more than one hundred miles beyond the Overhill Towns. These Lower Cherokees reportedly moved "for the sake of better Land and fresh hunting Ground" and to also trade with the Virginians. Although this new settlement proved short-lived, Carolina traders worried about the implications of a Cherokee country without the Lower Towns. James Beamer, whose economic life depended on keeping the Lower Towns intact, feared that if the Virginia traders were successful and "these two [remaining] Towns breaks up, Carolina loses the Cherokees."[4]

Although the refugee crisis conveyed the realities of war beyond individual towns and regions, Cherokee localism remained strong. Headmen from the remaining Lower Towns informed Beamer in 1752, "They don't care to go over the Hills. They had rather joyn with the Cutobas [Catawbas]." Other refugees who temporarily resettled in the Overhills, according to Edmond Atkin, "at first talked of removing to live with the Nottowegas." Atkin added that a Lower Cherokee delegation even traveled to the Lower Shawnee Towns on the Ohio River to acquaint them "that 1400 of their People intended to come and live among them." While certainly an exaggeration, the fact that Lower Cherokees considered refuge among non-Cherokee peoples speaks to the centrality of town and regional differences within Cherokee country.[5]

Still, the Lower Town refugee crisis, more than any other development during the Cherokee-Creek War, transformed the conflict into a cross-regional affair. The unusually intense attacks by the Lower Creeks threatened the very existence of the Lower Towns and spurred Cherokees from other regions not only to seek revenge for lost clan members but also to fear the geopolitical consequences of a weakened Lower Cherokee region. The war subsequently escalated. Overhill leaders declared they were "at War with the Covetas, and Cussitas, and [all] the Lower Creeks" because they were "daily doing us some Mischief," since "they cut off the Town of Tugolo and the Rest of the Towns on that River." Peace with the Upper

Creeks also collapsed. Previous reports indicated Overhill and Valley Cherokees and the Upper Creeks had ceased hostilities. In 1750 a Creek trader found that Upper Creeks and Upper Cherokees mixed peaceably "in their hunting ground." The Raven of Hiwassee seemed pleased when they "made Peace again," and to better avoid misunderstandings in the future, the warring parties "parted the Ground that we are to hunt." But all this changed in just two short years. Acorn Whistler, an Upper Creek headman from Little Okfuskee, was implicated in the ambush of Estatoe warriors near Charlestown. He afterward "went against the Town of Hywasse" in the Valley, whereupon the Raven lost two sons and a brother "and then he thought off Nothing but War." The prominent Overhill leader Ostenaco likewise confirmed the war had reached his towns and requested that Carolina "trouble themselves no more" with mediating a peace. Indeed, peace seemed like a distant memory, as subsequent reports from Creek country indicated the "War continues very hott between these People and the Cherokees."[6]

By the spring of 1752, both the Upper and Lower Creeks became embroiled in a general war with the Cherokees. From Creek perspectives, many reasons existed for this escalation. The history of their long-standing conflict played a crucial role. The memory of the Tugaloo Incident remained strong even forty years after the attack. Atkin observed in 1755 that the Creeks continued to "have an old Grudge against the Cherokees, for joining the Carolina Army in the Indian War in 1715, and falling on them unexpectedly." Imperial rivalries also mounted as French agents pushed their Indian allies to destabilize Anglo-Cherokee relations. A general war between two of Britain's steadiest trading partners in the Southeast, the Cherokees and Creeks, certainly served French interests. The most immediate cause of renewed hostilities, however, was intimated in a talk delivered by the Raven of Hiwassee to Governor Glen: "Formerly the Norards used [to come] here and assisted us, but now none comes here as usual to our Assistance." The Raven had touched upon the central impasse in Cherokee-Creek relations: the "Northward" Indians, who often attacked Creek townspeople after "being harboured, provided, and assisted by the Cherokees."[7]

Native Americans from the north, particularly those living in the Ohio country, Great Lakes, and mid-Atlantic hinterlands, were particularly active in the southeastern borderlands. Unfortunately, reports from Cherokee country rarely specified to which towns and ethnic groups these northern Indians belonged. The term "Nottawega," for instance, was known to be synonymous with "Northern Indian." Yet some speakers, including the Cherokees, used it to identify the Nottoways, the Six Nations (and Senecas more specifically), the Delawares, and various other Indians near the Susquehanna and Ohio Rivers. The term held such ambiguity that Governor Glen asked two Cherokee messengers in 1754, "What do they mean by the Indians called the Nettawegees?" They replied, "The French [Indians]"—a response that further obscured the outsiders' identities.[8]

In addition to Nottawega (and its variant spellings), a more common moniker was simply "Northward" or "Norward" Indians. General Thomas Gage wrote that Cherokees and other southeastern Indians "call them all *Northwards* without distinguishing any particular Nation." Similar uncertainty existed about the "Western Nations," some of which included the Chippewas, Illinois, Piankashaws, Miamis, Kickapoos, and Ottawas, but who were at times labeled Northward or French Indians. Such confusion partly stemmed from the inability of southeastern Indians and Europeans alike to clearly identify the "Multitude of strange Indians" who traveled south. Governor Glen was one of the few contemporaries who attempted to get beyond ambiguous labels. "Under the name of Northward Indians," he wrote, "I include not only the Six Nations, the Dellaware and Susqueehanna Indians, but all the different Tribes who may be in Friendship with them, particularly those on the Onis River." Glen's description does not comprise all Indian groups variously identified as "Northwards," but it does recognize a few of the major players.[9]

It is easy to oversimplify the complexities of Cherokee-Northward interactions. John Reid asserts, "If any external factor gave the Cherokees a sense of national unity, it was fear and hatred of their Iroquois cousins." While the Cherokees often found themselves in conflict with northern Indians, particularly the Six Nations, their associations with the Iroquois, Shawnees, and others were much more ambiguous and varied than such statements allow. On the one hand, Cherokee leaders repeatedly affirmed their abhorrence of the Northwards. On the other hand, Cherokees not only sheltered and abetted diverse groups of Northwards, but they also considered them staunch allies and kinsmen. Speaking for the Overhill Towns, a headman named Long Jack said of the Shawnees: "We look on them as on our own People, as they always come with Peace Talks, to our Nation." Another Overhill leader informed British officers that "his Town belongs to the Nuntuways and the Nuntuways belong to him."[10]

Other Cherokees besides the Overhill people, whose towns lay at the exposed northwestern fringes of Cherokee country, displayed ambivalence toward northern Indians. Juxtaposing two incidents, both of which occurred in 1748, reveals the ways in which Cherokees from other regions also divided over how to deal with the Northwards. They additionally testify to both the strength and limitations of the Anglo-Cherokee alliance as codified by the Treaty of 1730. The first incident involved the death of a packhorseman named Edward Carrol by a notable Tugaloo warrior. The murder violated the treaty's sixth article, which stipulated that if any Indian killed an Englishman, the said Indian should be delivered to the governor for punishment by English law. Governor Glen accordingly demanded satisfaction from Tugaloo and the Lower Cherokees. He advised his interpreter, James Beamer, to "speak with a pretty strong Mouth," to deliver it in "a formal manner," and to not be "put off with their Shifts & Evasions, that the fellow was in Liquor, or that he is removed to some other Towns or gone to War." As expected, some Cherokees (most likely clan relations) balked at the governor's request, saying "It would be hard to take the life of one of their Warriors for what was nothing," meaning that Carrol was "but an ordinary Man."[11]

The Tugaloo warrior's supporters also challenged their village headman and the Raven of Hiwassee who warned them about the potential loss of trade if they did not give satisfaction. If they had no occasion for the English, the two leaders argued, "they might go & live Separately among themselves," and if other Tugaloo townspeople "found that they Lived happier & better than they who were supplied," then perhaps they would join them, "but as that cannot be the Case it is necessary to put the Person to Death who had killed the White Man." The opposition continued to resist, until word arrived there had been "a general Consultation of the 7 Towns, when it was agreed to destroy that Town, Men, Women, & Children & to Burn it unless they put the Murderer to Death." The death of the Tugaloo warrior quickly followed, as his assailants shot him and then "cut off his Head with a Hatchet."[12]

Although it may seem in this instance that Lower Cherokees were slow to fulfill their treaty obligations, it stood in stark contrast to another murder involving George Haig and Northward Indians. Haig, unlike Edward Carrol, was no "ordinary Man." He was a well known and much respected Carolinian who dabbled in the Indian trade. In 1748 Nottawega Indians captured Haig near the Catawba trading path and then passed through the Lower Cherokee Towns. According to the second and third articles of the treaty, the Cherokees were obligated to assist Carolina in redeeming the captured Englishman and to "fight against any Nation . . . who shall dare to molest or hurt the English." How did the Lower Cherokees respond? In a way befitting their sociopolitical divisiveness.[13]

Beamer, whose primary trading town was Estatoe, first appealed for Haig's release to the Keowee people, among whom the Northwards currently stayed. He failed, as did other traders at Keowee who "tried all that was in our Power" to win Haig's freedom. Neither the threat of an embargo nor the promise of presents swayed Keowee leaders. Beamer had more influence and more success at Estatoe, however. The trader convinced three principal men of his town and fourteen warriors to travel to Keowee "with a full intent to kill the Nottaweegas." But Keowee headmen had been apprised of their plans the previous night and "ordered all to be armed ready to stand in defence of the Nottawegas if either Whites or Indians should assent to attack them." When the Estatoe party arrived, Keowee warriors appeared under arms and declared they "would all Die before they suffer" the Nottawegas to be captured or killed. If South Carolina stopped the trade or sent an army, then the Keowee people threatened to kill the traders and "go & Live with the Nottaweegas."[14]

The Lower Cherokees were divided over the Haig and Carrol affairs because they, like villagers in other regions, balanced competing and often conflicting agendas of their Indian and white neighbors. The threat of temporarily losing the British trade compelled many Cherokees to acquiesce to English demands, as seen in the general consultation of the seven towns to destroy Tugaloo and the quick military response of the Estatoe people to defend Haig (which proved unsuccessful, for the Nottawegas later killed him). But the Anglo-Cherokee trading alliance had its limitations. The possibility of an embargo was not a stronger deterrent for Keowee townspeople than was the consequence of offending the Northward Indians. Northwards came south to fight. If Cherokees could deflect their search for scalps and slaves to other southeastern Indian communities, then the dangers posed to their own villages lessened. Equally important, Cherokees found in the Northwards a potent ally in their long-standing war against the Creeks.

The relationships that existed between the Cherokee and Northward Indians proved a remarkable impetus to the continuation and intensification of the Cherokee-Creek War. Creeks were especially enraged when

Cherokees harbored and assisted hostile Iroquois, Shawnees, and other northern Indians. James Adair later wrote that "the true and sole cause of the last war between the Muskohge and Cheerake" resulted from Shawnee warriors killing two Creeks before escaping "to the northern towns of the Cheerake." Although more complicated than Adair allowed, the renewal of hostilities was exacerbated by the encouragement Cherokees gave to Northward Indians. A group of Shawnees had lately settled among the Overhill people, and the beloved town of Chota also recently "made Peace with the Nottowagas," who frequently warred against all southeastern Indians. The Overhill Cherokees encouraged peace with the Northwards to lessen attacks on their own villages. As one headman noted, many of these northern Indians had been "their enemies" until they diverted them "to go to Warr against the Cowetas."[15]

Cherokees from other regions also found the Northwards a useful ally against the Creeks. A Lower Town headman informed Northward warriors in 1751, "If you go to War with the Creeks we will thereby perceive you are our Friends." Reports indicated this union of convenience temporarily flourished. In March "a great Body of the Natawagees and Lower Cherokees" went against the Lower Creeks "to cut them off." Two months later "there was three hundred Notewegas in the Lower Cherokees," presumably at Keowee, since that town was known as "the principal Rendezvous of the Northern Indians." Additional intelligence from New York specified "the northerly French Indians have sent an Army" to attack the Creeks "and if they can utterly to destroy them." The Six Nations compounded the situation. Their insistence on not making peace with the "Caw, we, tas, alias Creeks ... on any Terms" prompted Governor Glen to alert Creek headmen that the Iroquois "made a Declaration of War against your Nation."[16]

Northward incursions against both the Lower and Upper Creeks, and Cherokee countenance and support of these war parties, elicited large-scale retaliatory offensives that nearly wiped out the Lower Cherokee Towns by the end of 1752. The Creeks, however, were not the only southeastern Indians antagonistic toward Cherokees for their Northward connections. "Settlement" Indians also pressed the Cherokees to deal with the Northward problem. Much like the generalized label many colonists attached to diverse northern peoples, Settlement Indians were likewise a varied group. The designation usually described those remnants of formerly substantial Indian communities, or *"Ancient Natives,"* as Atkin called them, who remained within, or near to, white settlements. Governor Glen—ever busy with Indian affairs—noted, "There are among our Settlements several small Tribes of Indians, consisting only of some few Families each." He listed some of these "Tribes" more specifically as the Cheraws, Yuchis, Natchez, and Pedees, many of whom he looked upon "as Branches of the Catawbas." These "friendly Indians, a quiet and inoffensive People who are at War with no Nation whatever," provided a constant target for northern war parties.[17]

Numerous reports near midcentury indicated the frequency and intensity with which Northwards traveled south to "steal a Scalp or make a Slave of some of the Settlement Indians." Diverse reasons accounted for these attacks. Besides the taking of scalps and slaves, embittered feelings also stemmed from a long history of conflict between northern and southern Indians. Northern raiders likewise knew less chance of reprisal existed from those who were few in number and lacked extensive kin networks. Another possible motive related to the cultural ambiguities and blurred identities of Settlement Indians. Those Indians living "within the boundaries of the British settlements," one observer noted, "are in many respects changed . . . from their original customs and moral habits." The clergyman Andrew Burnaby further commented that because their dress emulated that of the English, "I have sometimes mistaken them for the lower sort of that people." If "feared identity" is a primary component of self-identification, as some anthropologists argue, perhaps the Northwards and their Cherokee supporters had particular distaste for those Indians who, in their eyes, had been "domesticated."[18]

Settlement Indians, as well as the Catawbas, Savannah Chickasaws, and other Piedmont peoples, recognized that Cherokees sheltered and assisted their northern assailants. A multiethnic war party consisting of Mohawks, Delawares, and Susquehannas took two Catawba scalps in the summer of 1751 after having been "amongst the Cherokees all Winter." A "Cheerake guide" the previous year led a Shawnee party to attack Yuchi women and children near Savannah. In another encounter, Shawnees captured a Yuchi headman whom they "carried up to the Cherokee Country." Numerous southeastern Indians, in response, threatened the Cherokees. Savannah Chickasaws, a branch of the western Chickasaws who had relocated to the environs of Augusta, avowed they "might break out War" with the Cherokees "for suffering the Northward to pass through their Nation." They further declared that if "the Cherokees are so very desirous of maintaining a good Understanding with the Chickesaws," they must accordingly cease to "entertain and encourage" the Northwards and instead "drive them all away from their Nation." Cherokees listened to such talks more intently as worsening relations with southeastern Indians generated fears of war on all sides of their unstable borderlands. When rumors circulated that a combined force of Creeks, Choctaws, Yuchis, Catawbas, Chickasaws, and "all the Settlements Indians was coming to cutt off" their towns, many Cherokees began to rethink their close connections to the controversial Northwards.[19]

While Settlement Indians and their more powerful indigenous neighbors pressured the Cherokees to disown the northern Indians, the government in Charlestown provided equally forceful encouragement toward that end. Carolina had good reason to fear and loathe the Northwards. The colony had offered its protection to Settlement Indians, largely because they were, according to Glen, "upon many Accounts very serviceable to us." Settlement Indians destroyed "Vermin, and Beasts of Prey," procured skins for the trade, provided venison to colonists, and pursued runaway and maroon slaves. They also formed a thin but important buffer against hostile French Indians. When Northwards attacked Carolina's Settlement Indians, therefore, they not only threatened a serviceable ally but also affronted the government's authority. A lowcountry militia captain expressed outrage after northern Indians arrived at a settler's house "and with great Insolence entered with their Arms . . . asking for Indians they supposed kept there." Scalping and slaving raids in the distant borderlands was one thing; such activities within British settlements was another matter altogether.[20]

Northwards targeted Indians within British settlements, but they also abducted plantation slaves, destroyed settlers' property, and killed unsuspecting colonists. Atkin recorded that Northwards carried off "half breed Slaves, Mulattoes, and Mustees," while Governor Glen added the northern Indians captured "such of our Slaves as had the least Tincture of Indian Blood in them." This "carrying [off] of Slaves that are [our] Property," Glen continued, was matched by the loss of other types of property through the plundering of houses and the rustling and killing of livestock. Northwards additionally harassed and intimidated colonists and, at times, committed murders. Carolinians frequently complained about "these flying Parties" of enemy Indians who went "in large Companies and openly threaten[ed] white as well as red People." In the spring of 1751, Shawnees killed the Gould family near the Congarees, which was soon followed by further reports of confrontations and killings. Northwards were likewise implicated, along with some Cherokees, in many of the incidents that led to the Panic of 1751.[21]

The Carolina backcountry braced for "an open War" that never came. Threats from northern Indians and their Cherokee supporters prompted some colonists to abandon their settlements and "betake themselves in Forts with their Wives and Children, and their most valuable Effects." The government in Charlestown responded with attempts to exert its authority in the colony's hinterlands. Glen ordered existing militia and ranger units to patrol "the Woods, where these Norwards or French Indians seem now to have taken Possession." The governor also established a new troop of rangers that was to include "five Indians from the Settlements." If these patrols engaged "any Northward Indians" or any "such Indians by whatever Name they are called," they were authorized to "seize and apprehend them."[22]

Carolina's efforts to "clear the Country of these French and Northern Indians" centered most directly on the Cherokees. Glen chastised the Cherokees for harboring Northwards who attacked Settlement and Piedmont Indians. "You have fed and nourished them in your Country and have supplied them sometimes with Arms and Ammunition," he insisted, and then they "go through our very Settlements to attack and destroy those our Friends and Allies." Glen additionally reprimanded the Cherokees for acting "as their Conductors and Guides . . . into the innermost Parts of our Province" to rob and kill colonists, and "after all those Scenes of Blood and Barbarity you have received [them] back into your Country." The governor concluded his strong talk by reminding the Cherokees it was "in Vain to pretend to be Friends while your Practice is so inconsistent with your Professions."[23]

The Creeks, too, reminded the Cherokees, as they had many times before, that peace was unattainable as long as they "sheltered and protected" the northern Indians. Malatchi, a Lower Creek headman from Coweta, acknowledged this as one of the "greatest Grounds" of their quarrel with the Cherokees, a view seconded by other Creeks who "attributed the present Difference that now subsists betwixt them" to Cherokee-Northward connections. Cherokee leaders replied they held little control over the vast numbers of northern Indians who passed through their towns. Headmen alleged "themselves incapable without Assistance to withstand a Body of them," and they thus "permitted some Gangs of Northern Indians . . . to pass through their Country" to war. Cherokee reasoning did not convince their Creek neighbors. While working toward a general Cherokee-Creek peace in May 1753, Malatchi again reiterated that "such a Peace cannot take Effect" as long as the Cherokees "encourage these Northern Indians to come through their Towns to make War upon us."[24]

Eventually peace did come about between the Cherokees and Creeks. It did not happen overnight, as some headmen sent peace talks while others sent warriors. But as tensions mounted with their southern neighbors, Cherokees from all regions worried about the escalating Creek War. The depleted Lower Towns pressed especially hard for an end to hostilities. These Cherokees had suffered most from the fighting, as few towns remained in the summer of 1753. Even this was misleading, noted Skiagusta, who lived at Keowee: "I call it a Town, but there are so few People in it that it scarce deserves that Name." Initially against peace because of their exposed position vis-à-vis the Northwards, the Overhill Cherokees likewise came to realize they had been "deceived" by the Senecas, Shawnees, and other northern Indians. Old Hop of Chota declared the Northwards "have been seeking our Distruction," just as Skiagusta of Keowee found them "the Cause of all the mischief that has lately happened in our Nation and every where."[25]

While such assurances were well noted, Creek leaders demanded that Cherokees take firm action against the Northwards to end the war. They insisted that two Cherokee delegations travel to Creek country, one to Okfuskee (Upper) and the other to Coweta (Lower). Each delegation was "to bring a Northward Slave with them" so that both the Upper and Lower Creeks could ritually burn the captives, and then "they will think it is all straight." Although it is uncertain whether or not the delegations brought the slaves to Okfuskee and Coweta, Cherokees nonetheless demonstrated their disposition toward peace by altering their relations with northern Indians. Lower Cherokee headmen promised the Creeks "they would immediately send Runners to give you Notice" if Northward war parties arrived in their towns. Overhill Cherokees also confronted the Northwards who "come over the Mountains" to war "against the Southern Indians."

The "People of Chote" in particular rejected the Northwards, "for they knew they were Rogues" who pretended peace in order to kill and enslave them.[26]

The Cherokees also changed their disposition toward the Creeks to ensure peace. An Estatoe warrior promised a Coweta messenger that he had "forbid his People to go any more to War" and then loaded the emissary with "Presents as usual amongst Indians, Pipes, Beads, and Tabacco in Token of Peace." A Joree headman from the Middle Towns likewise stopped "some young Fellows" from "going to War against the Southwards," whereupon they "turned back to their Towns on Stecoe River." Numerous other reports from traders, government agents, and headmen confirmed the beginnings of a general Cherokee-Creek peace by 1754. Malatchi informed Glen he believed "it is a firm Peace" with the Cherokees, "for my People and them has met together in the Hunting Ground and eat and smoked together." An Upper Creek headman also related his people and the Cherokees met "in the hunting Ground" and "eat, drank, and smoked together in a very kind of friendly Manner." Delegations from both peoples additionally made "mutual Visits" to each other's country and to Charlestown to "confirm and strenthen" the peace. During one of these visits, Cherokee leaders assured their former enemies that if any of their people should be found "killed in the Woods" with "Tokens left as if done by the Creeks," they would not suspect their Muscogean neighbors, "but they would always attribute it to the French and Northward Indians."[27]

Cherokees and Creeks enacted stronger measures against the Northwards, which reshaped the geopolitical dimension of Cherokee country. Headmen from the Overhill and Valley Towns proposed joining the Creeks in a war against the Northwards. Old Hop of Chota and the Raven of Hiwassee in particular sent messengers to Coweta to obtain assistance "against the Nottawages." Creek leaders seemed pleased with their new Cherokee "Friends," but joint raids "against the common Enemy, the Norward Indians" helped create a rupture between Cherokees and Northwards that ultimately led to open warfare. Governor Glen forewarned Cherokee headmen of these consequences upon hearing their intention to join the Creeks and Catawbas against the Six Nations. "I know you are as brave as the Nittawagees and are much more numerous," he warned, "but they have Friends no doubt who will joyn them, and so it may become a very general War."[28]

Glen therefore must not have been surprised when trader Ludovic Grant reported in 1754 that the Cherokee-Creek peace was "unanimously confirmed," but it was "now a general War between this Nation and the Northward Indians." As it turned out, peace with the Creeks translated into war with the Northwards. Unlike the Cherokee-Creek War, which decimated the Lower Towns, the conflict Grant alluded to fell hardest on the Upper Cherokees. Overhill headmen alerted Glen in the fall, "the Enemy is like great Snakes lying on our River Banks ready to devour us." Other reports indicated that "the Over Hills Towns are much infested with the Enemy"—so infested, noted Old Hop, "they cannot stir out to hunt for them." Similar intelligence arrived in Charlestown from the Out Towns. A Tuckasegee headman found the Northwards "as bad against us as the People over the Hills," whereby they "can hardly go from Town to Town." And in the Valley, which had earlier been targeted by Creek warriors, the "Northward Enemy lately came upon [H]iwasee River" to kill and capture those people.[29]

It is difficult to identify exactly which northern and western Indians warred against the Cherokees. In addition to the Senecas, the attacks most likely came from groups living in the Mississippi River Basin, particularly the environs of the Great Lakes and Ohio country, who were closely connected to the French. The Shawnees were especially active against the Cherokees following the Creek peace. Although a group of Shawnees lived among the Overhill Towns and more peace-minded headmen attempted to strengthen relations between the two peoples, some Shawnees sought to unsettle the Anglo-Cherokee alliance. Perhaps even more significant to the rapid breakdown in Cherokee-Shawnee relations—and a key reason why the Overhill people repudiated the Northwards in favor of the Creeks—was a seemingly minor incident between South Carolinians and a small party of Shawnees in 1753.

During the summer of that year, Governor Glen imprisoned six Ohio Shawnees in Charlestown. These captives had been taken while "in the white People's Country" on suspicions of killing settlers near Saluda. The prisoners proclaimed their innocence, telling the governor that "their Business was with red and not white People." Nevertheless, the interrogation and imprisonment lasted for more than two months, and though they proved "very false Men," the governor released them on insufficient evidence. But the damage had been done. The imprisonment greatly affronted the Shawnees, who thought themselves "used like Dogs." Their anger was thereafter directed toward both the British and the Cherokees, which, in turn, led to open warfare against both peoples.[30]

Cherokee leaders later testified to the detrimental consequences of the Shawnee imprisonment. At the height of the Seven Years' War, in which the Shawnees and their confederates had for several years targeted Cherokee and British settlements, Lower Town headmen reminded the English they "brought this war upon themselves by putting the Savvanas in Prison some Years ago in Charlestown." Old Hop likewise attributed "the Occasion of the War to your Excellency in putting and detaining in Prison those Savannahs." On "that Account," he continued, the Shawnees warred against the Cherokees "because they, when in Charles Town, did not procure the Freedom of the Savannahs from your Excellency and send them Home." Equally important and damaging, noted Old Hop, the incident did not unbalance relations only with the Shawnees. Once the prisoners returned to their towns, "all the Head Men of the Savannahs met" and declared war. They then sent war belts and the "barbecued Flesh" of British captives to "fifteen different Nations to the Northward," who all agreed to join the French against the British and the Cherokees.[31]

The Cherokee-Northward conflict was similar to the latter stages of the Creek War in that significant cross-regional activity transpired. When fears mounted that Northwards would "drive the Over Hills People from thence," Chota sent runners to the Valley Towns "desireing their immediate Assistance," urging the "Valey People to repair over the Hills with all Expedition." They more specifically asked warriors from Hiwassee, Conastee, and Little Tellico to aid Great Tellico, and those from Neowee (Noyowee), Tomatly, Cheowee, and Natalee to assist Chota. The Valley headmen responded by sending warriors to the Overhills "to hunt the Enemy." As depredations continued and rumors circulated of Northward plans "to cut them off from being a People," Overhill Cherokees widened their search for allies, including exploratory missions to the French in Louisiana.[32]

The Northward conflict, while distressing to the Overhill Cherokees, did not achieve the level of severity experienced by the Lower Towns people during the Creek War. Creek attacks had generated widespread displacement among the Lower Cherokees as they dismantled their towns and relocated to other regions. The Cherokee-Creek War therefore represented a shift in regional power within Cherokee country. Once the gateway to

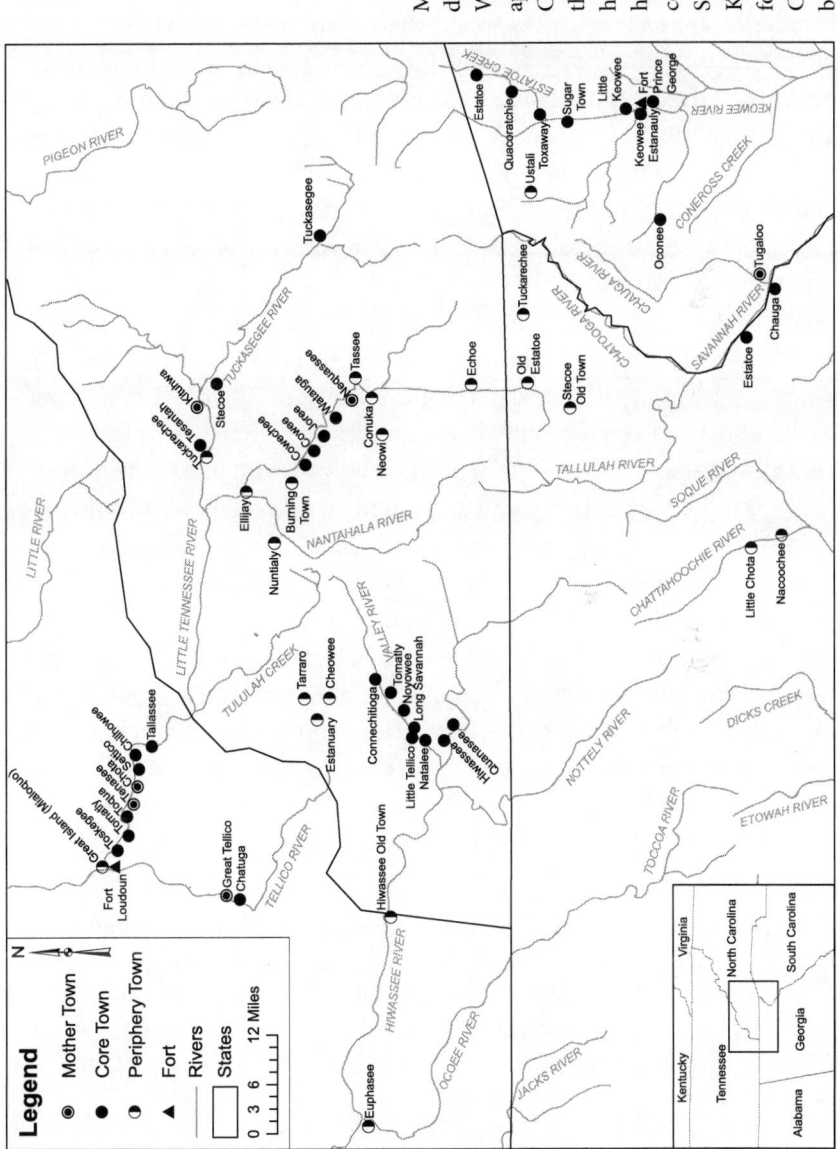

Map 4. Cherokee Country during the Seven Years' War. This map depicts the approximate location of Cherokee towns during the Seven Years' War. Note how the Lower Cherokees had shifted many of their core towns from the upper Savannah River to the Keowee River watershed following the Cherokee-Creek War. (Map designed by Isaac Emrick.)

Carolina and the British trade, the Lower Towns had been relegated to lesser importance in the immediate aftermath of the war. One reason is that many towns remained abandoned. George Chicken, for instance, counted as many as twenty-one Lower towns in 1725, but reports immediately following the Cherokee-Creek War found just five of these towns had been resettled. This decline in the number of towns was equaled by a comparable reduction in population. Though reports varied, ranging from as high as 500 warriors to as little as 160, James Beamer's account in 1756 is likely the most accurate. The Estatoe trader found the Lower people could raise a total of 240 warriors from his town, Keowee, Sugar Town, Toxaway, and Qualatchee (Quacoratchie). These figures put them well below the population of the Overhill, Middle, and Valley Cherokees and slightly less than the Out Towns.[33]

Beamer's report reveals even more about shifts in local and regional influence stemming from the Creek War. The Lower Towns people rebuilt their villages chiefly along the Keowee River and its tributaries, thereby avoiding more precarious locations nearer to the Creeks (see map 4). Towns that had once stretched along the Tugaloo, Chatooga, and upper Chattahoochee River watersheds were either abandoned or slowly reoccupied. In 1764, for instance, Tugaloo could raise only twenty warriors, while Keowee, Sugar Town, and several other Keowee River towns each boasted ninety or more warriors. Other considerations also drew the Lower Cherokees to this area. In 1753 South Carolina made good on its promise to build a fort in Cherokee country. They chose a site adjacent to Keowee, opposite the river from the town, which they named Fort Prince George. The new fort played a decisive role in returning the Lower Cherokees to a regional power. The fort became a political, diplomatic, and economic magnet that attracted villagers from all corners of their mountain homeland. The Lower Cherokees nearest to Keowee subsequently benefited from this new hub of Anglo-Cherokee activity as they regained some of their former influence following the Creek War. Nevertheless, the geopolitical circumstances of the Southeast and all of North America had noticeably changed with the onset of imperial warfare in 1754. The diplomatic and military importance of other Cherokees, particularly the Overhill people, increasingly attracted the attention of Carolina, her sister colonies, and the French.[34]

4

"the disaffected people of Great Tellico"

The Struggle for Empire in a Cherokee Town

In the fall of 1756, twenty-five Cherokees undertook a furtive diplomatic mission that would ultimately thrust Cherokee country into the heart of the Seven Years' War. Conducted by a French agent and three Shawnee guides, the envoy consisted of men and women primarily from the Overhill town of Great Tellico. Their journey took them through the Upper Creek Towns to Fort Toulouse among the Alabamas, from which a smaller contingent proceeded to New Orleans to visit Louis Billouart de Kerlerec, governor of Louisiana. The ensuing conference between the Tellico people and Governor Kerlerec must have appeared unusual to those who knew the history of Franco-Cherokee relations. The Cherokees had been dependable British allies and trading partners for more than a generation, and many Cherokee war parties had wreaked havoc on the French and their Indian allies equally as long. The French reminded "their lost Children" of this fact, lamenting they had been "Fathers to all the Indians on the whole Continent . . . except the Cherokee Nation which had been lost from them for a long Time." The Tellico emissaries sought to change this by establishing "a strong bright Chain" from New Orleans to Tellico "and from Tellico they would extend it as far as Chota."[1]

Initial reports about the "disaffected People of Great Tellico" heightened fears among an already unsettled British population in the colonial South. The American phase of the war had raged for two years, witnessing major British setbacks with General Braddock's defeat near Fort Duquesne followed by recurrent raids on the Virginia and Pennsylvania backcountries by Shawnees, Delawares, Mingos, and other French-allied Indians. By the fall of 1756 it seemed as if the French strategy of connecting their inland empire from Canada to Louisiana was succeeding in the Ohio country. If a Franco-Cherokee alliance could be secured, then the fate of the southern colonies would also be precarious. Governor Kerlerec believed peace with the Cherokees would "put Carolina within an Ace of its ruin," while Carolinians themselves recognized "the whole Fate of Carolina and Georgia both depends greatly on the Friendship of this Nation." The Tellico peace envoy was therefore no trivial matter to either the British or French Empire in North America.[2]

The Tellico affair was likewise no trivial matter to the Cherokees. Their alliance with Britain, although far from a perfect union, ensured a steady supply of goods to many mountain villagers. The Overhill Settlements, however, were the most distant from Carolina, which hindered British efforts to keep Tellico and its neighboring towns sufficiently supplied. The Tellico mission in large part reflected a search for new trading outlets, but it also signified the rise of the Overhills, with its beloved town of Chota, as the dominant regional force within Cherokee country. The debilitating effects of the Creek War in other regions and a renewed imperial conflict elevated the strategic importance of the Overhill Towns to both empires. Chota subsequently emerged as the regional center from which a capable cadre of leading Overhill men, in the words of one trader, was "always commanding the whole Nation."[3]

Other Cherokee towns challenged the ascendancy of the Overhill people. Recognizing that the Tellico maneuverings threatened to destabilize Anglo-Cherokee relations and interrupt British trade, many in the Lower, Middle, Valley, and Out Towns mirrored the British backlash to the Tellico incident by outwardly rejecting those Cherokees in the French interest. Such reactions did not cut only along regional lines; they were also indicative of deepening political divisions within the Overhills and especially within the conjoined towns of Tellico and Chatuga. As events unfolded, it became apparent that these twenty-five emissaries acted not only for their own town but also at the behest of the most influential headmen in the Overhill country. The Overhill Settlements, and more particularly the town of Tellico, therefore became a key locus for the struggle for empire as well as the future direction of Cherokee policy.

Although the Cherokees did not replace their English Brothers with a new French Father, the response of many Cherokees to pro-French maneuverings effected as much. For as warriors from all regions joined the British war effort to the north, it was here, in the Virginia backcountry, where the Anglo-Cherokee alliance unraveled, ultimately bringing the realities of imperial warfare to the very heart of Cherokee country.

One of the most distant Cherokee towns, at least from a British coastal perspective, Tellico had nevertheless long played a central role in Anglo-Cherokee relations. In the immediate aftermath of the Yamasee War, South Carolina's factor for the Cherokee trade placed one of his five assistants at Great Tellico. The Overhill town received even greater attention from Alexander Cuming fifteen years later, when the emboldened Scot pressed mountain villagers to select Moytoy of Tellico as "emperor" of all the Cherokees. Cuming also recognized Tellico as one of the "seven Mother Towns." As a beloved town, the people of Great Tellico were empowered to choose a "King" who was "elected out of certain Families." And Tellico had no shortage of these family connections. A British officer reported in 1756 that "the Tellico People stands very much on their Families as being the best and most ancient in the Nation," as they were related to the "great Men [in] the Nation by Birth, Marriage, &c." Tellico clan connections extended beyond their own village to include "a great many Relations in the Upper Towns as well as the Middle and Lower Towns."[4]

Tellico's mother or beloved town status, however, should not obscure its position on the geopolitical margins of Cherokee country. It was, in short, a border town. Colonel George Chicken recorded in 1725 that Tellico was "very Compact and thick Settled" to prevent being "Cut of[f] by the Enemy who are Continually within a Mile of the Town lurking about." To counter enemy movements, the Tellico people fortified both their town and individual houses, which they made "Muskett proof." So, too, had the conjoined town of Chatuga. In an unusual but not entirely unknown move among the Cherokees, the people of Great Tellico and Chatuga had "settled together." Eighteenth-century observers found their houses "mingled together indistinguishably," yet the Tellicans and Chatugans did not form one town; they maintained "two different councils" that met in two distinct townhouses. These "two Towns at Talico," as one Overhill headman described them, possessed strength in numbers. One British officer estimated that Tellico-Chatuga had 110 warriors in 1757, making it one of the larger settlements in Cherokee country by his calculations.[5]

The exposed position of Tellico and Chatuga affected local settlement patterns and complicated interactions with Europeans. Tellico was one of the nearest Overhill towns to Louisiana. One French captive among the Cherokees listed it as only a thirteen-day journey to the Alabamas, thus situating it closer to Fort Toulouse than to either Virginia or Carolina. Proximity to the French meant that Tellico and other Overhill towns became a strategic battleground for imperial rivalries. Both the French and British remained uneasy about the loyalty of the Overhill Cherokees, continually fearing their allegiance had been won by the other. Thus, just as the French believed "the eight [Overhill Towns] which are along the river are our enemies," the British were likewise convinced "the Indians over the Hills are greater Friends to the French than to the English."[6]

The communications of British and colonial officials throughout the Seven Years' War reflected this insecurity about French maneuverings in Cherokee country, albeit not without reason. The more distant town of Tellico generated the most concern. Major Andrew Lewis of the Virginia regiment observed that French and Indian agents had "a constant Correspondance" with the Cherokees, "more especially with the great town of Tellico." Similar sentiments were echoed in South Carolina, where Governor Glen expressed his concerns about French intrigue just months before the war began. In an especially tense conference with Cherokee headmen, Carolina traders, and his Council in Charlestown, Glen wished to know if the Cherokees had "any Correspondence with the French." The governor was particularly disturbed by reports he had received about licensed trader Anthony Dean of Tellico and his connections to the French. Addressing James Beamer, Glen inquired whether Dean was "a violent Roman Catholic," but the Estatoe trader could not or would not give a definitive answer. The governor then asked John Butler, a trader among the Valley Towns, "Do you know Anthony Dean? What kind of Man is he? Do you take him to be a Jesuite?" Butler skirted the issue, but Glen pressed him once again: "Do you think him to be a Jesuite?" Butler only accused Dean of being "a very learned Man," although he added that Dean did employ a French-speaking Spaniard from Havana. More damaging, both he and Beamer associated Dean with "one L'antignac."[7]

Anthony L'antignac, otherwise known as Antoine Lantagnac, was a Frenchman who seemingly deserted to the British in 1745. Convincing the government in Charlestown of his newfound loyalty, L'antignac secured a license and for the next ten years immersed himself in the Cherokee trade. In addition to establishing a trading post among the Overhill Cherokees, L'antignac served as a soldier in the South Carolina Independent

Company. As the British eventually learned, however, he was not a deserter but a French agent who possibly had kinship ties to the marquis de Vaudreuil, former governor of Louisiana. Carolina officials first became aware of the scheme when a Creek trader reported in 1755 that Frenchmen had "flattered" L'antignac to Mobile "with Hopes of a Pardon." A British officer the following year found the former trader was a lieutenant at Fort Toulouse who actively recruited Indian allies to serve French interests. L'antignac purportedly planned to return with an assistant to trade among the Cherokees, though some suspected "they will come as Traders and Agents both." These suspicions proved correct, but it appears the British had no idea just how long L'antignac had been working for the French. In October 1755 Governor Kerlerec forwarded L'antignac's memoirs to Paris, requesting his promotion as reward for nine years of service among the British and the Cherokees. Thus, it appears L'antignac had been a French agent from the beginning, recording in his own words that his main objective was to conduct trade and ascertain for the French how the British managed their Indians.[8]

L'antignac remained active in Cherokee country after his identity and intentions were exposed, particularly in the town of Tellico where he had earlier formed a close relationship with two local headmen, the Mankiller of Tellico and his brother Kenoteta. It was therefore no surprise to the British that when a number of "disaffected" Tellicans led by the Mankiller and Kenoteta traveled to the French in 1756, L'antignac was reportedly "the principal Manager of the whole Affair." The French lieutenant was not alone in his machinations, however; he also had the assistance of a very capable intermediary: French John.[9]

French John was a Canadian who had lived "some considerable time" among the Overhill people by 1756 along with his Cherokee wife who spoke the Shawnee language. The British naturally considered him "a very dangerous Fellow" and attempted repeatedly to have him captured or killed, even offering "500 Wt. of Leather" for such services. Neither the English nor Cherokees, however, seemed eager to apprehend French John, for all knew him to be "a Slave to Old Hop," the beloved man of Chota. Contrary to the term's modern-day connotation, it appears French John was no bound laborer but rather a cultural broker whose slave status afforded him protection. Old Hop considered the Frenchman "as his own Child," which forced Captain Raymond Demere of the Independents to concede, "I could not have him killed, it would have been the same as if

I had killed one of them." This certainly frustrated the aging captain who well knew that French John was Old Hop's slave "by Way of a Cloke to transact the French Affairs in this Nation."[10]

Demere's fears were realized when the first reports reached him at newly constructed Fort Loudoun in the Overhill country. French John and his Shawnee-speaking wife had guided the Mankiller's party from Tellico to Fort Toulouse and then, with L'antignac's assistance, taken a smaller contingent to New Orleans. Demere, in fact, had obtained such intelligence prior to the mid-October meeting at Fort Toulouse. On his march from Fort Prince George to the Overhill Towns in late September, Demere happened upon the Emperor of Tellico (Moytoy's son) working the fields near his home. According to Demere, the first words uttered by the Emperor were, "What do you think of our having given up one of our Towns to the French?" The officer responded that he "was very sorry to hear it," to which the Emperor replied, "it was good to be at Peace with all Kings."[11]

The Emperor's response at first seems rather vague, but it essentially speaks to a primary motive behind his townspeople's diplomatic maneuverings: the search for multiple allies and trading partners. Even before the Tellico crisis, villagers made it plain to the British that trade, or the lack thereof, was the reason for their French connections. In the fall of 1754, the people of Great Tellico "made a heavy Complaint" about Robert Goudy, a licensed trader for Tellico and Chatuga. Goudy only visited his towns seasonally rather than having a permanent residence, and he refused to extend sufficient credit to his Indian trading clients. This contrasted sharply to the days when Tellico was a center of Carolina trade and influence. As the Mankiller of Tellico later noted, "The Town of Tellico is not as it formerly was. That they used to have a Sufficiency of Goods amongst them, but now they have not one Trader sent to that Town."[12]

The Mankiller and Kenoteta accordingly sought to reorient their diplomatic and trading paths toward French Louisiana. The meeting with French officers at Fort Toulouse in October 1756 generated great expectations of trade for the Tellicans. After lavishing his guests with presents, one French officer agreed to visit Tellico to "see what Kind of a Trade they had." He then promised to "supply all the Nation of the Cherokees with all Kinds of Goods and Necessaries, and that he would undersell [the English]." The delegation that later met with Governor Kerlerec at New

Orleans, on the other hand, encountered a less indulgent host. Although Kerlerec kindly received the delegates and genuinely believed they desired peace with France, he remained unconvinced that these Cherokees spoke for the entire nation. The Tellicans assured the governor they represented "the Nine principal Villages of the Nation, settled on this side the Appalachian Mountains [Overhills]," but Kerlerec wanted more; he could not commit to a trading alliance without knowing that all Cherokees would abide by the agreements made at New Orleans.[13]

The outcome of the conference was therefore an unofficial peace, one that promised a reliable French trade only if all Cherokees agreed to the alliance and only if the Cherokees demonstrated their allegiance by first attacking the English. Kerlerec further specified that he did not want to "hear of such pityfull Doings as two or three Scalps." Rather, he pushed the Cherokees to engage in "some *Coup d'Etat*," such as attacking "some Fort of Strength." The Tellicans subsequently inquired as to how they could supply themselves once they turned on their British trading partners, to which Kerlerec assured them that if they "Knock on the Head 5 or 600, then you will get Slaves and Plunder in Plenty, and we can come into your Towns and supply your Wants without Dread or Fear." The Preliminary Articles of Peace signed in New Orleans thus revealed a cautious Kerlerec who was seasoned enough to know that once these Cherokees returned to their towns, "Different parties Excited by the English" would attempt to undermine any Franco-Cherokee alliance.[14]

Indeed, the return of the Tellico people from Fort Toulouse and New Orleans unleashed a political firestorm within the Overhill Towns. A heated dispute arose over whether Tellico and its headmen acted independently. Oxinaa, a Cherokee woman present at Fort Toulouse and New Orleans, revealed to Captain Demere that Tellico deputies had accepted the war hatchet from Governor Kerlerec. This French hatchet was destined for Chota along with gifts designated specifically to Old Hop. Old Hop subsequently denied any involvement in the affair to both the British and Cherokees. Although everyone knew the shadowy and active French John was his "slave" and that Old Hop earlier admitted to sending "some of his People to several different Nations of French Indians," the beloved man of Chota claimed that Tellico went "in an underhanded Manner to the French." The other Overhill Towns favored the British, he publicly maintained, and would "not be actuated by the Tellico People." Again emphasizing the village-based rather than regional dimension of the Tellico mission, Old Hop assured the British that the pro-French envoy was "but of one Town."[15]

Kenoteta and the Mankiller, however, immediately contradicted Old Hop by declaring that their mission was in fact a regional affair. "I did not go to the French of my own Accord," insisted Kenoteta. "'Tis Old Hop and the Little Carpenter's both which perswaded me to go there." To make his claim more convincing, Kenoteta showed Demere a string of small beads that served as evidence of "Old Hop's Commission." The Mankiller corroborated his brother's assertion. In a large gathering at the Chota townhouse, the Mankiller of Tellico turned to other Overhill leaders and vented his frustrations: "Well you have made me a great Rogue," he charged. "Is there any one amongst you . . . that dare deny that he did not know what I did; did you not put in my hands the War Hatchet? . . . Did you not advise me . . . to go to the French?" Other Tellicans later affirmed the Mankiller's words by noting that "it was true they had all the blame but the Indians of other Towns were as guilty as they."[16]

The intraregional tensions exacerbated by the struggle for empire, and in particular the Tellico affair, became more than a war of words among Overhill leaders. Sensing the British backlash to the Mankiller's French dealings, which many Overhill leaders countenanced initially, Old Hop and other headmen sought to create political distance between themselves and the Tellico people by utilizing the power of trade. When Captain Demere delivered a large supply of goods to the Overhill people in late December, he observed they "would give none to the Town of Tellico." Calling the Mankiller "a Rogue," Old Hop resolved that the Tellicans "must have no Presents for their bad Behaviour." Even more punitive was the Chota headman's determination that all traders should stay in the neighboring Overhill Towns, to which the Tellico and Chatuga people must inconveniently travel "to buy their Goods." Governor Arthur Dobbs of North Carolina later testified to the purpose and effect of this policy against Tellico, noting the Overhill people "would not suffer them to receive any Goods from the Traders, but obliged them to send a very considerable way for every thing they wanted, and omitted no Persuasion to bring them to a due sense of their Interest, and a Love for the English."[17]

The Tellico proceedings agitated Demere, but he differed with Old Hop about the best means to redeem the Mankiller and his followers. Demere believed that if the few traders remaining in their town moved elsewhere, "the Tellicoe People would have been ten Times worse." Recognizing the significance of gift-giving to the Anglo-Cherokee alliance, he also diverged from Overhill leaders over the distribution of British gifts. Demere argued that Tellico loyalties could be reclaimed only "by giving them Presents in Proportion with the other Towns." The Mankiller agreed. The Tellico headman told Demere in private that the lack of presents "grieved them very much.... That if Presents had been given to them they would prove as true Friends to the English as any of the other Towns." Demere accordingly shifted the burden of guilt from the British to the Overhill leadership, reminding the Mankiller it was not his fault "they had no Presents; he said he knew of it."[18]

Using British goods as a means to marginalize Tellico was facilitated by recent developments within Cherokee country, in which nearly all Overhill trade channels flowed through Chota. Such notable leaders as Old Hop, Attakullakulla, Oconastota, Ostenaco, Kittagusta, and Willinawaw—most of whom were related to one another—had gradually strengthened Chota's connections to Charlestown and Williamsburg, thus shifting the Overhill power base from Tellico to Chota by the onset of the Seven Years' War. The days when the British had taken great notice of Tellico and its "emperor" had come and gone, and so too had its plentiful trade. The Tellico diplomatic mission to New Orleans in 1756 should therefore be understood within this context. The Mankiller most likely sought not only a new avenue of trade with the French—and perhaps the reestablishing of old ones if the British countered appropriately—but also the regaining of Tellico's former regional and even national prominence. As Captain Demere later informed the governor, the Mankiller and his town "wanted Nothing else but I should take Notice of them in the Manner I did."[19]

The Mankiller's seemingly autonomous actions to reacquire trade and status for his town should not obscure the fact that Old Hop and other Overhill leaders either directly supported or at the very least countenanced his initial proceedings. Though Demere at first confessed it was impossible "to find the Particulars of their Designs," he quickly became convinced that "All the principal Men were certainly concerned in it without Exception." It was no secret, Creek trader Lachlan McGillivray later agreed, that the "Great Tellico affair was but a sham excuse, to hold correspondence with the French." Yet Tellico, Chota, and their respective leaders increasingly diverged over how to continue and control the events set in motion by the initial visit to Fort Toulouse and New Orleans. The greatest difference that emerged between the Mankiller and his Chota-based rivals was that he continued to openly maintain contact with the French, while the latter headmen openly disavowed such proceedings, regardless their true political leanings.[20]

The Chota-Tellico fallout over the Mankiller's diplomatic endeavors was not solely an intraregional struggle either, for it also drove a wedge between the conjoined towns of Tellico and Chatuga. One of the agreements reached between the Mankiller and French officers at Fort Toulouse was that Tellico and Chatuga were to relocate to Hiwassee Old Town, an abandoned Cherokee settlement thirty miles closer to the French. At first, it appeared Chatuga planned to "joine the Tellico People," but the reverse soon became apparent. Central to this reformation was the role played by the Chatuga women to influence village politics. An early report indicated, for instance, "all the Women of the Town of Great Tellico were gone" to meet the Mankiller, but "none of the Women of Chatuga went with them." Chatuga women, including several from Tellico, further served as informants to Raymond Demere, even after members of the disaffected party threatened their lives. The influence of these women ultimately prevented Chatuga from following the path laid out by the Mankiller of Tellico. Word reached Demere in January 1757 that "the whole town of Tellico, Men, Women and Children," had left for Hiwassee Old Town. He likewise learned that "Not a Man of the Town of Chatuga is gone with them." To the contrary, the Chatuga people had discussed removing to the other Overhill Towns and leaving "the Tellico People to themselves."[21]

In an effort to both redeem Tellico and ensure Chatuga's reformation, Demere dispatched Lieutenant Robert Wall to Tellico in early January. Not surprisingly, the dialogue that followed centered almost exclusively on gifts and trade. Demere worried that the redeemed Chatugans, or "the honest Town of Chatuga," as he described them, had been unfairly and injudiciously included in the Overhill leadership's embargo of British presents. He consequently challenged their authority by distributing presents to Chatuga. Although Tellico remained openly intransigent, Demere encouraged Lieutenant Wall to heed their complaints to see if similar action was needed for Chatuga's brother town.[22]

Wall arrived at Great Tellico on the evening of January 10, and a ceremonial gathering of three hundred Cherokees followed the next day in the townhouse. The Mankiller, Kenoteta, and the Emperor of Tellico seated Wall at its upper end, all the while observing "Nothing but the greatest Order, Decorum and Attention." After exchanging greetings and small tokens of peace, the Mankiller described their prior "bad Thoughts," adding that "the very Breath that came out of their Mouths" had been "infected and bad." He explained to Wall that their motives were actuated by their belief "that the great King George did not regard them as his Children," for they "never received any Presents from him." When the British did send gifts, he continued, "they were always distributed without any Notice taken or Provision being made for them." Alluding to a lack of status derived from their geographic disconnect and the recent power shift within the Overhill Towns, the Mankiller concluded that "they were looked upon as a different People because their Town was separated from the others."[23]

A lack of "Notice" and gifts from the British had also been accompanied by a sharp drop in trade, as witnessed earlier with the "heavy Complaint" against Robert Goudy. The Mankiller reiterated these grievances in the Tellico townhouse, as his talk was "much about a Trader they want in their Town" to get "Things pretty cheap." Wall empathized with the Mankiller, informing his superiors there was "not more Goods in both these Towns than one Packhorse can carry." Ever since Goudy "left off storekeeping there," another officer later concurred, Tellico had not "been properly supplied." The known correlation between trade and alliance made such reports especially alarming to British officers. "If there is not some Alteration and Amendment made therein," Lieutenant Wall cautioned, "those Towns will always be uneasy and dissatisfied."[24]

Captain Demere was therefore unexpectedly pleased when Wall sent an express from Tellico with news that the Mankiller and his townspeople displayed the most sincere professions of faith toward the British. After the Tellicans "hoisted the Union Flag" atop the townhouse, all the men and women of the village engaged in ceremonial dance to publicly affirm their attachment. Even the Mankiller, who told Wall "he never danced but upon some extraordinary Occasion," performed before the lieutenant. The Mankiller and other villagers then observed the most "profound Sylence," whereupon they promised to immediately "dispatch Runners to their Brothers at Chottee and all the seven Towns" to let them know "their Hearts were streight."[25]

Reaffirming attachment to the Chota leadership reflects an important reason as to why the Mankiller and his party orchestrated such a public display of peace. The withholding of presents and traders by Overhill leaders certainly played a part, but equally significant to the redeeming of Tellico and Chatuga was the effectiveness of Cherokee social control mechanisms. Although speaking in general terms of southeastern Indians, James Adair wrote at length about the "severe sarcasms" used by family members and townspeople to shame miscreants out of their ill habits. "I have known them to strike their delinquents with those sweetened darts," he observed, "so good naturedly and skilfully, that they would sooner die by torture, than renew their shame by repeating the actions." While we do not know the specific language used to marginalize Tellico and its leaders, we do know that the Mankiller, by his own admittance, felt "hated and disliked by every Body in the Nation." Raymond Demere attempted to feed these insecurities by telling the Mankiller that "his bad Behaviour had rendered him despicable in the Eyes of every Body and despised even by his own Relations." Indeed, the Tellico affair had become a town, regional, and family matter as the Mankiller's brother, Kenoteta, "fell out with him upon that Account." Initially involved in the diplomatic mission to Fort Toulouse, Kenoteta quickly altered his policies, saying to his brother, "I am determined to stand by the English . . . and I will be the first amongst them to dye and if you have a Mind to dye with the French you may." Kenoteta thereafter joined other Overhill headmen in denouncing the Mankiller, at one point making him "cry bitterly by reproaching him [for] his bad Conduct." The fraternal split had become so acute by Lieutenant Wall's visit to Tellico that rumors spread that the Mankiller's "own Brother will be persuaded to kill him, if he insists much longer in his Opinion."[26]

Trade embargos and neighborhood scorn had their limitations, however, one of which being that each method took time. The political leanings of the Tellico people therefore remained ambiguous for most of 1757. Particularly problematic for the British and their Cherokee supporters was the influence of French-allied Shawnees on Tellico and the Overhill Towns in general. Reports from Cherokee country indicated, for example, that both the French *and* Shawnees had "seduced the Tellico people." A British agent among the Creeks gave these anonymous seducers an identity: "I find the Channel through which the bad Talks run is by Means of two French Incendiarys, Peter Chartee and Mr. Lantanniact."[27]

Peter Chartier was a well-known leader of the Ohio Shawnees. About the year 1750, he led a contingent of his people to live among the Upper Creeks. Sometimes referred to as the Southern Shawnees, Chartier's band worked to strengthen connections between the French, Upper Creeks, and Overhill Cherokees. This was not a novel development, of course. The Shawnees and other Northward Indians had complicated Cherokee relations with both Carolina and the Creeks during the long war from 1715 to 1755. Their roles as French go-betweens continued throughout the Seven Years' War, even as Shawnee-Cherokee hostilities escalated following Glen's imprisonment of Shawnee warriors in 1753. Chartier and the Southern Shawnees frequently visited Tellico and the Overhills, while a detachment of this band lived among them for several years preceding the Tellico incident. The British and Cherokee backlash to Tellico's French connections was correspondingly a backlash to their Shawnee associations. As the Blind Slave Catcher of Chatuga noted after his town returned to the British fold, "There is none of the Towns in the Cherrockee Nation that has such bad Thoughts as the Town of Tellico, for they and the Savannahs are alike."[28]

With Tellico's allegiance still in doubt, especially after the Blind Slave Catcher implicated "every Man in Tellico" for being "concerned in the Affair," Captain Demere prompted Overhill leaders to enact stronger measures against the disaffected town. Demere's efforts were facilitated by the stationing of his company of Independents at Fort Loudoun, where he was able to maintain regular contact with the Chota leadership. Demere was particularly unsettled about those Shawnees who fled from Tellico upon his arrival at the fort but who thereafter visited that town for extended periods. In order to effectively complete the marginalization of Tellico and return them to the British interest, Demere promoted a scheme to attack and kill any Shawnees who returned to Tellico.[29]

His chance came in June 1757 when messengers reported seven Shawnee men and two women had arrived in Tellico from the Upper Creeks. Whereas Demere had earlier questioned the Overhill headmen's strategies of withholding gifts and trade to redeem Tellico, he had no qualms in exploiting another Cherokee approach for uniting town and regional factions—the creation of a common enemy through warfare. Demere believed an attack on these Shawnees would "certainly spoil any bad Schemes left in the Tellico People" who "must take up the Hatchet against the Savannahs in their own Defence." Working within Cherokee political structures to effect pro-British policies, Demere approached Old Hop, Standing Turkey, and two of the Mankiller's relations, Kenoteta and their father, the Smallpox Conjuror of Settico, to carry out the attack.

The Overhill headmen were against Demere's scheme, arguing that these Shawnees came in a "peaceable" manner.[30]

Old Hop was especially concerned with how an attack on these Southern Shawnees would destabilize Cherokee-Creek relations—a valid concern when the costly forty-year Creek War had just ended. The Chota beloved man had in fact already sent messengers to Okchai, an Upper Creek town, to discuss the Overhill Cherokees' dilemma with the Shawnees. Not only could an unprovoked attack on the Shawnees in Tellico spark another Creek War, since Peter Chartier's band was under Creek protection, but the immediate result might mean the death of Old Hop's messengers. Demere nevertheless pushed the headmen to act by reminding them the Shawnees were the "mortal and inveterate Enemies" of the English. Weighing its implications for relations with both the Shawnees and Creeks, the Overhill headmen likewise perceived the potential British backlash if they did not consider Demere's request. Ultimately, the Smallpox Conjuror of Settico promised to take charge of the affair, claiming he was a warrior and that Tellico was his town.[31]

The support Demere expected from the Smallpox Conjuror never materialized. Only two Overhill warriors—and those of little note—joined the detachment of Independents who waylaid the Shawnees near their "favourite Town" of Tellico. They killed three of Chartier's band, which brought about fears of immediate reprisals. Old Hop recommended that Demere "acquaint the out Settlements" of Carolina about a forthcoming Shawnee attack because of British involvement, while the Cherokee "out Town" of Chatuga recognized they were also in danger and "pleaded much for Guns" and ammunition. This danger appeared rather quickly, as a runner from Tellico "came riding very fast" to Fort Loudoun "and gave several Times the War Hoope, and cried Savannah, Savannah." The messenger told Demere that a Cherokee from Tomatly had been either killed or captured by the Shawnees. Demere outwardly lamented the loss of this Tomatly man, but he privately wrote to the governor that it was "one of the best Things that could have happened for us, that the Savannahs should have begun with one of the Cherokee Indians," which would "put an End to all, and will bring [in] those bad Men of Tellico too."[32]

Unfortunately for Demere and his hopes of putting "an End to all," the effects of the Tellico affair still lingered. Savannah Tom, a Shawnee working in the French interest, arrived at Tellico with French John and his party, and he killed the wife of a soldier stationed at Fort Loudoun. His accomplice in the slaying was the wife of a Tellico warrior called "the Thigh." Formerly a prisoner among the Shawnees and fluent in their language, the Thigh had strong connections to his former captors and other French-allied Indians. Thus, as many Overhill people increasingly distanced themselves from the Shawnees and French, a minority of Tellicans continued to harbor Shawnees in their village throughout the summer and fall of 1757. These ambiguous but alarming associations prompted the newly arrived captain of the Independents, Paul Demere, to look upon the "Tellico People almost as the greatest Enemies we have." Raymond Demere shared his younger brother's views. After being relieved by Paul to tend to his health and troubling financial situation, Raymond returned to Charlestown by a lesser-used and longer route to avoid the disaffected town of Tellico.[33]

By the time Paul Demere arrived at Fort Loudoun in August, a number of Overhill headmen under the guidance of Attakullakulla and Ostenaco had openly cast their lot with the British and sought to further marginalize the Tellico people. When sentries fired at two unidentifiable Indians "creeping along" the fort at night, Overhill leaders alerted the new captain that "they were not Savannah Indians, but Tellico, and wished they had been killed." Attakullakulla likewise assured Demere he and the other "great Men" in the Overhills looked on Tellico "as our and their Enemies, and would destroy them as much as laid in their Power." Realizing that clan revenge limited that which "laid in their Power," headmen continued to shame the Tellicans and prevented British presents (including rum) from entering that town.[34]

The Overhill leadership's increasing commitment to the British by the fall of 1757 should not be dissociated from the interregional dynamic of the struggle for empire in Cherokee country. Although Tellico's maneuverings and its reverberations within the Overhill Towns reflected the localism of Cherokee politics, headmen and townspeople from other regions also had a decided impact on the ultimate outcome of the Tellico affair. Rather than through direct political confrontation, which did at times occur, the most effective means by which other Cherokees effected policy change was through their involvement in the Seven Years' War as military allies of the British. Thus, just as Raymond Demere believed that attacking the Shawnees would end the Mankiller's schemes and return the "bad Men of Tellico" to the British fold, Cherokee leaders sought to use warfare as a means to direct cross-regional policy. The two most important venues wherein Cherokee headmen and warriors pushed their agendas were the Ohio country and the environs of the Mississippi River valley.

Following George Washington's escapades into the Ohio country culminating in the Fort Necessity debacle, the British war effort only worsened. General Edward Braddock lost his life and his army near the forks of the Ohio River in 1755, as the French and their Indian allies successfully defended newly constructed Fort Duquesne. These failures in part opened a window of opportunity for Shawnees, Delawares, Mingos, and other Ohio Indians who challenged British expansion into western Virginia and Pennsylvania by attacking backcountry settlements with repeated success. One of the most destructive border wars in American history resulted, as thousands of British settlers were captured, killed, or displaced. To stem the onslaught, Virginia sent frequent appeals to the Cherokees to scout and defend the colony's western borders. Cherokee responses early in the war, however, provided little encouragement to the beleaguered Virginians. No Cherokees joined either Washington or Braddock in 1754–55, although great promises had been made of sending hundreds of warriors to their assistance. A few Cherokees did join the Great Sandy River expedition against the Lower Shawnee Towns in early 1756, but the disastrous failure of the campaign generated great concern among the Cherokees about Virginia and British capabilities in woodland warfare. Nevertheless, many Cherokees increasingly recognized the potential offered by stronger connections to Virginia.[35]

The Virginia government promised the Cherokees not only a ready supply of gifts but also the possibility of increased trade in return for services rendered in that colony's defense. As a result, Cherokee warriors traveled north—a trickle at first, then by the hundreds. By the fall of 1757, between 150 and 250 Cherokees effectively scouted the Virginia backcountry, which "kept the Enemy's Parties out of its Settlements." Most of these early recruits came from the Lower and Middle Towns. Unnerved by the Tellico mission and the Mankiller's continued correspondence with the French and Shawnees, headmen and warriors from other regions found an opportunity in Virginia to acquire a new trading outlet, challenge the ascendancy of Chota, and deflate the Overhill-centered French faction. Lower Town leaders testified to these regional divisions when they assured the British that "the Overhill Towns may do whatever they please but if they incline to turn to the French they will divide the Nation and be true to the English."[36]

Sending warriors to Virginia to take French and Indian scalps, particularly those of the Shawnees, had the desired effect. The most influential Overhill headmen found it increasingly difficult to openly engage the French while maintaining their preeminent position within Cherokee country. Strong political messages were sent, for example, when the Chota leadership called national councils and "very few of the Leading men came from the Valley and Lower towns and but a few from the Middle Settlements." Overhill leaders subsequently encouraged their warriors to join other Cherokees in Virginia as well as to conduct raids on the French and their Indian allies in the trans-Appalachian west.[37]

These strategies of creating common enemies through warfare culminated in October 1757 with a more sincere and binding profession of faith from the Tellico people than that which had occurred with Lieutenant Wall the previous January. The all-important Green Corn Dance had commenced, which was the most consequential ceremony in terms of alleviating dissention between towns, regions, and clans. The Tellico people arrived at Chota for the five-day event but at first kept their distance from other Cherokees. Attakullakulla approached them, saying he was ashamed of their behavior toward the English and for their harboring the Shawnees in their town. He then called the Tellicans his "Brethren" but warned they would "be always Naked, and despised" as long as they hearkened to the French and their Shawnee emissaries. The Tellico people replied it was not entirely their fault, as "some of their headmen was the Creation of it."

Prompted by their own villagers, the Mankiller and other Tellico headmen entered the Chota townhouse the next day and admitted that "they were ashamed of themselves . . . & that they were very sorry for what they had done." They then presented a belt of peace and pleaded with Attakullakulla to give a talk in their favor to Demere. Attakullakulla received the belt but held it at length before speaking: "I have been for a long time asham'd of the Conduct and Behaviour of the Tellico People," but they have now promised "they would stand by the English, Like the rest of the Cherokees." The Tellicans should be forgiven, Old Hop concurred, whereupon he raised the belt over his head and reminded all present in the townhouse that the Tellico people "are our Neighbours and Children of our Fathers the Cherokees." When the Green Corn Dance ended, Attakullakulla spoke to Demere on behalf of Tellico, whereupon the officer pleasingly wrote to the governor "that the Talico People was quite reformed."[38]

William Henry Lyttelton, the new governor of South Carolina who had replaced James Glen the previous year, remained skeptical. He informed Demere that, before Tellico could expect a trader in their town, "they must prove that their repentance is Sincere." The best method of doing so was by their "bringing the Scalp of some Frenchman or Savannah," an act of political support that Cherokees from other towns and regions had already demonstrated to the British. Although the Mankiller and other Tellicans had warred sporadically against the French and their Indian allies following Lieutenant Wall's visit, the aftermath of the Green Corn Dance marked a turning point in the Tellico affair. Tellico and other Overhill war parties increasingly attacked their former "friends" with the purpose of convincing both the Chota leadership and the British, in the words of one village headman, "that Tellico Town is as much attached to the English Interest as any other Town." The Tellico people upheld their rhetoric, for by the onset of the new year, Attakullakulla notified Demere that "the French Indians now know that wee are in open War with them." Other signs that Attakullakulla and Old Hop believed the sincerity of Tellico's conversion could be found in their redistribution of goods. Whereas Overhill leaders earlier withheld gifts and traders from Tellico to marginalize the disaffected town, they now "interceded for it, that it might have goods." Demere therefore confidently repeated his assurances to Lyttelton in February 1758 that the town of Tellico was "Entirely Reformed," particularly when Tellico warriors and others from the Overhills returned with French and enemy Indian scalps.[39]

The ritual redemption of Tellico during the Green Corn Ceremony took place as a result of a tense, drawn-out political struggle within the Overhill Towns and throughout Cherokee country. The conflict centered largely on access to trade. Although South Carolina remained the indisputable Cherokee trading partner throughout the Seven Years' War, mountain villagers increasingly pursued other sources of goods. Tellico, with the initial support of influential Overhill leaders, searched for allies and trading outlets among the French. The Mankiller and his adherents, however, failed to shift Cherokee trading alliances toward French Louisiana primarily because headmen and warriors from all regions relied on the British for a steady supply of goods. The marginalization of Tellico and the French faction subsequently resulted. Overhill leaders sought to deny Tellico both presents and traders while townspeople used well-entrenched social control mechanisms to convert the Tellicans. As one Tellico headman later cited as a reason for his return to the English fold, "We were despised by the Rest and always naked." Other Cherokees responded to the Tellico affair by working within the British alliance and strengthening their ties to Williamsburg. Headmen and warriors from the Lower and Middle Towns in particular responded to Virginia's call for assistance by traveling north to war against the French and their Indian supporters. But promises of gifts and a steady trade failed to materialize. The resulting disappointment, combined with a hostile reception by Virginia's backcountry population, prompted Cherokees to once again reconsider the nature of the Anglo-Cherokee alliance. As events spiraled increasingly out of control in the Virginia backcountry, the alliance would not stand.[40]

5

"in a discontented mood"

The Crisis in Virginia

Endeavoring to reinvigorate the alliance following the Tellico affair, many Cherokees demonstrated their political and economic attachment to Britain by warring against the French and their Indian allies. Overhill and Valley peoples, situated on the western fringes of Cherokee country, frequently targeted those enemies beyond the Appalachian Mountains. Warriors from these settlements also joined Cherokees from other regions in western Virginia, Maryland, and Pennsylvania. Judging by numbers alone, the Cherokees proved the most committed Native American ally of the British throughout the early stages of the Seven Years' War. The best estimates ranged from 600 to 1,200 Cherokee warriors at the peak of their involvement, prompting General John Forbes to rightfully observe, "They are by far the greatest body of Indians that we have ever had to join us."[1]

Cherokee experiences in Virginia, however, steadily undermined "the antient Friendship and Union" they had long held with South Carolina. British officers at times treated warriors contemptibly, while negligence in following established norms of gift-giving compounded an already volatile situation. Relations worsened as Cherokees and frontier settlers eyed one another with certain mistrust, which led to thefts, confrontations, and murders on both sides. Although resentment was initially found only in a few towns, the conflict quickly widened when Virginians killed headmen and warriors from the Lower, Middle, and Valley Settlements. The emerging crisis thus became an interregional affair, but vengeful Cherokees limited their attacks to Virginia to maintain stable relations with Carolina and its traders.

Efforts to contain the conflict appeared to work. The Overhill people did not support other Cherokees in their raids against Virginia, and the

Chota-based leadership rebuked hostile towns for their actions. Without the support of the Overhill Settlements, headmen in other regions attempted to defuse the crisis by utilizing their South Carolina connections. The winter of 1758–59 seemed promising as Cherokee delegates successfully negotiated with Governor Lyttelton in Charlestown. But hopes for peace collapsed the following spring. Moytoy of Settico, an Overhill warrior and headman, broke with the Chota leadership and orchestrated the killing of nineteen settlers in the Carolinas. Moytoy's actions accordingly brought both South Carolina and the Overhill Towns more directly into the conflict. Political disputes sharpened throughout Cherokee country, much like those witnessed during the Tellico affair, as headmen from all regions distanced themselves and their people from the offending parties. Peace-minded Cherokees also organized two cross-regional delegations to keep the path open to Carolina and put an end to what had become more than just a crisis in Virginia. The government in Charlestown had other ideas.

The early Anglo-Cherokee alliance rested upon trade, but it was strengthened through warfare. Cherokees assisted the English in the Tuscarora War and seemingly rescued South Carolina from the throes of disaster during the Yamasee uprising by massacring the Creek delegation at Tugaloo. Carolinians thereafter spoke of the Cherokees as "our first Friends" and vowed to defend their indigenous neighbors if attacked by the French or enemy Indians. The Treaty of 1730 further bound the two peoples militarily. The second article required Cherokees to fight Great Britain's enemies, and the seven headmen then in London affirmed "the Great King George's Enemies shall be our Enemies, his People and ours shall be always one, and shall die together." The fulfillment of these promises after 1730 was more rhetoric than reality, but the Seven Years' War brought significant changes to the military alliance.[2]

Perhaps the most consequential change was the emergence of Virginia as a key player in Cherokee country. Virginians had long maintained trading connections to the Cherokees, but Williamsburg never mounted a serious challenge to Charlestown's hold on the southeastern deerskin trade. Nevertheless, Carolina remained in constant vigilance against "those Interlopers." The Treaty of 1730 added to this potential trading rivalry with its ambiguous language. The first article required "the English in Carolina" to trade with the Cherokees. The fourth article, on the other hand, was less restrictive, stipulating the Cherokees "shall not suffer their People to trade with the white Men of any other Nation but the English." The treaty was therefore primarily a contract with South Carolina, but it permitted the Cherokees to deal with other English colonies. Speaking in a localized context that every Cherokee could understand, one savvy trader reminded village leaders that "the English [in Carolina] was but one Town, & that there was more Towns for them to go to at Virginia"[3]

It was not until the imperial crisis began anew that a Virginia-Cherokee alliance became a real possibility. With Virginia reeling from enemy Indian incursions and many Cherokees pursuing trade outlets beyond Carolina, the two peoples strengthened their economic and military ties. Overhill leaders in particular utilized their geographic proximity to the Commonwealth to secure a Virginia alliance. In March 1756, Overhill headmen and commissioners from Virginia conducted treaty negotiations near the Broad River in South Carolina. During the proceedings, Overhill representatives sought to reaffirm their regional supremacy, which suffered throughout the Tellico affair, by controlling Cherokee dealings with Williamsburg. Attakullakulla welcomed the commissioners to their hunting grounds but requested that subsequent agents and communications instead travel "the *Northward* Path, it being the nearest" to their towns, rather than "the *Southern* Path," whereby he and other Overhill leaders had to "cross the Mountains." Attakullakulla then informed the Virginians that his people were the most capable of providing assistance against the French and enemy Indians. "I must tell you," he noted, "that all our People, who, by their Situation, can be most useful on this Occasion, live in the upper Towns." When Virginia's agents pressed their counterparts to dispatch warriors to the north, headmen insisted they first build a fort in the Overhill Towns to protect their women and children.[4]

An English fort in the Overhill country had been a matter of consequence prior to 1756. Overhill headmen had long petitioned South Carolina to establish a garrison for their protection, and these appeals appeared more frequently once Fort Prince George became a reality within the Lower Towns in 1753. But Charlestown was slow to act, which prompted village leaders to believe Governor Glen had "forfeited his Word." In urgent need of manpower, Virginia sent Major Andrew Lewis with sixty men to Chota. They built a small fort and then returned home. Although Overhill leaders wanted troops to man the structure, they were at least pleased with Virginia's efforts to fulfill their treaty obligations and accordingly encouraged warriors to travel north. The number of warriors increased substantially once Carolina built and garrisoned Fort Loudoun shortly thereafter. These developments marked important changes in the Anglo-Cherokee alliance, as British and Cherokee peoples directly involved themselves in each other's military affairs to an unheralded degree. The trading alliance, in short, became more martially oriented as the Seven Years' War progressed.[5]

From 1756 to 1758, Cherokees from every region crisscrossed the southern and mid-Atlantic borderlands in search of scalps, prisoners, and presents. Headmen and warriors provided valuable services to the British, not only protecting colonial settlements but also gathering intelligence by scouting Fort Duquesne and capturing French and Indian prisoners. Cherokee war parties likewise killed many of the enemy, which placed French-allied Indians on the defensive and made them more willing to sue for peace. British and colonial leaders readily understood the significance of the Cherokee alliance to their military success. Captain Raymond Demere called them "the best feather in our Cap's," while Colonel George Washington of the Virginia regiment found the Cherokees "indispensably necessary in our present circumstances." Although relatively inexperienced in Indian affairs, Washington recognized that Cherokee assistance might determine the outcome of the British drive to the Ohio. He was particularly impressed with the advantages Cherokees brought to woodland warfare. "I can not look upon strength and Success in the Woods to be the Consequence of Numbers," he wrote, which made the Cherokees (and Catawbas) "the only Troops fit to cope" with the enemy's "Sculking" way of war.[6]

General Forbes, commander of the expedition against Fort Duquesne in 1758, agreed with Washington and sought to avoid the mistakes made by General Braddock three years earlier when he did not utilize Indian auxiliaries. Forbes believed "the Cherokees of such Consequence" that when the number of colonial recruits failed to meet his expectations early in the campaign, the general declared, "Necessity will turn me a Cherokee, and don't be surprised if I take F: du Quesne at the head of them; and them only." Forbes's comments perhaps reflected more his frustration with the lack of colonial support than his faith in Indian fighting capabilities, yet he understood the importance of Cherokee military assistance. Upon hearing of Cherokee restlessness in the midst of the expedition, Forbes felt nothing could prevent his success against the French except "the defection of the Cherokees." Colonel Washington feared much worse than failure at Fort Duquesne if their disaffection proved general. Realizing the Cherokee alliance was "of the last importance to the colonies in general, and this in particular," the Virginia officer worried that a break with those people "may be productive of the most destructive consequences to the British Affairs in America, and terminate in the ruin of our Southern Settlements."[7]

Washington's anxiety portended a future crisis in Anglo-Cherokee affairs. Virginia mismanagement of its newfound allies was partly to blame. Doubts about Virginia capabilities in Indian affairs surfaced immediately after the colony's initial call for Cherokee assistance in 1754. Governor Glen, who was apprehensive of South Carolina's tenuous situation as a frontier colony and protective of Charlestown's special position in the Cherokee trade, bluntly informed Lieutenant Governor Robert Dinwiddie of Virginia that Carolina "is [extremely] jealous of any other Colonies intermeddling [with] our Indians." Glen asserted that Carolinians "by long Experience" had become acquainted with the "Nature and Inclinations" of the Cherokees and therefore managed "to keep them steady in the British Interest." The governor was so certain of his management of the Cherokees that he promised Dinwiddie to "answer for their good Behaviour with my Life, if your Province does not interfere." To the contrary, if Dinwiddie continued to lure the Cherokees to Virginia, Glen cautioned, "I fear it will have an Effect in the End to withdraw them from the British Interest." Sir William Johnson of New York agreed. The recently appointed superintendent of Indian affairs in the Northern District wrote to the governor of Pennsylvania in 1757 that the "Scheme" to recruit the Cherokees, if handled improperly, "may be attended with Effects very much to the Disadvantage of yours and the neighbouring Southern Governments."[8]

These concerns proved prophetic. Of particular importance to both Cherokees and informed British officials was the interconnectedness of gift-giving, trade, and alliances. Cherokees looked toward the war in the north with a diplomatic and economic gaze, as many desired to not only reaffirm their alliance with Britain but also to enjoy the benefits of stronger gift-giving and trading partnerships with both Charlestown and Williamsburg. The allure of material rewards for military service held great promise. Captain Paul Demere recorded that Cherokee warriors were typically given two pounds of powder, four pounds of bullets, a knife, paint, flints, and sometimes a hatchet for a longer warring expedition. Enemy captives and scalps also brought tangible benefits, as when Virginia paid the Second Yellow Bird and his party £30 for a Canadian prisoner taken in 1757.[9]

But going to war also held economic risks. The loss of a hunting season meant that warriors did not accumulate skins to repay their traders, which discouraged traders from extending further credit. To encourage Cherokee participation in the face of such obstacles, Virginia pledged forty weight of leather to each man in the spring of 1758 "to make them amends for the loss of the summer-hunt." The Cherokees appreciated such assurances of reimbursement, but in the meantime they looked "upon all their [past] Accounts as settled" by the act of going to war—a view not shared by traders, who were themselves indebted to merchants. These diverging views complicated relations between the Cherokees and their traders and placed a heavy burden on the Virginia government to make good its promises.[10]

This burden increasingly appeared too much to bear. As hundreds of Cherokee warriors arrived in the Virginia backcountry insisting upon presents, inexperienced officers in the Virginia regiment acceded to their demands. Captain George Mercer was one such officer who, according to Washington, promised a large supply of gifts to prevent Cherokees from returning home "in a discontented mood." Maintaining that Mercer had not been given proper orders to deal with the matter, Washington also admitted that the captain, "(nor are any of us who are now here) is but little acquainted with the proper manner of treating them."[11]

Washington must have therefore felt relieved when Superintendent Edmond Atkin arrived at Winchester, a backcountry town in Virginia that served as the general rendezvous for Cherokee warriors and British presents. Atkin soon confirmed Glen's initial fears when he alerted Governor Lyttelton of the Virginians' inexperience in Indian affairs. Displeased by the incident involving Cherokee warriors and Captain Mercer, the superintendent was both humored and annoyed by the extent of their demands for presents, relating to Lyttelton that it "would make you laugh to see how they rack'd their Brains to make it out." Once Mercer and others caved to such requests, other war parties increased their demands for services rendered. This situation became increasingly problematic for Anglo-Cherokee relations, which was reflected in the frustrating correspondence of those involved in the business. Even Atkin, a supposed expert in the management of Indians, quickly became overwhelmed by Cherokee demands and encountered much criticism for his own inabilities.[12]

Presents therefore became a point of contention between the British and Cherokees. As the Seven Years' War intensified, the cost of fighting a global imperial contest hindered British effectiveness and willingness to satisfy Native American demands for presents. The gifts offered to Cherokee warriors rarely met their expectations, and headmen of note bitterly denounced Virginia officials as "liars." Cherokee warriors were additionally concerned about the cumbersome nature of the British war machine. With hundreds of Cherokees ready to assist the British in the spring of 1758, few signs existed of an organized army preparing to march against Fort Duquesne. General Forbes wrote to his superiors about the Cherokees' displeasure "at not seeing our Army and Artillery assembled." They "begin to weary, and languish after their own homes," he noted, which prompted many to leave before the campaign materialized. This piqued the general, who became increasingly frustrated with his allies. Whereas the general had earlier commended the Cherokees for being "fully as good as their Promise," he now derided "their natural fickle disposition." They "are most certainly a very great plague," he wrote, for "putting us, to a very great expence and doing of nothing for it."[13]

Cherokee disaffection in the spring of 1758 resulted from other forms of British mismanagement in Indian affairs. Especially disturbing were peace talks carried on between Virginia, Pennsylvania, and the Ohio Indians, which culminated in the Treaty of Easton later that fall. As Forbes prepared to move against Fort Duquesne, many on both sides had become war-weary. Teedyuscung, a Delaware from the Wyoming Valley in Pennsylvania, worked diligently to bring about peace between the British and Ohio Indians. This proposed peace—and the health of Teedyuscung's unpopular pro-British platform—could only survive if the Cherokees ceased attacking the Shawnees, Delawares, and other Ohio peoples. The Delaware leader accordingly entreated Governor Denny of Pennsylvania to prevent Cherokees from continuing the war. If the killings continued, he counseled Denny, the Ohio Indians will not say the Cherokees did it, "but that You have done it; who hired & Sent them, and this will undo all what we have done."[14]

Teedyuscung rightly feared the Anglo-Cherokee military alliance would ruin his peace efforts. In turn, some British and colonial officials, even those in the war-torn Mid-Atlantic, worried less about peace with the Ohio Indians and more about offending the Cherokees. Officers stationed in Virginia believed British policies should not affront those who "have always been our Friends, to oblige those who revolted from our Friendship & have been our professed Enemies." These officers recognized the benefits of Teedyuscung's proposals, which sought to include the Cherokees in peace negotiations, but they nevertheless advised their superiors not to lay the plan before the Cherokees, else it "may be productive of Consequences as fatal to the prosperity of the southern Colonies as a Peace with those Indians, would be serviceable to the Northern." But Cherokee headmen had their own diplomatic channels and were fully aware of what was afoot. Finding their supposed British allies pulled different ways in Indian affairs, Cherokees imagined their worst fears had been realized: as soon as the British encouraged them to attack the many Indian nations in the French interest, they would make peace and thereby leave the Cherokees alone "to be destroyed."[15]

The return homeward of disgruntled Cherokee warriors and headmen did not bode well for Virginia. Some Cherokees had earlier threatened to plunder settlers as they headed south. Such threats proved genuine as accounts from the Virginia backcountry detailed how the inhabitants were "robbed and other ways ill treated." Horse stealing generated the most concern, and since free range was a common practice in the colonial South, acquiring the animals by dubious means was not difficult. Cherokee warriors often did little to conceal their acquisition of "great Gangs of Horses" from Virginia. One settler espied a small party of Cherokees who "stopped in an open, convenient Part of the Road to try the Horses they had but just stolen and continued there some Time paceing up and down the Road diverting themselves." Cherokees also confiscated horses using threats of force, making the possibility of armed confrontation increasingly likely as settlers sought to protect their property.[16]

Anglo-Cherokee relations worsened when robberies gave way to murders. Backcountry settlers responded to horse thefts by killing two warriors from Estatoe. The Estatoe people retaliated by killing two Virginians in March 1758. The conflict at first remained limited to only a few towns in the Lower Settlements. When confronted about the murders, Estatoe leaders attempted to divert blame away from their town. They first accused the Raven of Toxaway, another Lower Town headman, and then an Overhill warrior who they claimed led the attack. Overhill leaders responded in kind, telling British authorities, "It was not an over the Hills man that headed the Gang that killed the White People but some of the Lower Towns."[17]

The conflict quickly became a cross-regional matter, however, when Cherokees from other towns were murdered. In three separate incidents, backcountry settlers from Bedford County, Virginia, killed more Estatoe people as well as warriors of great rank from the Valley and Middle Settlements. The death of these "fellows of Great Note" prompted headmen from the Valley, Middle, and Out Towns to organize war parties. Lower Town warriors from Estatoe, Qualatchie, and Toxaway also left for Virginia to seek revenge for lost clan members and town leaders, which numbered perhaps as many as thirty-seven killed from all Cherokee towns. The conflict seemed to have become so widespread by the fall of 1758 that Thomas Beamer, the Cherokee son of trader James Beamer, reported that townspeople "all over the whole Nation in general say that it will be a War."[18]

Young Beamer's observation, however, applied to those Cherokees primarily in the Lower, Middle, Valley, and Out Towns. The Overhills had not lost any people in Virginia. Attakullakulla, Old Hop, and other Overhill leaders accordingly distanced themselves from the guilty parties, blaming it all on the "Rogues in our Lower Towns." When runners came to Chota from the Lower and Middle Settlements requesting assistance, Overhill headmen forbid their warriors to go against Virginia. Old Hop and Attakullakulla sent instead "a Strong Talk to the lower Towns Indians" and further assured Captain Paul Demere that if other Cherokees killed the traders and soldiers in their villages, the Overhill people would join the English "and destroy them all." James Adair later testified to the significance of these regional differences when he recalled that "a misunderstanding had subsisted some time, between several distant towns, and those who chanced to lose their people in Virginia." There "were seven northern towns," he continued, "who from the beginning of the unhappy grievances, firmly dissented from the hostile intentions of their suffering and enraged country-men, and for a considerable time before, bore them little good will." The trader ventured this could "soon have been changed into a very hot civil war, had we been so wise as to have improved the favourable opportunity."[19]

Adair's understanding of Cherokee regional differences—although far from becoming "a very hot civil war"—partially explains why the crisis in Virginia remained a limited border conflict. Lower and Middle Town leaders found that Overhill nonparticipation in the conflict undermined their efforts against the Virginians. It was therefore no surprise when rumors surfaced that these headmen hoped Virginians would "kill the Little Carpenter or some of his gang and then that they may have the over Hills People to Joyn them." Attakullakulla had in fact put himself in harm's way by traveling to Virginia in the fall of 1758 to join the British assault on Fort Duquesne—at least that is what General Forbes believed, which led to a troubling incident that worsened relations between the Overhill Cherokees and Virginia.[20]

Before Forbes made his final push toward the French fort in October and November, nearly all Cherokee war parties in the British interest had returned home. Still mindful of the benefits that Indian auxiliaries could provide to the expedition, Forbes was delighted when the "famous Cherokee warrior" Attakullakulla and "about 60 of the best warriors of the nation" arrived at the English camp. The French, however, had abandoned the fort before the British attacked, and feeling their assistance was no longer needed, Attakullakulla and his warriors took leave of the army without notifying Forbes. The general was "astonished and amazed" at this "villainous desertion" during "so very critical a time." Fearing they might join other Cherokee warriors then attacking backcountry settlers in Virginia, Forbes had the party pursued, arrested, disarmed, and stripped of all presents they had been given for their services. The British commander chastised Attakullakulla before ordering his release, whereupon the insulted Cherokee leader sent a heated message to the Overhill people informing them of this mistreatment. Although Attakullakulla later downplayed the incident to promote peace, he disagreed with Forbes over the intent of his original mission, especially when defending his actions to the governors of Virginia and South Carolina. Attakullakulla told them he did not travel north to join Forbes's expedition but to make up all differences that existed between the Cherokees and Virginians. Forbes, however, thought the Overhill party would be more useful to his campaign and thus prevailed on Attakullakulla to go to war, which he did until just days prior to the British capture of vacated Fort Duquesne.[21]

Attakullakulla's subsequent efforts toward peace in Williamsburg and Charlestown demonstrated a lack of unanimity within Cherokee towns and regions concerning the crisis in Virginia. For just as some headmen led war parties against backcountry Virginians, others attempted to restrain their people until they learned whether or not the British intended to give satisfaction. Since the Cherokees' strongest diplomatic and trading connections reached to Charlestown, the response of Governor Lyttelton was particularly important. Lyttelton previously received messages from Lower and Middle Town leaders whose people were most involved in the Virginia incidents. Informing the governor that only a few of their people were then out to war, these headmen warned Lyttelton, "That is nothing in comparison of what will go, if we have not a favourable Answer." Lyttelton responded with equal determination by threatening to withdraw the trade if Cherokees did not "make up the Matter in an amicable way." Reminding Cherokee leaders that "the Armies of the Great King are strong and mighty," Lyttelton also tempered such threats with promises of presents to the affected clan members that would "hide the bones of the dead Men & wipe away the Tears from the Eyes of their friends."[22]

Lyttelton's carrot-and-stick approach worked, largely because a bigger stick rested in Creek hands. Edmond Atkin used the threat of a renewed Cherokee-Creek war to serve British interests. Upon learning that Cherokees expressed great apprehension about his upcoming visit to the Creeks, Atkin deliberately played on these fears, falsely telling Thomas Beamer his mission was to elicit Creek support against the Cherokees. The superintendent further claimed he had fifty horse loads of goods to engage Creek warriors "to Cut them of[f] Root and Branch." Young Beamer returned to Cherokee country with this startling news. Later reports indicated Cherokees swallowed Atkin's bluff, especially after a party of Creeks killed two villagers from Little Estatoe in the fall of 1758. This act of aggression unsettled the Cherokees, prompting the Little Estatoe people to remove to "Big Estatoe," while at the same time encouraging Lower and Middle Cherokees to suspend their attacks against Virginia for fear of a potential war with the Creeks. James Beamer believed the Estatoe killings "Squashed their Pride and Insolence" and brought them to the peace table. Governor Henry Ellis of Georgia likewise found this "unexpected Blow" threw the Cherokees into confusion and "gave an immediate turn to all their plans." Lower and Middle Town headmen subsequently communicated to Governor Lyttelton that their fourteen towns "have Hearts as one," and they were glad the "Path is not bad but good to the Governor of Carolina." Regional leaders also organized a delegation to visit the governor in mid-November. Headmen at the meeting pledged to restrain their people from taking satisfaction in Virginia, while Lyttelton fulfilled his earlier promise of sending presents to "the Relations of the Slain."[23]

The winter of 1758–59 held great promise for the Anglo-Cherokee alliance. Relations had been stretched to the breaking point by the murders in Virginia, but peace efforts by leaders on both sides seemed to prevent a widening of the conflict. Equally important to isolating the conflict was the initial selectivity of Cherokee retaliation to the Bedford County murders. Contrary to British misconceptions that Cherokees would revenge their losses "where Ever they can find it"—a view often maintained among scholars of Cherokee history and the Seven Years' War in general—headmen and clan members demonstrated extreme precision in their efforts to obtain satisfaction. Not only did they target settlers in Virginia, but their initial attacks centered on the local community of Bedford County. These retaliatory raids were even more exact in that they had an ethnic and cultural component. Cherokee warriors specifically attacked German settlers in Bedford County whom they believed the most culpable. When Lower and Middle Town Cherokees requested Overhill assistance, for example, they appealed for help against those people "whom they call Dutch" (i.e., German). Overhill headmen declined, and later reports indicated warriors from other regions "went of[f] to Warr against the Dutch in Virginia."[24]

The targeting of German settlers in Bedford County reflects the importance of place, politics, kinship, and ethnicity to Cherokee understandings of community. That Cherokees were adeptly aware of the multilayered identities and polities of their Euroamerican neighbors should generate little surprise, since Cherokees themselves structured their own communities and identities along the same lines. Thus, when the legal historian John Reid argues for the idea of "corporate responsibility," whereby Cherokees held the "manslayer's nation collectively liable," greater caution is needed in how we evaluate both Cherokee and British conceptions of "nation." As the attacks on Bedford settlers demonstrate, Cherokees did not randomly revenge their losses on just any British subject in America. This desire to restrict clan retaliation to a specific community testified to the political sophistication of Cherokees who sought to limit the conflict to Virginia.[25]

Yet Cherokees were increasingly aware that the British represented a distinct people. The rhetoric of British and colonial officials contributed to these understandings. Governor Horatio Sharpe of Maryland told Cherokee warriors in 1756 that all British inhabitants in America were "one People ... Subjects of the Same great King." Atkin likewise stressed that colonists living "under the several Governours in different Colonies, were like so many different Families only, of whom he [George II] is the common Father." This spirit of unity particularly surfaced following Cherokee attacks in Virginia. Since "all the King's Children upon this Continent were Brothers," warned Governor Lyttelton, the Cherokees would incur "the resentment of this Province" if they continued to take revenge in Virginia.[26]

Perhaps this recognition of British collectivity influenced Moytoy of Settico. The Overhill leader expressed his confusion as to why Cherokee warriors traveled "so far for hair, (meaning Sculps) when they could get it nearer [to] home." In the spring of 1759 Moytoy acted upon these words when his party killed nineteen settlers near the Yadkin and Catawba Rivers. An early British historian claimed the site of the attack resulted from Cherokees being "unacquainted with the provincial boundaries, [who] frequently mistook North Carolina for Virginia." Colonial boundaries in the interior were vague to Indians and colonists alike, but Moytoy may have considered the Virginians and Carolinians "one people." Furthermore, the Settico attacks indicated a continuation of clan revenge based on ethnic and cultural qualifications. Settico warriors may not have retaliated against Germans in Bedford County, but they did return with "some White scalps, from the Dutch Settlement" in western North Carolina. Moytoy of Settico "made no scruple" of telling British officers "he had taken Eight Dutch Scalps" in the raid. James Adair later wrote about these scalping parties going "against those Germans," while also noting that "contrary to the wise orders of their seniors," they had killed "Dutch" settlers not in Virginia but in North Carolina.[27]

The attack on Germans and other settlers in North Carolina revealed that Moytoy's agenda involved more than straightforward clan obligations. Evidence indicates the Settico headman also intended to widen the war and unbalance the Anglo-Cherokee alliance. This strategy was countenanced and perhaps instigated by pro-French Creeks, particularly Mortar of Okchai, who arrived in the Overhill Towns just weeks prior to the attacks. Mortar found in the Virginia killings an opportunity to cultivate anti-British sentiment among some Cherokees. The Upper Creek leader met with Overhill headmen and "Passioned" them against the British with

French talks. Although some leading men refused to hear Mortar, Captain Paul Demere found that Moytoy and Mortar "stayed all Night in the Town House," whereupon the next morning three war parties from Settico "set out . . . against the back Inhabitants."[28]

Mortar received an audience because many Cherokees increasingly mistrusted British intentions. Some "expect to be attacked from Carolina and Virginia," wrote Governor Ellis of Georgia, while others believed the British "would prevail on the Creeks Catawbas and Chickesaws to Join and cut off the Cherokees." Village leaders responded by making "what friends they could," and for some this meant strengthening ties to the Creeks, in spite of the recent killings at Little Estatoe. Ellis found in August 1759, for example, that Cherokee headmen had "for many months past been concerting measures for their defence with the Creeks." One strategy included securing Creek promises of "Assistance and protection" in case an Anglo-Cherokee war erupted. Another approach was to encourage Creeks to live among them as a safeguard against either British or Creek attacks. A party of Creeks successfully petitioned the Lower Cherokees to settle at Old Estatoe, an estimated thirty miles from Fort Prince George. Mortar likewise obtained Overhill and Valley support to form a new settlement along the upper Coosa River. This "new Settled place Ettuea [Etowah]" generated concern among the British who feared French intrigue. When Oconastota assured Captain Demere that Mortar only wanted "a spot of Ground to plant, and Settle, and to go hunting," the officer recognized his deceit, finding instead from a Cherokee woman named Buffalo Skin that Mortar planned to serve as a go-between for the Cherokees and French. Demere subsequently pressed Wawhatchee to attack Mortar's gang at Etowah, but the Lower Town headman adamantly refused, noting the Creeks "were their friends."[29]

As the Creeks became further involved in Cherokee affairs, the Settico attacks forced the Overhill Towns and South Carolina to more directly engage in the conflict. Moytoy's actions, in short, subverted the efforts of those leaders who wished to stabilize relations with Charlestown during the Virginia crisis. Similar to the Mankiller's maneuvers three years earlier, the Settico murders unleashed a political firestorm throughout Cherokee country. Much of the language emanating from Cherokee leaders in different towns and regions mirrored that which transpired during the Tellico crisis. When the Settico people attacked settlers in North Carolina, for instance, Wawhatchee of Keowee assured the English that the Lower Towns "were of a quite different Way of thinking." Tistoe of Keowee likewise confirmed the good intentions of the Lower and Middle people, declaring, "The Mischief that has been done, it was alone the outside Town over the Hills, Setticoe. We are all quiet and think well in these Parts." A talk from thirteen towns in the Middle Settlements denied involvement in the affair by notifying Governor Lyttelton that those "in other Parts of the Nation" seemed "not to set any Regard by us no more than we were a different People," since they "don't care to lead us into the Light of their private Affairs." These regional distinctions emphasized by Cherokee leaders reflected a continued effort to prevent the conflict from spreading to South Carolina. Attakullakulla stated this point clearly when he "acknowledged the kindness of the English of Carolina, but complained much of the usage his people had met with from Virginia." Lower Cherokees also desired to contain the conflict, informing Lyttelton there was a "stumbling Block in the Virginia Path," but the "Path from us to you in Carolina, we desire to be kept free from any Disturbance, or Blood."[30]

Maintaining a clear path to South Carolina grew increasingly difficult as tensions mounted in late summer and fall of 1759. A small number of warriors mostly from the Lower Towns followed Moytoy's attacks with raids of their own against settlers in South Carolina. Settico and Tellico warriors also killed three white people in the Overhill Towns and attempted to block all communication between Forts Loudoun and Prince George. As events spiraled out of control, the Chota leadership pursued familiar policies of isolating the offending towns. In a series of meetings between Oconastota and Captain Demere, the two leaders debated the extent of anti-British sentiment. Demere asked the Great Warrior "why the Cherokees killed the white People, and had so suddenly declared War." Oconastota explained that not all Cherokees condoned the killings, particularly in the Overhill Settlements, since the "Towns of Chote, Tenesee, Toqua, and Tomotly were not guilty of any of the Outrages complained of." When Demere expressed his doubts, Oconastota further assured the captain that "the Town where he lives, and the rest of the [Overhill] Towns, are your Friends, except Settico." Demere at last seemed satisfied that the recent murders were not national acts, but he nonetheless vowed to "never forgive the Barbarity, and Cruelty of the Towns of Settico, and Teliqua."[31]

Other colonial leaders interpreted the murders as a sign the war had indeed become general. Believing their former allies had finally "declared war against the English," William Byrd III of Virginia was the first in a long line of British and Americans to label the conflict "the Cherokee War." While open war did not yet exist, rumors of war abounded, many of which intensified when Lieutenant Richard Coytmore of Fort Prince George confiscated a large supply of ammunition destined for the Overhill Towns. "This News was no sooner heard," Captain Paul Demere of Fort Loudoun wrote, "but all the Indians were in an Uproar," saying the English intended "to starve them, by stoping their Amunition and so hindering them going a hunting." As the ammunition lingered within the confines of the fort, longtime traders within Cherokee country feared "the Consequence will be an open & declared War."[32]

The Anglo-Cherokee alliance seemed stronger than ever at the onset of the Seven Years' War. Hundreds of warriors led by the most notable headmen in Cherokee country joined the British war effort between 1756 and 1758. Their services in the Mid-Atlantic and Trans-Appalachian West helped Britain protect her colonial settlements and ultimately defeat the French in North America. Yet not all was well with the alliance. Dissatisfaction with the Carolina trade prompted village leaders to look beyond Charlestown for new trading alliances. In need of assistance against the French and Ohio Indians, Virginia presented a viable alternative, one that appeared safer and more reliable than what the Tellicans had hoped to secure from French Louisiana. Overhill leaders were especially active in strengthening ties to Williamsburg. Located closer to Virginia, keen on maintaining their regional dominance, and mindful of the threat posed by hostile Shawnees and other Northward Indians, the Overhill people eagerly supported the Cherokee-Virginia alliance. The plan backfired, however, following repeated hostilities between warriors from other regions and backcountry settlers. Headmen from these towns sought to limit revenge killings to Virginia, thereby preserving the "antient Friendship" they had established with South Carolina. These attempts failed as Moytoy of Settico and his adherents brought Overhill Cherokees and Carolinians more directly into the widening conflict. As villagers dispatched two cross-regional delegations to Charlestown to avert war, Governor Lyttelton readied his troops to march against the Cherokee towns.

6

"every Town wept for some"

The Anglo-Cherokee War

On August 26, 1756, Captain Raymond Demere and the Independent Company of South Carolina prepared to march from Fort Prince George to the Overhill Towns. Their mission was to construct and garrison Fort Loudoun near the town of Toskegee, thereby protecting the Overhill people from French and Indian incursions and consequently strengthening the Anglo-Cherokee alliance. While encamped near the Lower Cherokee fort, Demere issued explicit instructions to his men regarding their conduct toward the Keowee people. He told them not to go into their "Fields or to do any Kind of Damage to the Indians by pulling or destroying their Corn, Watermellons &c." Five years later, Colonel James Grant expected a different kind of behavior from his troops. Leading an expeditionary force of more than 2,500 British Regulars, Carolina provincials, and Indian auxiliaries, Grant recorded in his journal at the Middle town of Nequassee: "We halted. Corn about the town was destroyed. Parties were sent out to burn the scattered houses, pull up beans, peas, and corn, and to demolish everything eatable in the country." The Seven Years' War had unmistakably arrived in Cherokee country.[1]

Between 1759 and 1761, the southeastern borderlands exploded as Cherokee war parties attacked English settlements from Virginia to Georgia, and British and provincial armies in turn burned and destroyed Cherokee villages. The Anglo-Cherokee War held lasting consequences for South Carolina–Cherokee relations, but it also provided the most direct challenge to Cherokee localism and regionalism yet. The war against the British and their colonists enabled Cherokees to achieve a greater degree of collective action than had been known in prior conflicts. Whereas one eyewitness noted earlier that Cherokees from different regions "seldom take part in each others Wars," townspeople from Keowee to Chota now joined in the defense of their kinsmen and neighbors. The event therefore marked a new epoch in Cherokee history, as mountain villagers witnessed a level of dislocation and cross-regional resistance rarely found in earlier conflicts with neighboring indigenous peoples. This is not to say that local identities and allegiances wilted under the strain of war, but many Cherokees nonetheless found common ground against a common enemy. The killing of warriors in the Virginia backcountry, the imprisonment and massacre of a cross-regional peace delegation by Carolinians, and multiple invasions of Cherokee country by British and American forces prompted James Adair to assert, "We forced the Cheerake to become our bitter enemies, by a long train of wrong measures." Adair's comment speaks to more than just a breakdown in Anglo-Indian relations, however; it also alludes to the effects of the war on Cherokee notions of themselves as a distinct "people." Although the war against the British did not erase localized identities, it did foster a stronger ethnic consciousness and commitment among diverse Cherokees by creating a legacy of shared experiences and memories that effectively crossed town and regional boundaries.[2]

The Anglo-Cherokee War also altered the dynamic of Cherokee regionalism. Perhaps the most noticeable change was the rise and fall of the Out Towns as a regional power. Prior to midcentury, the Tuckasegee River towns received little attention from South Carolina. Often labeled the "Back Settlements or outside Towns" by the British, they were, according to John Reid, a "vague, backwater region of the nation." But the Out Towns emerged as a distinct region during the war, recognized as such by both British and Cherokee peoples. Influential headmen like Round O of Stecoe, whose familial networks stretched directly to the Chota-based leadership, garnered a large following among Cherokees beyond their own villages. These headmen proved instrumental in the events leading up to the war, but their influence and that of their towns waned as a result of British invasions, the death of notable leaders, and the permanent removal of the Kituhwa people to the Overhills. Nevertheless, the prominence of Round O and other Out Town leaders challenges Reid's other assertion that "the Out Cherokees had little impact on eighteenth-century history, too removed from the war paths and too separated from the other regions to assume a leadership role." While certainly true for much of the colonial era, the Out Cherokees and their headmen did emerge—even if only temporarily—as an influential regional force during the Seven Years' War.³

Unlike the ephemeral nature of the Out Towns' political influence, the Overhill Settlements and their leaders played a dominant role in cross-cultural negotiations and resistance throughout the Anglo-Cherokee War and beyond. Most of the Chota-based leadership fervently supported the war effort, particularly during the two British invasions of Cherokee country in 1760 and 1761. Attakullakulla, however, cast his political fortunes with the British, as he worked tirelessly throughout the crisis to reestablish the Anglo-Cherokee alliance. Repeatedly marginalized by the militants for his peace platform, Attakullakulla tried to protect the garrison at Fort Loudoun, often by encouraging village women to resupply the fort with victuals. His diminished political standing proved short-lived as Cherokees from every region tired of war. War-weary villagers relied on the Overhill headman to repair the broken alliance, which was effectively concluded in the winter of 1761–62. Although tensions remained within the Overhill leadership following the war, Attakullakulla and other regional- and national-minded headmen increasingly dominated Cherokee affairs until the American Revolution rearranged the geopolitical landscape of Cherokee country.⁴

The alarming reports from officers, traders, settlers, and Cherokees during the crisis in Virginia prompted Governor Lyttelton to forcefully reassert South Carolina's primacy in Indian affairs. Lyttelton initially used the power of trade to obtain satisfaction. Rather than isolate those towns most accountable, the governor enacted a trade embargo against all Cherokees. Although embargos had been implemented before, land encroachments, an imperial war, and escalating border incidents produced a powder keg for Anglo-Cherokee relations. The trade with Britain, which in earlier times reinforced local and regional interests, increasingly became a point of contention for all Cherokees. In order to resolve the crisis that now extended to South Carolina, mountain villagers organized two peace delegations to visit Charlestown. Oconastota led the first delegation, which included leaders from the Overhill, Valley, and Lower Towns. These headmen arrived in Charlestown and began negotiations with the usual exchange of diplomatic greetings and tokens of peace. Lyttelton, however, refused to accept the deerskins and white beads of peace. He then dismissed their authority to treat, implying they were unofficial spokesmen who only came "in Consequence of being refused Ammunition at Keowee" by Lieutenant Coytmore.[5]

Lyttelton's terse dismissal of Cherokee peace proposals largely resulted because the governor had already decided upon war. On October 6, 1759—before the delegation arrived in town—the South Carolina Assembly had requested that Lyttelton raise a "sufficient Force" to repress Cherokee "insults & Barbarities." Although the Assembly later softened its tone, expressing a wish to avoid war "until all hopes shall be lost of obtaining a reasonable and adequate satisfaction from them," Lyttelton dismissed their fears and reiterated his expectations of a "speedy grant of the supply" for military preparations. The Assembly acceded by allocating money for the provisioning of 1,000 men. In the official "Declaration of War against the Cherokees," South Carolina listed its many grievances, beginning with the Bedford County murders in May 1758.[6]

Lyttelton initiated his campaign against the Cherokees by placing the first peace delegation under house arrest. The governor then forced these headmen to accompany his newly formed army of South Carolina militia as they marched toward Cherokee country. At the Congarees, near the confluence of the Broad and Saluda Rivers, Lyttelton encountered the second envoy led by Round O of Stecoe. Alternatively referred to as the Mankiller of Stecoe, Tacite of Stecoe, Shonguttam, and Rondeau, the Out Town headman was usually identified by his "trading name," Round O. Throughout the Seven Years' War, Round O represented his towns along the Tuckasegee River, but he also spoke for the Middle Cherokees (and to some extent the Lower Towns people). In 1759 he declared that he had "13 Towns under him," many of them in the Middle Settlements, which prompted John Stuart to call him "the Leading man of that part of the Nation."[7]

Round O became a village and regional headman by proving himself as a warrior and diplomat. He also spoke English, an invaluable asset in cross-cultural exchange that assisted his rise as an intertown leader. Support from the British additionally buttressed his authority, as officials often utilized him as a go-between. Equally important, Round O and other Out Town headmen enjoyed close kinship connections to the Overhill leadership. Round O's brother was a headman in Toqua, while another Stecoe leader was reportedly the brother of the influential Ostenaco. Villagers from the Out Towns and those from other regions therefore relied on Round O's capabilities and connections to negotiate with South Carolina in 1759–60.[8]

The Lower, Middle, and Out Cherokees who selected Round O to lead their peace delegation wanted no association with the envoy headed by Oconastota. Holding these Cherokees responsible for the recent troubles, Round O's constituents desired the British to know they "have behaved in a manner Quite Different from the Other Indians, nor have [they] ever been Guilty of the Insolent & Treachery the Others have." They then expressed their unwillingness to conduct negotiations with Lyttelton in the presence of Oconastota's party and accordingly traveled to Charlestown at a later date and by a different path. At the Congarees, however, Round O's delegation became unnerved when they saw Oconastota and the others surrounded by armed guards. Lyttelton also detained these headmen by confining them "in the Middle of the Army's Encampment," which the governor unconvincingly explained was "to prevent the common white People being troublesome to them." More likely, Lyttelton feared the consequence of these Cherokees returning to their villages in a hostile disposition. His concerns were realized when four headmen from Keowee, Stecoe, Watauga, and Nequassee escaped. A large meeting at Keowee followed, attended by the Lower Towns people, and all present took note as the headmen recounted how Oconastota, Round O, and "all their People" were treated "like Slaves." Those in the Keowee townhouse subsequently dispatched runners with black wampum to villagers in other regions with news of their headmen "coming like Slaves of the white People," adding that Lyttelton intended "to destroy all their Towns and make Captives of their Women & Children."[9]

The headmen's loss of liberty tore not only at accepted notions of diplomatic protocol but also at the insecurities many Cherokees and other southeastern Indians experienced as the colonial plantation system spread inland. Claudio Saunt effectively demonstrates how Creeks and Seminoles responded with alarm to these developments, and the Cherokees were likewise fearful of the English having "a Mind to make Slaves of them all." James Adair later wrote of the hostage crisis, "It was well known, that the Indians are unacquainted with the custom and meaning of hostages; to them, it conveyed the idea of slaves." The suspicions many Cherokees held toward British intentions of enslavement also directly related to the two forts that had been constructed in Cherokee country: Fort

Prince George at Keowee in 1753 and Fort Loudoun among the Overhills in 1756. Although many on both sides of the emerging divide had reasons for wanting the forts, their presence increasingly agitated the Cherokees. They thus listened more intently when the Shawnees, Creeks, and French warned that the soldiers in the forts intended "to kill all the Men and to take their Women and Children Slaves." More disturbing and prophetic were insinuations that Cherokee women would "be taken into the Fort before their Husbands' Faces and used by the Soldiers." Before being taken hostage in Charlestown, Tistoe of Keowee complained to Lyttelton of the conduct of the officers at Prince George. Lieutenant Richard Coytmore, along with Ensign Bell and Alexander Miln, had intensified Cherokee dissatisfaction when they forced their way into a house in Keowee and reportedly raped the women who were inside.[10]

When Lyttelton and his troops finally reached Fort Prince George in late 1759, the Cherokees were alarmed, confused, and hesitant to spark a confrontation with so many of their headmen in custody. The long march, harsh weather, and many strange Indians about them similarly unnerved the Carolinians. After encamping near the fort, Lyttelton's force became further weakened by an outbreak of smallpox. News of the disease first appeared in the environs of Augusta the previous year. It spread among the Savannah Chickasaws, killing ten villagers within the year, and then northward to the Catawbas, where it reportedly "raged with great Violence" and "carried off near one Half of that Nation." Six Catawba warriors thereafter joined the governor's expedition, and though "they had Passes of Health" from a local justice of the peace, the disease nevertheless became lodged within the army near Keowee.[11]

As disease and desertion took its toll, the governor sought a diplomatic end to his military expedition. Attakullakulla, assisted by Round O and other headmen, concluded a "Treaty of Peace and Friendship" with Lyttelton on December 26. Although the two parties had reached an impasse over the Virginia killings, they eventually agreed the hostages would remain in custody at Fort Prince George until Cherokees delivered the guilty individuals. In what he thought to be a show of good faith, Lyttelton released four of the more influential headmen: Oconastota, Tistoe, Saluy (Young Warrior of Estatoe), and Round O. But such gestures were too late, for as Adair noted, "The Indians reckon imprisonment to be inslaving them, [and] they never forgive such treatment." Indeed, those headmen who had been held hostage became the bitterest enemies of the English. Even in the aftermath of the bloody war that followed, British officers noted, "There still seems to subsist among them a discontented party headed by the Great Warrior Ouconastota, who still resents his imprisonment at Fort Prince George by Gov. Lyttelton." Saluy likewise revealed that his fight with Carolina began with the "ill usage my People & I got several times at the fort." Almost immediately after the Lyttelton expedition ended, reports indicated the Young Warrior of Estatoe "was gone with all his People against the back Settlements."[12]

Round O did not initially join his enraged countrymen. Rather than war against the English, the Stecoe headman stayed voluntarily among the hostages, which included his two sons. He then worked to free the prisoners by peaceful means and repair the Anglo-Cherokee alliance. Round O often left the fort for nearby towns to give good talks and deliver white beads of peace. Such efforts seemed increasingly futile, however, as restless villagers demanded the release of their headmen. Round O found that British support, which previously buttressed his authority, now became a political liability as his followers turned against their former allies. The once-staunch British advocate reversed course. Appearing in the Sugar Town council house, he "Absolutely Pleaded ignorance" to the contents of the treaty he had signed, particularly the article relating to the hostages. Round O also blocked the efforts of village women to provide intelligence to the garrison by driving them away and "chiding them for telling any thing." One report even implicated him in a failed scheme to overthrow the fort by subterfuge.[13]

Despite the initial efforts of such peacemakers as Round O and Attakullakulla, the hostage crisis emerged as the breaking point in Anglo-Cherokee relations. Throughout the short-lived affair, leaders from several towns and regions attempted every means to free their people. Headmen typically sought to secure hostages "belonging to their Parts" only, taking little notice of prisoners from other regions. Leaders from Chota demanded the release of the five Overhill headmen, while the Mankiller of Nequassee and other Middle Cherokees related "their Towns were never Guilty of molesting the white People &c. and that they desired to have their Hostages." Round O likewise reminded Coytmore that his people "had never behaved ill." Since the Stecoe headman represented more than one region, he asked the lieutenant to "sett at Liberty the Middle

Settlement People, if not all the Hostages." Coytmore dismissed these entreaties by informing Cherokee leaders he had no such authority; only the governor could free them. Lyttelton, however, failed to act upon these long-entrenched regional divisions, believing instead that all Cherokees were involved in the recent troubles and all Cherokees must therefore be held accountable. Lyttelton also intended to use the prisoners as leverage to exert Carolina's authority and obtain satisfaction for the recent murders. The strategy ultimately backfired, for the way in which the crisis ended held disastrous consequences for the alliance.[14]

The smallpox outbreak that weakened Lyttelton's expedition did not retreat with the Carolina militiamen but instead lodged itself among local villagers. A Keowee man who had visited the Catawbas earlier that year died the first week of December. Other townspeople became infected and "mov'd at some Distance from the Town" to recover. Such preventive measures failed as accounts from Keowee revealed the disease "destroyed a great many of the Indians there." Predating the germ warfare controversies during Pontiac's Uprising, Lieutenant Coytmore admitted, "I cant help being so unhuman as to wish it may spread through the whole Nation." His inhuman wish came true. By the end of January, smallpox had reached the Valley Towns, particularly Quanasee and Tomatly, and then "among the Middle Settlements People." The Overhill people bought time with their efforts to not "allow a single Person from the above named Places to come amongst them," but they too ultimately suffered.[15]

The smallpox epidemic also included the soldiers and hostages within Fort Prince George. On February 6, 1760, news of the first headman's death surfaced when the Warrior of Stecoe succumbed to the disease. Almost immediately the "Death Hoop was given three Times over the River opposite the Fort," and at midnight a large fire "was made in the Middle of the Square at Keowee and Indians heard all round the Remainder of the Night." Those from all regions participated in this public display of mourning and enmity, which became more heated and more collective as an Overhill and a Middle headman, along with two others, died over the next six days. Round O to his detriment remained within the fort throughout the ordeal. The Stecoe leader earlier proclaimed "he was ready to Die for his two sons" to secure their release, but he never got the chance, for "he catched the Smallpox" and died. Coytmore immediately warned Lyttelton that the death of Round O and the Warrior of Stecoe would bring the Middle Cherokees to attack his garrison. Overhill warriors beat them to it.[16]

When news spread of a raging sickness within the fort, Attakullakulla, Oconastota, and Little Raven of Chota arrived at Keowee to inform Coytmore "they come for their Hostages." The three leaders threatened the lieutenant that "the Overhill Indians had hitherto behaved quietly" but "would join with the Rest" if their fellow headmen were not released. Coytmore responded in the negative, and rumors quickly circulated that "all the Overhills People were coming down . . . to War against the back Settlements." The Overhill people also targeted the fort itself. Oconastota returned days later to feign a parley with the officers. When Coytmore, Ensign Bell, and an interpreter came to the river, Oconastota gave a signal and "off went about 25 or 30 Guns from the Indians that had concealed themselves under the Banks of the River." The incoming bullets grazed Bell and the interpreter but fatally wounded Coytmore. Upon seeing the Cherokees' treachery, the soldiers inside the fort "fell to work" on the hostages and "laid them all lifeless."[17]

The soldiers' hasty actions, more than any other incident up to that point, drove villagers from all corners of Cherokee country to favor war. "By this Massacre," one observer later wrote, "most of the Head-Warriors lost Relations and Friends." Even the people "of those friendly towns," Adair recounted, had "been changed wholeheartedly by the misdeeds Carolina did to them." This "uniform misconduct . . . fixed the whole nation in a state of war against us—all the families of those leading men that were so shamefully murdered, were inexpressibly imbittered against our very national name." The eighteenth-century British historian Alexander Hewat agreed. He recounted there "were few men in the Cherokee nation that did not lose a friend or a relation by this massacre, and therefore with one voice all immediately declared for war." The leaders "in every town seized the hatchet" and subsequently encouraged their followers to revenge "the spirits of murdered brothers." The conflict thereafter became an "open war" as "large parties of warriors" from nearly every town and every clan "took the field."[18]

In the aftermath of the Fort Prince George massacre, numerous "scalping Gangs" from all corners of Cherokee country descended on Carolina to kill "swarms of white dung-hill fowls," as they insultingly labeled the English. Many of them returned to their villages with scores of white and black captives. This outbreak of hostilities partially shifted British strategies for success in their war against France. Although British armies had enjoyed remarkable victories in the north in recent months, most notably the capture of Quebec in September 1759, General Jeffery Amherst recognized that "our business to the Southward is not near done." As Virginia appointed a day of public thanksgiving for the fall of Quebec, Amherst ordered Colonel Archibald Montgomery and 1,300 Highlanders to Charlestown with orders to act offensively against the Cherokees "by destroying towns, and cutting up their settlements."[19]

Unlike Lyttelton's ineffectual show of force in 1759, Montgomery's invasion wreaked havoc on the Lower Cherokees before British forces withdrew. The Lower Towns were "left in ashes" as troops destroyed homes and council houses throughout Estatoe, Qualatchie, Toxaway, and Sugar Town and killed an estimated eighty Cherokees. These towns, Montgomery observed, were "more considerable than could be imagined," with Estatoe and Sugar Town consisting of above two hundred houses and "not less than a hundred houses in any of their other towns"—a testament to the Keowee River towns' speedy recovery following the destructive Cherokee-Creek War. They were also well provisioned. Lieutenant Colonel James Grant, second in command of the expedition, found "Plenty of Ammunition . . . and every where astonishing Magazines of Corn, which were all consumed in the Flames." Before turning the army north toward the Middle Settlements, Montgomery proudly informed General Amherst of his soldiers' thoroughness, noting, "Every town in their Nation [Lower Towns] is burnt."[20]

The lay of the land between the Lower and Middle Towns was, as Captain Raymond Demere once observed, "a dismal and wild Kind of Country." He prophetically wrote in 1756 that on the road from Keowee to the first Middle town of Etchoe (Echoe), "I may assure you that twelve resolute Men by Way of Ambuscade might cut of[f] 100, there being such Mountains, narrow Passes, dismal and dangerous Places." The Cherokees used this difficult terrain to their advantage four years later, for when Montgomery's men traveled through Etchoe Pass, they were attacked by a cross-regional force consisting of warriors primarily from the Lower and Middle Towns but including small detachments from other regions. The British advance faltered as the army incurred approximately eighty casualties, but the soldiers regrouped and continued their march to Etchoe, which they burned the following day. Unable to proceed and believing he had fulfilled Amherst's orders, Montgomery withdrew to Fort Prince George and then quickly returned to Charlestown.[21]

Cherokee forces at Etchoe Pass, which one estimate held to be more than six hundred warriors, most likely incurred a similar number of casualties as the British. Although unable to stop Montgomery's army from reaching Etchoe, Cherokees inflicted enough damage to force the colonel's hurried return southward, thereby preventing the destruction of the Middle Towns. The perceived outcome of this campaign in the eyes of the British, Carolinians, and Cherokees was as contested as the battle itself. Montgomery believed he "succeeded in everything we have attempted," particularly the burning of the Lower Towns, which he found "the most guilty." Some Carolinians disagreed by emphasizing the incompleteness of British victory. Christopher Gadsden criticized at length Colonel Montgomery for "the lamentable retreat from Etchowih" that followed his army's slight "brush" with the Cherokees. Gadsden was especially concerned with its effects on the thinly protected backcountry as well as the beleaguered garrison at Fort Loudoun. The colonel, Gadsden asserted, "never intended to go to Fort Loudoun at all," a failure which left the garrison in a precarious state.[22]

Cherokees agreed that Montgomery's expedition achieved little in terms of military success. Lower and Middle Cherokees boasted "they were not beaten by the White Warriors," specifically referring to the engagement at Etchoe Pass, while two Cherokee messengers traveling in the Ohio country told a party of Iroquois they "had a battle with part of the Armey to the Southard, and had beat the English." Overhill Cherokees displayed similar confidence when they informed soldiers at Fort Loudoun that British troops "had been attacked, defeated and driven out of the Cherokee Country." Attakullakulla believed the battle made hostile Cherokees "flush'd with success," warning Colonel William Byrd they "must not expect a peace" until they could "beat them into it." The British quickly realized, as did one of South Carolina's earliest historians, that the "great majority of the nation spurned at every offer of peace" following Montgomery's campaign.[23]

Most Cherokees did reject peace in the summer of 1760. Cherokees from every region had warred against the British in the aftermath of the hostage crisis and massacre, and the failed invasion of Colonel Montgomery did little to induce headmen to restore the broken alliance.

Nevertheless, Cherokee policies were neither uniform nor one-dimensional, a point most effectually demonstrated by scrutinizing wartime responses of the Overhill people and their most prominent leaders. Of particular relevance is the townspeople's differing treatment of the Fort Loudoun garrison. Prior to the Montgomery expedition, Cherokees had blocked off all communication with the fort. Some messages seeped through, especially those carried by Abraham, the slave of trader Samuel Benn who later obtained his freedom for such dangerous exploits. These and other communications brought word that Overhill Cherokees besieged the garrison and attempted to prevent both messages and supplies from entering the thinly provisioned fort. This policy was not unanimous, however. An early report by an escaped trader held that four of the Overhill Towns—Chota, Toqua, Tomatly, and Tenasee—"stand by Fort Loudoun & supply it with Necessaries." Of even greater significance was the news that Attakullakulla was "visiting that Fort daily."[24]

Attakullakulla, one of the most influential cross-regional leaders, seems to have also been the most active British ally among the Overhill people during the Anglo-Cherokee crisis. Although doubts existed about his loyalties prior to the war, little evidence exists that points to anything other than a staunch proponent of the British trading alliance by 1759. Attakullakulla's following among the Overhill people and those from other regions temporarily waned, however, as the crisis mounted and British and colonial armies made inroads into Cherokee country. Following Oconastota's attack on Lieutenant Coytmore at Fort Prince George, Attakullakulla responded with his own political message: he vowed to retire with his family and those "he had any Influence over" into "the Woods ... separating himself from his Nation, and shewing his Detestation of their Breach of the late Treaty." Threats of self-exile seemed more akin to forced exile as an increasingly hostile Overhill population marginalized the peace faction. Militant Cherokees "threatened the Little Carpenter's Life," saying they "looked upon [him] as an Englishman" who "no longer [would be] admitted into their Councils." Attakullakulla confirmed these accounts when he informed Captain Demere that "he was no longer able to give Intelligence, as formerly, of what passed in his Countrymen's Councils."[25]

Thus entered the informal political power of Cherokee women who challenged those headmen and warriors who blockaded Fort Loudoun. Overhill women repeatedly brought intelligence and supplies to the beleaguered garrison, many of whom had husbands within the fort, which engendered threats of retaliation from the militants. Reports indicated that warriors "had Orders to kill all Women that should attempt to go to the fort," but upon considering that clan revenge made such threats unlikely, they turned to confining unruly women and threatening to have them "whipped through the Town" with their "Hair cut off, the highest Disgrace of an Indian." Theda Perdue argues that these women "did not defy the warriors out of rebellion or subversion—they acted according to long-established standards of behavior for married women." In short, women controlled food production and dispersed it as they saw fit. Such behavior, Perdue continues, also reflects the "corporate ethic" that guided Cherokee actions, since individuals "decided on the course that they thought best served community interests." In conjunction with these insights should be added the decided political dimension of women's activities. Often, women did not act as "rogue" individuals but as political agents of leading headmen. Attakullakulla, in particular, had "great interest among the Indian wenches." The Overhill headman used this influence to supply Fort Loudoun by "conveying Refreshments to the Garrison through Indian Wenches." In one instance, the soldiers were delighted when the "Indian Women, by Means of the Carpenter . . . brought us in 12 Days, Corn, a very seasonable Supply." Even more substantial was Attakullakulla's "Negotiation" with his pro-war antagonist Oconastota that procured over "300 Bushels of Indian Corn, and a Quantity of Bacon" for the fort in mid-June. The motives of Overhill women to provision Fort Loudoun therefore derived not only from long-established traditions but also from the desire to assert a political voice that had the backing of influential headmen.[26]

The sporadic provisioning of the fort failed to save the starving garrison. Perdue conjectures either the "war chief" halted the visits or the amount of supplies had little effect. Both seem logical conclusions, although the diminishing effectiveness of women's support should not be dissociated from the declining influence of Attakullakulla. Oconastota and other militant headmen intensified their efforts against Fort Loudoun following Montgomery's retreat, which had the support of most Overhill people. Intelligence revealed Oconastota effectively "invested the Fort" with warriors from Chota, Settico, Chilhowee, Tellico, and Chatuga. Hurried messages slipped through the cracks from Fort Loudoun to Charlestown expressing the soldiers' lamentations of being "abandoned and forsaken by God and Man" as they survived on "Horse flesh." Although

Attakullakulla continued to be "their Friend," the aging headman and his followers could "contribute little to their Support."[27]

The garrison finally surrendered in early August 1760. The articles of peace signed between Captain Paul Demere and "the headmen and warriors of the Overhill Cherokee towns" reflected the regional nature of the siege, but one that also had widespread support throughout Cherokee country. Perhaps revenging losses sustained in the Fort Prince George massacre, Overhill warriors later attacked the troops on their march toward the Lower Towns, killing thirty. Paul Demere seemed to attract the bitterest revenge, for the captain "was scalp'd alive, and made to run about bare headed for the diversion of the Indians; they then chopp'd off his leggs and arms, and left him to himself." John Stuart, another officer of the Independents, fared better, thanks in large part to the remaining influence of Attakullakulla. The Overhill headman persuaded Round O's brother to protect Stuart during the attack, whereupon Attakullakulla purchased him "at a very considerable Price" and safely delivered him to Virginia.[28]

The survivors of the ambush, numbering as many as 180 men and women, were held as captives. Eyewitnesses noted that headmen "dispersed the rest [as] slaves thro' their towns," especially among the Overhill and Valley Settlements, which had acquired fewer prisoners than Lower and Middle Cherokees during the attacks on the Carolina backcountry. Prisoner distribution served as a means for all towns and regions to share the burdens of war and peace. It also eased clan bereavement. While few captives were adopted into Cherokee clans for the purpose of replacing lost kin, some prisoners were ritually tortured to avenge the spirits of the slain. Cherokees also ransomed prisoners for rewards or as a strategy to redeem their own captives held by the British.[29]

Cherokees were by no means unanimous in how to deal with their British captives, and they were equally divided over how to continue the war following the Fort Loudoun massacre. Emboldened by their success in forcing a fortified British garrison to capitulate, many Cherokees looked to re-create this feat at Fort Prince George. Oconastota sent messages to the different settlements requesting warriors for the attack, hoping to use the ammunition and even cannon from Fort Loudoun in the campaign. Rumors quickly surfaced which indicated his appeals had been favorably answered. One report claimed "the whole Cherokee Nation the Overhills, Valley, middle Settlements, and lower Towns People" were joined by hundreds of Creeks and Northward Indians to beset the fort. While certainly an exaggeration, the besieged garrison at Fort Prince George could not fail to notice that warriors from all regions had in fact "blockaded and pent us up like a Parcel of Cattle for Slaughter."[30]

These efforts received encouragement from the French, who sent none other than Anthony L'antignac to the Cherokees. The French officer arrived at Chota with presents and petitions for the continuance of war. He also offered cannon and soldiers to assist in the reduction of Fort Prince George. The British believed L'antignac's arrival "destroyed all Prospect of an Accommodation" and hindered the exchange of prisoners. But not all Cherokees were receptive to French proposals. Attakullakulla later commented he would have "destroyed Lantiniac, and his Companions; but was told by the Indians, if he did so, they would destroy the white Prisoners." The small amount of gifts initially brought by L'antignac also encouraged many Cherokees to witness "the Poverty of the French, and their Inability to help them." With French assistance slow to arrive and the blockade of the fort equally slow in effecting its capitulation, many Cherokees grew more attentive to peace proposals.[31]

While more than a few Lower Cherokees continued their search for scalps and captives in Carolina, others showed their disposition toward peace by resettling the Lower Towns and assisting in the return of more than one hundred prisoners to the British. Similar divisions existed among the Overhill people. Some headmen and warriors attacked the frontier, while those wishing to end the war entertained peace proposals from the Virginians, who then had an army encamped near the Kanawha River. Led by William Byrd, the Virginia militia had earlier failed to coordinate their attack on the Overhill Towns with Montgomery's invasion of the Lower Settlements. Byrd now used threats of not leaving "one Indian alive, one Town standing, or one Grain of Corn, in all your Country" if British captives were not returned and if Cherokees spurned his efforts at peace. Although fully aware the Virginians could not execute these threats, Overhill leaders nevertheless traveled "thro' all the Towns" with talks of peace. Attakullakulla arrived with an embassy to negotiate with Byrd, and the two parties drafted preliminary articles of peace.[32]

Officials in Williamsburg, however, rejected peace in the winter of 1760–61. Lieutenant Governor Fauquier believed a separate treaty would alienate South Carolina. He also recognized terms "with the upper Towns only" would serve "no manner of purpose," for the Overhill people could continue the war and then lay all blame on "the Middle & lower Towns over whom they had not Authority." Fauquier's grasp of Cherokee regionalism and the difficulties this presented to a general peace found favor among those who believed the restoration of the Anglo-Cherokee alliance was "now attainable only by the Sword." The British accordingly looked to exploit the Cherokees' "Disunion among themselves," not with more peace talks but with a vigorous military expedition against their towns.[33]

James Grant, Montgomery's subordinate during the first invasion, commanded the redoubled British effort in 1761. With more than 2,500 British and colonial troops, Grant bypassed the already spoiled and mostly vacant Lower Towns and moved directly toward the Middle and Out Settlements. Once again, warriors attacked the invaders near Etchoe Pass. One soldier believed more than 2,500 Cherokees assaulted their force, a claim reinforced by another eyewitness who related "that the whole Warriors of the Cherokee Nation, (exclusive of a few) . . . had engag'd us." Gadsden likewise believed the attack had been executed by a "force of lower, middle, and upper Cherokees, I mean such as were disposed for war, which most of them were, excepting a few old men." One warrior who participated in the attack, the Mankiller of Nequassee, reasoned later "that he thought it was his duty to fight for his Country, & he should always be ready to do it." Apparently, the Mankiller was not alone in his sentiments, for if the above reports can be trusted, a force of 2,500 warriors corresponds with prevailing estimates of the Cherokee warrior population. In other words, most of the fighting men from all towns and regions participated in the battle in order to constitute such numbers.[34]

Regardless of the exact number, the attack failed to check the invaders. Following their successful repulse of Cherokee forces near Etchoe Pass, the British laid waste to twelve Middle Towns in the summer of 1761. They burned the remnants of Etchoe and then destroyed Neowi and Canuga, two towns that had been built in the Middle region by Lower Town and Etchoe refugees following Montgomery's expedition. Moving even farther into Cherokee country, Grant's men ruined four towns in the Out Settlements: Stecoe, Kituhwa, Tuckarechee, and Tesantah. By the end of the campaign, the army had destroyed an estimated 1,500 acres of "fine fields garden orchards etc." Thousands of Cherokees fled to less exposed regions. One account held that as many as 5,000 had been driven from their homes to seek shelter in the Valley and Overhill Towns. Attakullakulla related that "some of the Middle Settlements People have come amongst them. That they are dying, naked, and starving." Colonel Byrd, who led another unsuccessful invasion against the Overhills, informed General Amherst that the refugees "are all retreated into the upper towns."[35]

Although not all Cherokees took refuge in the Overhill Towns, Byrd's observations testify to the degree of displacement that occurred in the aftermath of the two British campaigns. The destruction of the Lower, Middle, and Out Settlements and the subsequent stress placed on the Valley and Overhill Towns resulted in Cherokees from every region sharing in the ravages of war. Through these experiences of resistance and dislocation, the Cherokee people found a degree of commonality previously unknown, even during the Creek War. While large-scale Creek attacks near midcentury displaced many Lower Towns people, the destruction wrought by British armies produced a broader and more intense refugee crisis that touched nearly every mountain villager. As Henry Laurens observed during the final expedition, "Every Town wept for some." This weeping peaked once British microbes effected what their armies could not: a significant reduction in the Cherokee population. The smallpox outbreak at Fort Prince George in the winter of 1759–60 surged beyond its walls, eventually reaching all corners of Cherokee country. After three years of conflict with population losses totaling perhaps 10 percent or higher, the Cherokees listened more intently to British peace proposals. Although not all Cherokees were equally ready to forgive and forget, even those still desirous of revenge wanted to end the destruction of the Cherokee homeland.[36]

Both British and Cherokee leaders realized that a firm peace could only be established if headmen from all regions participated. Grant accordingly agreed with Attakullakulla that Cherokees "from the Upper, the Valley, the Middle and Lower Settlements, shall come down to Charles-Town" to confirm the peace. As the most recognizable proponent of peace, Attakullakulla headed the cross-regional delegation that met Lieutenant Governor William Bull and his council in Charlestown. Attakullakulla produced "strings of wampum he had received from the different towns," informing his counterpart that he had "come to you as a messenger from the whole nation." The two sides tentatively agreed to the terms, which were transmitted throughout the Cherokee towns and later ratified by a second cross-regional delegation in Charlestown during the winter of 1761–62.[37]

Cherokee headmen also looked to secure peace with Virginia. Overhill leaders in particular attempted to undercut Carolina's influence by negotiating with the Virginians. But Fauquier and Byrd informed Cherokee leaders they "did not consider themselves as principals in this Cherokee warr" and therefore advised Overhill headmen to join deputies from other regions in Charlestown. They complied, but peace talks with Virginia continued nonetheless. Not only did they seek provisions and an outlet for trade, but Overhill leaders also recognized the need to formally end hostilities with that colony. The war began in the Virginia backcountry, a point admitted by all parties involved. Fauquier, for instance, initially held that Cherokees "were the Aggressors by their own confission," but he later acknowledged the policy of offering "Reward for Scalps may have done mischief." The "Reward for Indian Scalps," he wrote to the Board of Trade, "was found to produce bad Consequences, by setting our people on to kill Indians whether Friends or Enemies, for the Sake of the Reward; by which we much fear the Cherokee Nation are incensed against us." Officials in South Carolina agreed that their "expensive war with the Cherokee Indians" originated "principally by the disgust given them in the Northern colonies." In 1765, the most influential Overhill warrior, Oconastota, likewise remembered "the Virginians were the occasion of the last War."[38]

Virginia and the Overhill Cherokees reestablished peace following the Grant campaign. Henry Timberlake, a young officer in the Virginia regiment, conducted a small delegation to the Overhill Towns. Ostenaco then guided the lieutenant to the most hostile towns, particularly Settico, so those townspeople could ceremoniously reaffirm their attachment to Virginia and the British. It must have seemed rather ironic and unsettling to Timberlake as he witnessed four hundred Cherokees dancing to the beat of the drums—the very drums of "the late unfortunate Capt. Demere." Timberlake thus hurriedly concluded his winter visit, returned to Williamsburg with a Cherokee peace envoy, and then accompanied Ostenaco and two other Overhill leaders to London. Initially concerned about the expense of this trip to the metropolis, Fauquier ultimately concluded it would prove invaluable to British interests to show these headmen "the Grandeur of our Court, the great Warlike Stores, the number of our Shipping, able to Transport Warriors, all over the World, and the Infinite Number of our People compared to their Small Towns, [which] must give them great Ideas of the British power." As the English colonists faced increasingly hostile Indian populations following the Peace of Paris in 1763, the projection of British power on Cherokee peoples would have the desired effect. Although countless pan-Indian emissaries arrived in Cherokee country during Pontiac's Uprising, they failed to obtain Cherokee support, in large part because of British hegemony and the legacy of the Anglo-Cherokee War.[39]

The Anglo-Cherokee War held lasting effects for Cherokee peoples. Shared wartime experiences bound them more closely, as warriors from every region fought against a common enemy and the general population assisted each other during the scorched earth campaigns. Middle Cherokees welcomed Lower Town refugees, for instance, allowing them to settle their "New Towns" at Neowi and Canuga. They also helped the Lower people "gather in the Corn, and carry it to the Middle Settlements" following Montgomery's invasion. When agricultural fields along the river bottoms became crowded, the Middle Cherokees encouraged the newcomers to plant on higher ground. One soldier marching through the Middle Towns in 1761 recorded, "Some of the fields are new, and on the sides and tops of the hills, said to be those of the Lower Townspeople, while the former inhabitants reserve for themselves the possession of the large and fertile valleys."[40]

While commonality through crisis strengthened in 1760 and 1761, wartime experiences also testified to the endurance of Cherokee localism and regionalism. In both war and peace, Cherokees from different towns and regions held different ideas about the best interests of their people, and factions naturally resulted from such divergent perspectives. Lower Town headmen in particular embraced regional divisions to achieve the best possible peace. Tistoe of Keowee told a British officer the lands between Long Cane and Tugaloo should be the hunting ground of the Lower people only. "The middle Settlements People have no right to Hunt on this Ground," he related. "Let them Hunt a'twixt them & Virginia, & Over Hills to Hunt down their River." The Keowee headman further expressed his attachment to regional hunting grounds and ancestral village sites when he and his people returned to their former habitations: "I and my People are come home to our Native Land. . . . We have Dances all Night for Joy of coming home again. . . . We are going to make Houses, & Plant, as soon as we can. I have been Lost over the Hills: I am come down to hunt on my own Land." Tistoe was not alone in his sentiments. Saluy later informed Carolina's governor he had repeated wartime invitations from the Creeks to "come with my whole Towns, and Settle amongst them." He declined, simply answering, "I loved my Country."[41]

The Lower Towns people, similar to the aftermath of the Cherokee-Creek War, quickly reestablished themselves as a regional power following their subsequent conflict. The Out Towns were not so fortunate. Whereas both the Cherokees and British recognized the Out Towns as a distinct region throughout the 1750s, the documentary record indicates no such status in the war's aftermath. These towns diminished as a regional power partly for the same reasons that gave their rise: the authority of their headmen. Round O and other Out Town leaders enjoyed a wide following prior to the Anglo-Cherokee War, particularly among the Middle people, but this ended with the death of notable headmen. Round O and the Warrior of Stecoe died of smallpox in 1760, and Chickasaw warriors took the scalp of a Kituhwa headman the next year. The British-led invasions also cut into the demographic and diplomatic relevance of the Out Towns. Grant's men ravaged the Tuckasegee River settlements, not only disrupting infrastructure and agriculture, but perhaps reducing the warrior and village populations by half. Kituhwa, "the oldest Settlement in the whole Cherokee Nation" and "Mother Town" of the Ani-Yun-wiya, suffered particularly hard. Many Kituhwa people permanently withdrew from their ancestral home. According to Cherokee oral history as recorded by John Norton, Kituhwa refugees first moved to the Overhills, where they built a new town called Mialoquo (Great Island). Attakullakulla became their leading headman, and upon his death near the onset of the Revolution, his son Dragging Canoe assumed authority and led them "from that place to the Chicamauga." The town of Sawtee, in particular, was settled by the newcomers, for Norton found they spoke "a different dialect from their part of the Nation and are descended from the inhabitants of Kittowa." Although remnants of Stecoe, Kituhwa, and other towns remained along the Tuckasegee River, the Out Towns' brief emergence as a regional power collapsed as a result of wartime experiences.[42]

7

"now all our Talks are about Lands"

Unstable Borderlands

Although no European or colonial war touched Cherokee towns from 1763 to 1775, the interwar years were nevertheless trying times for the beleaguered Cherokees. A declining deerskin trade, hostile northern and western Indians, and unremitting land encroachments pressed the mountain villagers on all sides. The bitter legacy of the Anglo-Cherokee War continued to haunt the substantially depopulated Cherokees amid the burnt ruins of the Lower, Middle, and Out Settlements. Yet the basic structure of Cherokee localism and regionalism remained intact. Displaced villagers rebuilt many of their towns once the fighting ended, and, as Tom Hatley notes, the resilience of Cherokee farming promoted a postwar recovery that was "remarkably swift."[1]

This resilience allowed the Lower Cherokees to reclaim their status as a regional power. Lower Towns people returned to their homes, boasting approximately 520 warriors among a total warrior population of 2,700 by 1764. Although less numerous than other Cherokee regions, the Lower Cherokees and their leaders negotiated nearly all matters of consequence with outsiders in the war's aftermath. Surprisingly, interactions with British and colonial officials throughout this period involved few headmen from the Middle and Valley Towns. Troubled relations with indigenous peoples and subsequent attempts to end intertribal hostilities revealed a similar absence of Middle and Valley headmen. Instead, Lower and Overhill leaders served as the voice of the Cherokee people. The reasons for this change seem to rest on the quality of leadership within the two regions, the placement of British and colonial agents in the Lower and Overhill Towns, and the geopolitical positioning of these regions on the most contentious Cherokee borderlands. Headmen from the Lower and

Overhill Settlements thus became most directly involved in the economic, political, and diplomatic exchanges that involved all Cherokees.[2]

Postwar efforts to reestablish the Anglo-Cherokee trade occupied the attention of these Lower and Overhill leaders. Restoring dependable trade networks, however, proved difficult. South Carolina's temporary experiment with a public monopoly, which was then followed by an all too familiar decentralized and poorly regulated trading system, neither satisfied Cherokee consumer demand nor corrected trader abuses. More importantly, the Peace of Paris in 1763 removed France and Spain from eastern North America. While not steady trading partners of the Cherokees by any means, headmen at times used imperial competition and British insecurity to gain greater access to European goods. Added to these economic difficulties was a decline in the deerskin trade, resulting in part from intense competition with neighboring Indians and whites as well as dangerous borderlands that restricted Cherokee hunting opportunities.

Trade remained a common concern for Cherokees during the pre-revolutionary era, but they were not alone in their economic reliance on Britain and her colonies. Native Americans throughout the interior, many of whom were former French allies, became disaffected when the financially strapped British limited trading and diplomatic privileges to Indians following the Seven Years' War. These changing circumstances contributed to a massive uprising among Indians known as Pontiac's Rebellion. Although courted by anti-British deputies, Cherokees from every region refrained from joining the revolt due to trade concerns, recent wartime experiences, and long-standing hostility to the rebellious Indians. Conflicts with northern and western Indians intensified throughout the decade, prompting Lower and Overhill headmen to utilize their British connections to structure a peace with the Six Nations in 1768, which reflected cross-regional efforts to stabilize relations with northern and western Indians.[3]

Lower and Overhill leaders also became engrossed in the most pressing issue of the day: land. Unstable borderlands with the southern colonies emerged as *the* critical issue for all Cherokees, but especially for the Lower and Overhill people, who faced repeated demands for territory from Georgia, the Carolinas, and Virginia. From 1763 to 1775, settler encroachments placed the Cherokees under extreme pressure. As Attakullakulla complained at the Treaty of Lochaber in 1770, "We never had such Talks formerly but now all our Talks are about Lands." Subtle regional tensions emerged during discussions over land boundaries and cessions, but in general land became the focal point of cross-regional dialogue and cooperation, as Cherokees looked to manipulate land dealings to secure their borders and improve trade networks. Cherokees therefore displayed a degree of unanimity over land deals throughout this period that would be conspicuously absent during and after the American Revolution.[4]

Cherokee peace efforts following Grant's invasion largely resulted from a desire to reestablish trade with the British. The war disrupted the natural cycle of Cherokee farming and hunting activities which, coupled with a trade embargo, temporarily undermined the village economy. The Lower Towns in particular had been hit hard by invading armies and the stoppage of trade. More closely connected to South Carolina than other regions, the Lower Cherokees had become "very urgent for a Trade" by the spring of 1762. According to the new governor of South Carolina, Thomas Boone, Lower Town headmen had been the most active in fulfilling treaty obligations by securing and returning British prisoners held throughout Cherokee country. In return, they and other Cherokees expected traders to be "sent into their Towns as usual," but the government in Charlestown had other ideas.[5]

Aiming to improve Cherokee relations, the South Carolina Assembly dissolved the private trade and instituted a public monopoly by an act passed on February 6, 1762. Although both Carolina and the Cherokees hoped that a well-regulated trade would prevent trader abuse and supply villagers with goods at reasonable rates, a public monopoly was not the solution the Cherokees had in mind. The principal cause of complaint with the new system was the establishment of a single trading factory at Fort Prince George, which Cherokee leaders made well known at the Congress of Augusta in 1763. Held at Augusta, Georgia, in order to stabilize relations with southeastern Indians, the four governors of the southern colonies met with more than seven hundred Creeks, Catawbas, Choctaws, Chickasaws, and Cherokees along with a multitude of colonial inhabitants in early November. For the three hundred Cherokees in attendance, the issue of trade and the Fort Prince George factory quickly emerged as a key concern.[6]

Overhill leaders in particular objected to the recent changes in the Anglo-Cherokee trade. Attakullakulla, in an effort to obtain traders for his towns, stressed that Fort Prince George was "a long way from him, and it is very hard work to carry leather over the mountains, and a long way for the women to fetch any small matter." Unhappy with Carolina's public monopoly, Attakullakulla would not be content to have a comparable factory established among the Overhills. Rather, he wanted traders "placed in the towns" as before. Even the Lower Towns people, among whom Fort Prince George was situated, expressed their discontent. Saluy, a headman of Estatoe and Tugaloo, requested a proper trade from Charlestown on account that "people who live eight or ten miles distant" from the fort "find it hard to send or go to Keehowee for them." John Stuart, the new superintendent of Indian affairs in the Southern District, likewise recognized these inconveniences. "The Overhill Cherokees," he wrote, "could not be satisfied to travel 160 Miles, the Inhabitants of the Valley 90 & the people inhabiting the Middle Settlements 60 & 40, for such Necessaries as perhaps might be purchased with a few pounds of Leather."[7]

The public monopoly applied only to South Carolina, however. Traders from other colonies were allowed into Cherokee country, but this seems to have done little to satiate Cherokee demand for European goods prior to the Congress of 1763. Lieutenant Governor Fauquier observed earlier in the year that Virginia's Indian trade was "at present inconsiderable." The *Georgia Gazette* seconded this assertion when it informed its readers the Virginia-Cherokee trade was "not carried on to any great extent." Overhill headmen, who worked diligently to reestablish linkages with Williamsburg, voiced these same concerns at Augusta. Attakullakulla told the assembled governors it was "very rare at his town to see any goods brought amongst them." Some traders "did come from Virginia," he continued, but they had "exhorbitant prices." The several governors casually replied that traders must earn a profit from their goods, and Cherokees were "free to purchase them or not, as you approve of the prices set upon them."[8]

The Congress of Augusta did not end well for the Cherokees. Although peace had been reaffirmed with Britain and the southern colonies, trade disputes remained unresolved. The governors dismissed complaints about the public monopoly as they did for the private trade, leaving Cherokees "mortified at the refusal of traders from South-Carolina." Arguing that not only did the Fort Prince George factory have prices "lower than any private trader can afford," the governors also reminded the Cherokees that only the king could alter the current regulation of trade. George III did just that with the Proclamation of 1763. This act opened trade to all British subjects, thereby overturning previous colonial laws that pertained to the

Indian trade. South Carolina responded to this potential increase in competition with an ordinance that dissolved the factory system. Throughout the remainder of the prerevolutionary era, traders steadily returned to Cherokee country, but the British trade remained a point of contention for all Cherokees, regardless of the particular trading outlet sought.[9]

The Congress of Augusta dealt with other issues besides trade. Another reason for the meeting centered on relations among southeastern Indians. Such matters affected Cherokees from every village but not all regions were equally represented, as Overhill and Lower Town headmen took the lead in negotiating with outsiders. Although the commissioners indicated nearly "all the headmen in the upper and lower towns" participated in the peace discussions, in reality only one hailed from the Middle Settlements. The Valley Towns sent no representatives at all. Most important, Oconastota, one of the most influential leaders in Cherokee country, was not in attendance. The official reason given for his absence alluded to fresh disturbances with neighboring Creeks. Oconastota sent word "that the Creeks have bad intentions, and that his presence at home is absolutely necessary, to prevent his young men from going to war against them." Attakullakulla elaborated on this point following the meeting. Not only did the Creeks interfere with the Carolina trade, they also recently killed Cherokees in their hunting grounds. Even more alarming to both Cherokees and Carolinians were reports that Creek warriors killed fourteen settlers near Long Cane Creek in the immediate aftermath of the Congress.[10]

News of the Long Cane killings first arrived from trader Arthur Coodey. Warned by Cherokee hunters that Creek warriors intended to fall upon the inhabitants, Coodey fled to safety at Augusta. Local militiamen soon scouted the area and found fourteen bodies "cut and mangled," whereupon hundreds of settlers immediately fled to backcountry forts or toward the coast. As was often the case with such border incidents, the identity of the perpetrators was not entirely clear at first. Initial reports held the Lower Creeks responsible, but trader George Galphin dismissed this notion, maintaining it was most likely the Upper Creeks. Perhaps even "the Cherokees had a hand in it," wrote Galphin. Togulki agreed. The Lower Creek headman confirmed Galphin's suspicions when he revealed that seven Creeks—four from the Lower towns of Cussita and Coweta and three from the Upper towns of Tallassee and Okfuskee—committed the murders. To further complicate matters, Togulki also informed

Galphin these seven Creeks had lived among the Cherokees for more than five years and had assisted them during the Anglo-Cherokee War. John Stuart later specified they resided at the Lower Town of Estatoe with their Cherokee wives.[11]

The Long Cane murders, occurring just weeks after the Congress of Augusta, alarmed both Creeks and Cherokees. Lower Creek leaders immediately dismissed the seven "Renegadoes" by emphasizing their attachment to the Cherokees. A Coweta headman told Stuart, "If it was not for the Cherokeys there would not be all this done." Togulki was more specific when he blamed Saluy, saying if the Lower Town headman was not concerned in the affair then he should have his people kill those renegade Creeks who "harbor in his Nation." Saluy's limited authority, bounded by clan retaliation from those with familial ties to the seven Creeks, could effect no such order. Clan revenge, in fact, may have contributed to the Long Cane killings and the subsequent allegations leveled at Saluy by Creeks. This clan retaliation dated back nearly fifty years to the Yamasee War, in which Overhill Cherokees, at the instigation of South Carolina, murdered a Creek delegation in the Tugaloo townhouse. Handsome Fellow, an Upper Creek headman from Okfuskee, stated as much, and Saluy even believed the Coweta accusations stemmed from "an old Grudge they owe my Town . . . viz: of 14 of their head men having been killed in Toogola Townhouse when I was a Little Boy."[12]

Saluy, headman of both Tugaloo and Estatoe, responded in a way that best demonstrated his disapproval of the killings: he withdrew from Tugaloo to Estatoe. Although Stuart earlier identified Estatoe as the most culpable village, evidence suggests the guilty Creeks lived at Tugaloo. Speeches from Saluy in late January 1764, for example, expressed his intention to "remove with all my People to Estatoy." A few months later Saluy lamented he was obliged to retire "from his beloved Town of Toogola"—the place of his birth—to Estatoe, adding, "if he had had his will, [Tugaloo] should have been clear enough of Creeks." Saluy then admonished those Tugaloo people who "caress the Creeks, and will not quit the town" with him, and proceeded to accuse Cherokees from Little Chota, a border village in northern Georgia, of joining the Creeks.[13]

Beloved Chota in the Overhill Settlements, on the other hand, wished to avoid charges of duplicity at this critical juncture in Anglo-Cherokee relations. Although his towns were not directly involved in the Long Cane incident, Oconastota worried that the recent murders would interfere with the British trade—a trade Cherokee leaders had worked hard to reestablish at the Congress of Augusta. Oconastota offered to send guards to protect traders coming from Augusta, promising he would "give orders through my whole Nation to fall upon them" if Creeks harmed them. Oconastota may have voiced such assurances to the British, but his rhetoric did not meet the reality of peace that Cherokees from all regions wished to maintain with the Creeks.[14]

An Anglo-Creek war, however, might be more welcomed. Participants at the Congress of Augusta had no trouble recognizing that the Cherokees and Creeks "seem not to be upon the best of terms." John Stuart was less subtle when he observed that the Cherokees bear the Creeks "an Inveterate hatred" and "would gladly see them humbled to an Equality with themselves." The reasons for this were many. Balance of power likely played the most critical part, as the Cherokees had been much reduced by a smallpox epidemic, repeated attacks by northern and western Indians, and the Anglo-Cherokee War. The Creeks, to the contrary, had increased their numbers and become "Haughty and insolent to their Indian Neighbours." Many Cherokees were also incensed at the Creeks for their "Machinations, Messages and promises of Assistance," which encouraged the Cherokees to war in 1759 and then failed to deliver substantial military assistance during the British invasions of 1760–61.[15]

Cherokee headmen, especially those from the Lower and Valley Towns, fomented rumors of Anglo-Creek antagonism. The Rabbit of Tugaloo and Moytoy of Hiwassee pressed Arthur Coodey "to let the Governours know from them that the Creeks had broke out War with the White People and that now was the Time to humble them." The two headmen warned Coodey that the Long Cane murders were just the beginning and that more than three hundred Creeks were encamped above Augusta with the intention of ravaging the countryside. Saluy likewise related that Creek headmen were assembling "in order to concert proper measures to fall on the English." The Long Cane murderers, he continued, had returned to their Creek villages and were "much blamed . . . for beginning before their grand project was ready to take place." In order to encourage Carolina to demand immediate satisfaction for the recent murders and consequently escalate Anglo-Creek hostility, Cherokees from all regions promised military support.[16]

Colonial officials were attuned to such contrivances. Governor James Wright of Georgia believed the murders were "not a concerted Measure but done by Straglers and possibly promoted by the Cherokees with a View to involve us with the Creeks." A war with the Creeks, however, was not in Britain's interests, especially as their Indian affairs floundered in the north.

Just months prior to the Congress of Augusta and the Long Cane murders, the Ohio country and Great Lakes erupted with the commencement of Pontiac's Uprising. In the spring and summer of 1763, Indians throughout the region attacked British forts and settlers. Many reasons existed for this loosely coordinated revolt that lasted until the fall of 1765. Scholars typically attribute a marked shift in the balance of power following France's defeat in North America. To this they add settler encroachments, a tightening of British Indian diplomacy and trade, a loss in status, and a Native American spiritual awakening that provided a common bond to diverse Indians (which conveniently coincided with widespread anti-English sentiment). The British, of course, saw French intrigue in every Indian scheme and diligently sought to prevent the rebellion from engrossing the southeastern Indians.[17]

Cherokees showed little interest in joining the uprising. After two years of warfare with the British, villagers seemed more concerned with rebuilding their towns and restoring vital trade links. Further influencing "this postwar logic of recovery," Hatley argues, was the legacy of, and continued conflicts with, northern and western Indians. For much of the century, Cherokees had warred against French-allied Indians and other hostile natives from the north. Conflict with the Six Nations had been particularly acute, and these and other natives took advantage of the Anglo-Cherokee War to attack the beleaguered Cherokees. Some even joined the British expeditions into Cherokee country. Peace between the Cherokees and British did little to diminish these raids. Reports concerning northern and western Indian incursions against the Cherokees fill the documentary record throughout the 1760s. As Alexander Cameron, commissary to the Cherokees, observed, "Lord knows how many different Tribes are at War with them." It is important to note these intertribal conflicts were not limited to any particular town or region, but instead affected villagers throughout Cherokee country. Thus, when the Pontiac militants encouraged Cherokees to join their uprising, it is little wonder that Cherokees from all regions closed their ears to such talks.[18]

Cherokees proved slightly more receptive to British requests for assistance against the insurgents. Notable leaders such as Attakullakulla,

Oconastota, Ostenaco, Willinawaw, and Saluy led expeditions against hostile Indians during Pontiac's Uprising. These raids corresponded with obligations of clan revenge and provided Cherokees leverage for improving trade relations with the British. As with earlier campaigns against the Shawnees, Delawares, and Mingos during the Seven Years' War, the British lobbied hard for Cherokee assistance, but warriors made it perfectly clear "they have been naked a great while" and therefore needed ammunition and supplies before they could set out to war. Cherokees were especially concerned about how their military assistance would interfere with the hunting season. "We must hunt very strong," they declared; otherwise, traders "will never trust us again" with goods on credit. When Cameron attempted to prevail upon Cherokee headmen to attack enemy Indians in 1765, for example, he could only get Ostenaco to undertake the service, noting that other Cherokees could not be persuaded to leave off their hunting. Later, upon Ostenaco's return from war with captives, the Overhill headman reminded Cameron he and his party had "lost their hunting season by this expedition" and expected a reward sufficient to purchase "as many necessities as those that brought in skins or furs instead of prisoners."[19]

Cherokees needed to hunt "very strong" for other reasons: frequent attacks by enemy Indians often prevented them from taking deer except "in large Parties." Cherokee warriors responded by launching counter raids of their own, thereby demonstrating more a desire to act "by Principles of self defence" than from meager British encouragement. The focus of these raids also shifted as the nature of the rebellion changed. By the spring of 1765, most of the Ohio and Great Lakes Indians had ceased hostilities against the British, and what limited resistance still existed swung farther south and west to the Illinois country. Cherokees accordingly sent parties against their western enemies who, in turn, continued to harass Cherokees in their villages and hunting grounds well after Pontiac's Uprising ended.[20]

As the more general Anglo-Indian conflict subsided, Cherokee affairs took a turn for the worse in the Virginia backcountry. Augusta County inhabitants killed five Cherokees near the town of Staunton. Whereas the Long Cane killings in 1763 directly involved the Lower Towns, the recent murders most affected the Overhill Settlements and, in particular, the town of Chilhowee, "where the relations of the murdered Indians live." Fearing that Chilhowee and the Overhill people would immediately seek revenge, Fauquier issued a proclamation and reward for the murderers' apprehension. The governor and other officials also promised satisfaction as Virginia sought to avoid becoming embroiled in yet another Indian war.[21]

Bereaved clan members, however, did not take immediate satisfaction against the Virginians as they had prior to the Anglo-Cherokee War. This owed in large part to the efforts of Overhill headmen to quell calls for retribution throughout many Cherokee villages. Although the nearest relatives of the deceased lived in the Overhill Towns, clan connections extended throughout Cherokee country, making the murders in Virginia a cross-regional affair. Ostenaco accordingly traveled from the Overhill Towns to the Valley and Middle Settlements with a string of white beads, advising those villagers to mind their hunts and wait for satisfaction from Virginia. Overhill leaders also sent for Saluy, the Lower Town headman, who reassured all in the Chota townhouse he had persuaded "the relations of those Indians who were assassinated in Virginia to forbear taking revenge" until Attakullakulla returned from Williamsburg. Attakullakulla eventually returned home with good talks but no satisfaction, either in news of the offenders' punishment or in presents for clan members.[22]

With satisfaction not forthcoming, Virginians found evidence of Cherokee clan vengeance in almost every frontier report. In May 1766, trader James Welsh was killed in the Lower Towns. Shortly thereafter, a trader named Boyd and two others from Virginia were purportedly killed near the Overhill Settlements. Two more Virginians were found murdered later that fall near the Yadkin River. Just months after this incident, seven traders from Virginia met their end near Cowee in the Middle Towns. In every one of these and subsequent accounts, the British initially suspected "the relations of those Cherokees who were killed . . . in Virginia, [who] will, according to their inhuman custom, take every opportunity of revenge, at least till they have killed as many as they lost." Even the well-informed John Stuart initially believed the Cherokees had some hand in the killings. So, too, did Saluy, who sought to protect his Lower Towns people "from any part of the Charges" laid against the Cherokees. Speaking at the head of seven Lower Towns, Saluy assured the British that there wasn't "a Warriour of these lower Towns" involved in the murders. If the Overhill leaders "choose to Countenance such proceedings," he continued, "they may; they began the last war [Anglo-Cherokee War] and made their Road thro' our Towns to the Settlements [and] the Nation was thinned by it." Overhill headmen, for their part, denied any involvement in the murders.[23]

Although later reports indicated hostile northern Indians most likely committed the murders, warriors from Chilhowee eventually killed five Virginians in October 1768. That they waited twenty-nine months to do so testifies to the influence of Overhill leaders but also a consensus among Cherokee peoples to maintain stable relations with Britain. Preserving the alliance was particularly important because raids from northern and western Indians had increased in recent years. Villagers from every region found their "Enemys were too numerous" as they infested "all parts of our Country." A desire to stem these attacks prompted Cherokee leaders to seek peace with northern and western Indians, and they needed the British to act as intermediaries. No person was more fit for the task than Sir William Johnson.[24]

Johnson's close connections to the Six Nations gave him remarkable influence among the northern Indians. Cherokee headmen as early as 1765 requested that both Stuart and Fauquier ask Johnson for help in brokering a peace with the Iroquois Confederacy. Johnson, however, initially spurned such efforts, advising Stuart that encouraging intertribal peace was not good policy so soon after the pan-Indian uprising. But circumstances had changed by the spring of 1768. The British began to see the powerful Creeks as the more immediate threat in the South. Astute officials recognized the Cherokees counterbalanced Creek power and therefore worried that an increasingly besieged Cherokee population was not in their best interest. After "incessant" applications from the Cherokees via Stuart, Johnson finally agreed to mediate a Cherokee-Iroquois peace.[25]

Oconastota, Attakullakulla, Kittagusta (Prince of Chota), Tistoe of Keowee, and the Raven of Tugaloo headed the delegation that traveled to New York. Primarily from the Overhill and Lower Settlements, but representing villagers from every region, Cherokee headmen conducted negotiations with Johnson and more than seven hundred Indians over a period of seventy-nine days. The peace that resulted comprised more than just the Cherokees and Iroquois. In addition to the Six Nations were, among others, the Seven Nations of Canada, which included Iroquois, Huron, Algonquin, Nippising, and Abenaki peoples. This meeting was soon followed by an even larger gathering of more than 1,000 Indians at Fort Pitt, whereby Attakullakulla struggled to end their long-standing conflicts with Delawares, Shawnees, Mingos, and other Ohio and Great Lakes Indians. Although less successful than the New York peace talks, the Fort Pitt proceedings brought diverse Indians together to address another pressing matter, one that affected nearly all indigenous peoples at the conference: land.[26]

As Cherokee headmen attempted to stabilize relations with enemy Indians, they also had to contend with land pressures from the southern colonies. The issue first surfaced at the Congress of Augusta in 1763. While trade concerns inundated Cherokee speeches during the conference, land encroachments proved equally contentious. Settlers increasingly pressed against Cherokee lands following the Anglo-Cherokee War, particularly the Long Cane region, which threatened the hunting grounds of the Lower Towns people. Yet land ownership was not a town or regional prerogative, at least when it concerned those vast hunting grounds beyond the villages. A letter from John Stuart to the Board of Trade in March 1764 sheds more light on the subject. Stuart observed that each Cherokee "looks upon himself as Proprietor of all the Lands claimed by the whole Nation." No individual Cherokee, regardless his standing in the community, could "give away any more than his own right in any piece of Land; which in the Cherokee Nation would be no more than as One is to 13500." Leaders representing specific towns or regions, therefore, were not authorized to dispose of lands without first obtaining consent from Cherokees throughout the nation—at least in theory.[27]

Attakullakulla, for example, apparently had such authority when he negotiated a treaty with South Carolina to end the Anglo-Cherokee War, which designated Long Cane as the limits of British settlement. When it came to actually marking the boundary in 1765, however, local and regional tensions temporarily surfaced. Overhill leaders acknowledged the land was "the hunting Ground of our lower towns People," yet both they and Carolina recognized a strong Overhill presence would add legitimacy to the transaction. Some Lower Town leaders took umbrage at this, claiming that "the Land is theirs to give, the overhills people have no business with it." The Old Warrior of Estatoe and Wolf of Keowee in particular attempted to take charge of the affair and set out with officials to run the line. Other Lower Town leaders were furious at the actions of their fellow headmen. Saluy and Tistoe "called it a theft" and asked Ensign George Price if he thought "those two warriors with him could dispose of the Land which belong'd to the whole Nation." Foreshadowing internal

Cherokee divisiveness over land as both a regional and generational dilemma, Saluy and Tistoe warned Price that their young warriors "talked loudly" of the cession and "mischief would be done if the line would be attempted." Price appeared puzzled and annoyed at Cherokee contradictions and threats. Ostenaco dismissed such talks altogether. He reminded the Lower Towns people they had agreed to the boundary before Overhill leaders arrived, and they still had plenty of land on which to hunt. Alluding to the disruptions experienced during the recent war, Ostenaco advised them to "build good houses" and live in peace with the English.[28]

South Carolina and the Cherokees finalized the land cession on October 19, 1765, and ran the boundary the following spring. Twelve headmen signed the agreement: three from the Overhill Settlements and nine from the Lower Towns. The issue of landownership concerned all Cherokees, yet townspeople from different regions held varying levels of attachment to certain hunting grounds. Whereas only three Overhill headmen and no Middle or Valley leaders signed the document (though represented by other regions' deputies), headmen from the Lower Towns of Estatoe, Keowee, Sugar Town, Toxaway, and Qaulatchie were specifically identified. The Long Cane area had long been the Lower Towns' hunting grounds, and their voices accordingly became the loudest as land pressures from South Carolina mounted. These regional divisions pertaining to hunting grounds lessened, however, once white encroachment began to threaten all Cherokees.[29]

Of particular concern were encroachments from North Carolina and Virginia. Kittagusta informed Alexander Cameron at the running of the South Carolina line that his people also desired to mark the boundaries with those two colonies. Complaining of the many families who had "settled upon a great part of our best Lands," Kittagusta wished to "make a final Conclusion of the whole at once" by securing their borders with all the southern colonies. The line initially agreed upon ran from Reedy River in South Carolina to Tryon Mountain in western North Carolina and then to Colonel Chiswell's Mines near the New River in Virginia. North Carolina delivered on its promises in June 1767 after some hesitation and continued intrusions by settlers into Cherokee territory. But the real problem lay with Virginia. Lieutenant Governor Fauquier delayed and then died, all the while witnessing a massive tide of settlers edging ever closer to the Overhill Towns. In October 1768, it appeared the Cherokee-Virginia boundary would be settled by treaty negotiations held in the

South Carolina backcountry. More than three hundred Cherokees led by nearly all the principal men in the Overhill and Lower Towns attended the conference. With the resultant Treaty of Hard Labor, the boundary with Virginia continued north from Chiswell's Mines to the confluence of the Great Kanawha and Ohio Rivers (present Point Pleasant, West Virginia). Oconastota subsequently chose May 10, 1769, to meet the Virginians at Chiswell's to mark the line. Using firm and visual language, Oconastota declared, "I shall cut such a deep ditch round our Lands, that whoever shall attempt to cross it, will be in danger of falling in." Unfortunately for the Overhill headman, British settlers and rival Indian peoples did not find the ditch too deep.[30]

The Cherokees were not the only Native Americans that Virginians negotiated with over boundaries. Representatives from Virginia and other colonies met Sir William Johnson and more than 3,200 Indians at Fort Stanwix in upstate New York shortly after the Hard Labor proceedings. The central issue concerned competing land claims by Indians and whites, but negotiations exposed similar friction between Indian groups, particularly the Six Nations and Cherokees. The Iroquois declared their boundaries extended south along the Ohio River past its confluence with the Great Kanawha to the mouth of the Tennessee River, a tract of land that included Cherokee hunting grounds. This presented a problem for British officials. In December 1767 the Board acknowledged that the Iroquois claimed those lands "as part of their ancient dominion," but they were "in fact actually occupied by the Cherokees as their hunting ground." The Board therefore ruled initially in the Cherokees' favor by recognizing the mouth of the Kanawha River as the extent of Iroquois claims. John Stuart was pleased to notify the Cherokees of the Board's decision the following October. Sir William Johnson, on the other hand, wrote to Stuart that regardless of the Board's directive, the Six Nations "will insist on their Title to the Lands as far South as the Cherokee [Tennessee] River."[31]

Johnson proved correct. Iroquois headmen at Fort Stanwix argued they had "a very good and clear title" to those lands and could not allow other Indians' claims without "acting unworthy [of] those Warriors who fought and conquered it." Conquered is a relative term, however. Iroquois warriors and their confederates may have plagued the Cherokees prior to the peace of 1768 (concluded earlier that spring), but the latter people "never acknowledged themselves to be conquered by the Six Nations, or any other Confederacy or Tribe of Indians." Johnson, however, ignored

Cherokee entreaties and the Board's directive by allowing Iroquois claims at Stanwix. The two treaties of 1768 thus appeared to many to be only a temporary solution, since disagreements continued over the territory in question.[32]

These debates intensified after the delegates left Hard Labor and Fort Stanwix. The Iroquois held certain advantages over the Cherokees, one being their connections to Johnson and another their support from the expansionist Virginians who wanted to divest Cherokees of their hunting grounds. When British agents worried the Stanwix proceedings would "produce Jealousy & Disatisfaction amongst the Cherokees," officials in Virginia asserted the territory "was never justly claim'd by them." Johnson agreed it was "indisputably the Lands of the 6 Nations." If the Board denied Iroquois claims, he added, they would prove "Worse Enemys than the Cherokees." Tying these words of caution to recent pan-Indian maneuverings, Johnson warned General Thomas Gage, "Should the six Nations in general Attack us; all the rest would immediately follow." The Board eventually sided with Johnson, agreeing with the superintendent that an angry Six Nations and its confederates would defeat any attempt to run a final boundary in the west. Furthermore, the contested lands had already been purchased at Fort Stanwix, and the debt ridden British did not relish paying for the same territory twice by also compensating the Cherokees. Virginia was especially pleased with this decision because settlements had already been established west of Chiswell's Mines along the Holston and Clinch Rivers.[33]

Cherokee headmen were understandably alarmed when, just three months after the Treaty of Hard Labor, Stuart notified them of Virginia's request for a new boundary to include these recent settlements. Attempting to follow orders while also easing Cherokee discontent, Stuart explained to them that the Virginians wanted only "a little Land that you can easily Spare them without injuring yourselves." When communicating with the Board of Trade, however, Stuart was more forthright. The Virginia-backed Iroquois claims, he wrote, "will divest the Cherokees of every foot of hunting Ground they possess beyond the Mountains." Oconastota likewise recognized the economic setback of ceding more hunting territory. He reminded Stuart that Virginia had agreed to a line run by Chiswell's Mines, and any additional land cessions must be accompanied with substantial compensation. The Board subsequently ordered Virginia to purchase lands west of Chiswell's Mines from the Cherokees rather than defend their claims by way of prior agreement with the Six Nations. Accordingly, almost two years to the day of the Treaty of Hard Labor, over 1,000 Cherokees met Stuart and representatives from Virginia and South Carolina near Long Cane. With the ensuing Treaty of Lochaber in October 1770, Virginia's boundary with the Cherokees pushed west to the Holston River (near Long Island on the Holston) and then north on a straight course to the confluence of the Kanawha and Ohio Rivers. That Cherokees from different regions were willing to treat with the Virginians at Lochaber so soon after Hard Labor testifies to the extent to which land and trade had become interconnected to Cherokee policy making.[34]

The British trade was in a state of disrepair by the fall of 1770, and Cherokees from every region felt its effects. Unstable borderlands and dangerous hunting grounds interfered with the deerskin trade, which weakened village economies. Mounting debts owed to traders became one of the biggest problems. Traders explained to Governor Wright in 1771 that Cherokee debts grew exponentially in the immediate aftermath of the Anglo-Cherokee War. Because the Cherokees had been reduced "to nakedness and extreme poverty" during that conflict, traders had little choice but to "trust them, not only with ammunition, but with Guns and Cloathing also, before they could go out to hunt even for bare subsistance." Added to these Cherokee miseries were "the northern and western Indians [who] soon after fell upon them in Swarms." Ostenaco verified these difficulties when he informed Cameron that "being engaged" these many years in war, they had "little time to hunt" and therefore could not pay their debts. Overhill headmen also related that competition from white hunters contributed to their poor hunts. They accused colonists of coming in large parties to "the Middle of our Hunting Grounds," adding, "The whole Nation is full of Hunters, & the Guns Ratling every way." Settler encroachment exacerbated this competition from white hunters—a point not missed by headmen who found that frontier inhabitants "Steal our Deer & our Land too."[35]

These changing geopolitical and demographic circumstances had a direct bearing on regional hunting grounds. Highlighting the Lower Towns provides a case in point. Lower Cherokees frequently hunted the South Carolina and Georgia Piedmont prior to the Anglo-Cherokee War. Although they continued to do so once the fighting ended, settler encroachment and competition from both white and Creek hunters made these areas not "any use to them, as a hunting ground." By 1771 many Cherokees found the land below Keowee "entirely wore out," so that Lower Towns people were "obliged to go over the Hills to Hunt." Rather than initiate interregional conflict over designated hunting grounds, receding lands (and deer) instead encouraged cross-regional cooperation as Overhill headmen worked with Lower Town leaders to channel the latter's hunting expeditions toward the hinterlands of North Carolina and Virginia. Oconastota, for instance, explained to Stuart that as white settlements neared the Lower Towns, he reserved the lands beyond the mountains for their hunting. Intrusions from North Carolina and Virginia, therefore, not only threatened the Overhill and Middle Settlements; they likewise jeopardized the newly designated Lower Towns' hunting grounds.[36]

Poor hunts, debts, and a decline in trade subsequently provided key motives for Cherokee land cessions. The Lower Towns in particular used land to obtain outlets for trade beyond South Carolina. One method centered upon granting tracts of land to traders or their Cherokee offspring in return for improved trade or debt cancellation. Saluy was especially involved in schemes to grant Cherokee lands near South Carolina to Virginia trader Richard Pearis. Pearis had apparently promised Saluy an endless supply of goods from Virginia and an audience with King George III in exchange for land. None of the Overhill headmen were present at the transaction, and when Oconastota found out, he sent a heated talk to Stuart complaining of Pearis. Saluy, however, was "much of an Orator," and he and Pearis traveled to the Overhills to assure Oconastota of the deal's merit. Their visit paid off. In a letter to the Virginia Council in August 1770, a converted Oconastota explained they felt "much Cramped in their Trade which at present is only with Carolina." The Cherokees therefore granted lands to Pearis "with a View also of Future Trade" with Virginia.[37]

Saluy died before he could benefit from the Pearis land cession. A Lower Town leader with substantial cross-regional influence, Saluy was part of an older cadre of headmen who for the first time faced a growing multi-front threat to the Cherokee homeland. As seen with Pearis and again with the Broad River cession in Georgia consummated at the Congress of Augusta in 1773, a land-for-trade strategy provided temporary relief from increasing economic troubles and settler encroachment. But ceding land for trade and borderland security had its limits. Cherokee delegates at Lochaber, for instance, could not be persuaded to give up the sacred ground at Long Island on Holston. Other natives held similar views about their lands as white encroachment increasingly became a pan-Indian affair.[38]

Pan-Indianism—a movement that stressed intertribal unity and a common Indian identity—had accelerated in recent years. The Seven Years' War had spurred intertribal communication and cooperation to unprecedented levels, and Pontiac's Uprising continued this trend as a spiritually charged nativistic movement fueled militant pan-Indianism throughout eastern North America. Although the rebellion subsided by 1765, proponents of intertribal accord and confederacies remained active throughout Indian country. The Creeks had one such voice in Mortar, an Upper Creek headman who earlier encouraged the Settico people to attack British settlers in 1759. Mortar maintained strong ties to the Cherokees during and after the Anglo-Cherokee War. The Okchai headman reportedly assisted Cherokee warriors during the conflict, and some historians attribute his influence to the murder of several English traders in 1760. Later reports indicated his party was also involved in the Long Cane killings in 1763, which had been committed by Creeks living in the Lower Cherokee Towns. The following year Mortar articulated his deep connections to his mountain neighbors when he informed Stuart that "he looks upon the Cherokees as his people."[39]

Regional divisions among the Cherokees, however, meant that Mortar's policies were differently received. Saluy had become such an active antagonist to Mortar by 1765 that the Okchai headman claimed he "would never trust himself near any place where the young Warrior of Estatoe was." Overhill and Valley leaders, on the other hand, welcomed Mortar into their towns. Kenoteta, the Mankiller of Tellico, and Oconastota particularly countenanced Mortar. Oconastota had in fact employed Kenoteta and the Mankiller as ambassadors to Mortar to strengthen Cherokee-Creek connections, and Overhill headmen at some point during the interwar years appointed him as a Creek beloved man in Chota. His presence in Chota was particularly noticed following the murder of five Cherokees in Virginia in 1765. Stuart and Cameron observed that Mortar had been "very Busy" encouraging the Cherokees to take revenge, even "Offering to support them with 700 Men immediately" to "go to Virginia & fall on the back Settlements." These promises of assistance fit nicely with his and other pan-Indian efforts to "form a Confederacy among the great [Indian] nations" in the South to challenge the British. Although most Cherokees seemed unwilling to adhere to Mortar's vision in 1765, circumstances began to change as Cherokees and other Indians confronted an increasingly hostile and aggressively expanding colonial population.[40]

Whereas Mortar and other militant Creeks peddled pan-Indianism in the South, it was the Ohio Indians, particularly the Shawnees, who most aggressively sought to strengthen connections across tribal boundaries. The Shawnees had long been known as diplomatic go-betweens. Their strategic location in the Ohio country situated them on both a north-south and east-west axis that connected diverse and distant Native American peoples. One Hiwassee headman described them as "a People of no Settlement but rambling Place to Place with Nothing by Lyes." Although not an entirely accurate statement, it does testify to the mobility of Shawnee peoples as well as their significance to intertribal communication. This communication greatly intensified during Pontiac's Uprising but even more so in the wake of the Fort Stanwix Treaty in 1768.[41]

The Fort Stanwix land cession revealed conflicting claims of ownership between the Iroquois and Cherokees over the Ohio country. More importantly, it widened the growing chasm between the Ohio Indians and the Six Nations. Long held as "props of the Longhouse," in which the Shawnees, Delawares, Wyandots, Mingos, and other Indians in the region acted as subordinates within the Iroquois Confederacy, the balance of power had shifted to the Ohio and Great Lakes Indians following the Seven Years' War. These Indians had been marginalized during the Fort Stanwix proceeding, whereby much of their land was ceded without their consent. Many Shawnees and their confederates thereafter worked tirelessly to achieve intertribal cooperation directed against the Six Nations but more so against the British. Of particular interest to the Shawnees and other Ohio Indians were the western Indians, namely those peoples along the Wabash, Illinois, and Mississippi Rivers and western Great Lakes. The western Indians' willingness to participate in this new confederacy resulted not only from general anti-British sentiment but also from the recent Iroquois-Cherokee peace, which they felt had been directed against them. Cherokee deputies to the Six Nations, for instance, made it clear they desired to "unite their Arms against several of the Western and Southern Indian Enemys to both." The western Indians responded by strengthening their confederacy "to better oppose the Six Nations and Cherokees." Such intertribal hostility made it remarkably difficult for the Shawnees to establish a general pan-Indian confederacy.[42]

Shawnee deputies nevertheless traveled throughout eastern North America to promote intertribal peace. They labored particularly hard to end the Cherokee–western Indian wars. The Cherokees likewise sent their own agents to broker peace, first at Fort Pitt in the failed congress of 1768, and later throughout the different Indian nations. Both Shawnee and Cherokee diplomacy proved unsuccessful. Attakullakulla admitted in 1773 that the western Indians rejected their offers of friendship "with insulting Contempt," even cutting to pieces and burning their belts of wampum in the presence of Cherokee messengers. The confederacy continued to grow, however, thanks in large part to the westward expansion of British colonists. Pan-Indian proponents effectively utilized "the principle of defending their Lands" to strengthen their associations. As John Stuart noted, "For however Indians may Quarrel amongst themselves, yet an Encroachment upon the Lands of any Nation becomes Common cause & attracts the attention of the whole." Thus, even though Cherokees and western Indians did not bridge their differences and join together in the confederacy, they increasingly shared a "Common cause" in protecting their lands.[43]

The British recognized the potential danger of these maneuverings but were not fully aware of the details. Reports and rumors of Indian confederacies and rebellions abounded in the early 1770s. The Board of Trade received accounts through "almost every channel of correspondence from America" that a "union between the Northern and Southern Indians has been in agitation." The Board asked William Johnson to confirm the truth of such reports and, if they had certain merit, "to defeat and disconcert it." Johnson responded with a lengthy narration of intelligence he received from two Indian informants with ties to the Shawnees and Delawares. Entitled "Information Concerning an Indian Conspiracy," the report could not have pleased British officials. Apparently, the Six Nations denied any culpability in the Fort Stanwix treaty, telling the Ohio Indians the British had forced them to cede these lands. Deputies from the Iroquois Confederacy then expressed their desire to join and even lead the burgeoning confederacy. Once peace had been established with the western Indians, which they "fixed four Years for doing it in," the Indians would fall upon the English. With French and Spanish assistance, the Six Nations along with the Ohio and western Indians intended to attack all British posts in the American interior, while the Cherokees and other southern Indians would invade the Carolinas and Virginia. In order to deceive the British, the confederated Indians would speak well to the English, but it would be "from their Lips only, and not from their Hearts." Diplomatic envoys were subsequently sent throughout Indian country to implement the plan.[44]

Cherokee connections to these pan-Indian stirrings confused British agents. Everyone knew that Iroquois, Creek, Shawnee, and Delaware messengers (among others) frequented Cherokee towns, but John Stuart and Alexander Cameron could not decipher the purpose of these visits. "The Indians are very obscure in their messages," Stuart wrote, as their method of communication could only be "understood by the few who can decypher their Belt of whampum strings of Beads and other Tokens." Cherokees increasingly held closed session meetings, turning away traders and even their Cherokee offspring from their townhouses. Even plying Cherokee headmen with rum failed to produce intelligence, as when Cameron lamented after one such attempt, "I am not to day the wiser for it." These secret councils also had a regional dimension. The beloved town of Chota was the central location for pan-Indian meetings, which prompted other Cherokees and British agents to question the motives of Oconastota and the Overhill leadership. Cameron suspected Oconastota of "being a great politician" and "a great Planner of Congresses & Meetings." Although the Great Warrior of Chota denied duplicitous behavior, Lower Town headmen also worried about the true intentions of Overhill leaders. Suspecting the Overhill people held bad talks, Tistoe of Keowee asked, "Why did Oukonnastotah leave the tokens of Peace with us when he was lastly here? If a Bird of Peace should come from you amongst us, we shall be better Satisfied." The British and southern colonists, too, wished for "a Bird of Peace," but this became increasingly doubtful as colonial unrest turned to armed rebellion in the spring of 1775.[45]

The 1760s and early 1770s were rebuilding years for the Cherokees. Rather than retreat into isolationist tendencies, Cherokees were forced to engage their Indian and white neighbors through mediums of trade, warfare, and diplomacy. Land encroachments and the securing of boundaries emerged as the critical issue for most mountain villagers. Cherokee debates and deals over hunting territories in the immediate aftermath of the Seven Years' War were characterized by relative accord. This unanimity collapsed, however, at the onset of the American Revolution. Subsequent Cherokee fractures over land cessions had its roots in two key developments during the interwar years: the burgeoning of a pan-Indian confederacy and the colonial rebellion against Britain.

Cherokees were not the only indigenous people to feel the pressure of expanding backcountry settlements. Land provided a "union of interest" among diverse and often discordant Native Americans, many of whom worked tirelessly to strengthen intertribal alliances designed to protect Indian lands from British encroachment. Although pan-Indian efforts would not come to fruition until the American Revolution, these prewar stirrings represented a watershed for Native Americans by providing an outlet beyond the town, region, or even nation for anti-British sentiment. With the French ousted from North America, the embryonic confederacy constituted a new regional and potentially continental power that could challenge British hegemony. Coupled with the growing political rift between Britain and her colonists, pan-Indianism complicated Cherokee policies and generated discord between towns, regions, and generations. The approaching revolution would therefore test Cherokee peoples as never before.[46]

8

"half war half peace"

The American Revolution in Cherokee Country

The onset of the American Revolution forced Cherokees to engage in the conflict, and the result was far from unanimous. Although nearly all Cherokees were embittered by continual land encroachments from American settlers, not every mountain villager agreed upon the best means of safeguarding their homes and lands. Some favored neutrality and were reticent to become involved in the "white people's war." Others openly sided with the British to counter American expansion by force of arms. Perhaps the best known leader of this latter faction was Dragging Canoe, an Overhill warrior who led hundreds of Cherokees away from their ancestral lands to erect new villages further down the Tennessee River. These dissidents eventually became known as the Chickamaugas, and they continued fighting the Americans until 1794, more than a decade after the Treaty of Paris officially ended the war between Britain and the United States.

Standard interpretations of this period of Cherokee history are thin and unconvincing. The consensus among notable Indian experts is that the Chickamaugas organized "a secessionist movement" from the Cherokee nation. These scholars envision a sharp break between Cherokee peoples, arguing that the Chickamaugas created "a splinter tribe" that "broke completely with the Cherokee Nation." The two factions ultimately grew so disjointed that "the Revolution became a Cherokee civil war." None of these interpretations, however, accurately conveys the Cherokee experience during the last quarter of the eighteenth century. The Chickamauga "secession," for instance, denotes a formal withdrawal from the Cherokee political community. While hundreds and eventually thousands of Cherokees relocated to the Chickamauga Towns, these dissidents did not sever political or kinship ties to those Cherokees remaining on ancestral lands, but instead actively maintained these connections in both war and peace. There is likewise no record of Cherokees fighting or killing each other during the revolutionary era. Infrequent political assassinations did occur in the early nineteenth century, but even this political factionalism can in no way be construed as a civil war.[1]

Arguing for the formation of a new, even if short-lived, tribe is more problematic, because the assumption that the Chickamaugas partook in some form of ethnogenesis is untenable. Rather, the Chickamaugas from the onset of their removal forcefully projected their identity as Cherokees, even as they strengthened connections with non-Cherokee peoples. The Chickamaugas are therefore markedly different from the Seminoles in Florida whose withdrawal from the Creek confederacy during the eighteenth century translated into political and cultural distinction as well as a new ethnic identity. Instead of envisioning the American Revolution in Cherokee country as an example of secession, ethnogenesis, or civil war, the conflict should be more appropriately understood within the context of Cherokee regionalism. The failure to explain the Chickamauga experience from a regional perspective is surprising, since nearly every work on the prerevolutionary Cherokees identifies regional settlements as key to their sociopolitical organization. Scholars are usually quick to point out that towns and villages were clustered in the Lower, Middle, Valley, and Overhill regions, stretching from the Savannah to the Tennessee Rivers. Yet the Chickamaugas are viewed as outside this historical continuity, representing a war faction whose people cut ties to the Cherokees in order to carry out attacks against the Americans until they finally made peace in 1794.

The Chickamaugas were therefore not a new tribe but the founders of a new Cherokee region. Its origin can be traced to the more than twenty militia invasions directed against the Cherokee towns throughout the revolutionary era. Widespread displacement resulted, and the center of Cherokee population shifted away from ancestral lands to the environs of the Chattahoochee, Coosa, and Tennessee Rivers (see map 5). Nonetheless, Cherokee localism and regionalism remained intact, although the influence of older regions waned as those newly established gained power. The Chickamaugas of the Five Lower Towns in particular emerged as a powerful regional force within Cherokee country. They became the progenitors of the Lower Cherokees with their regional council center at

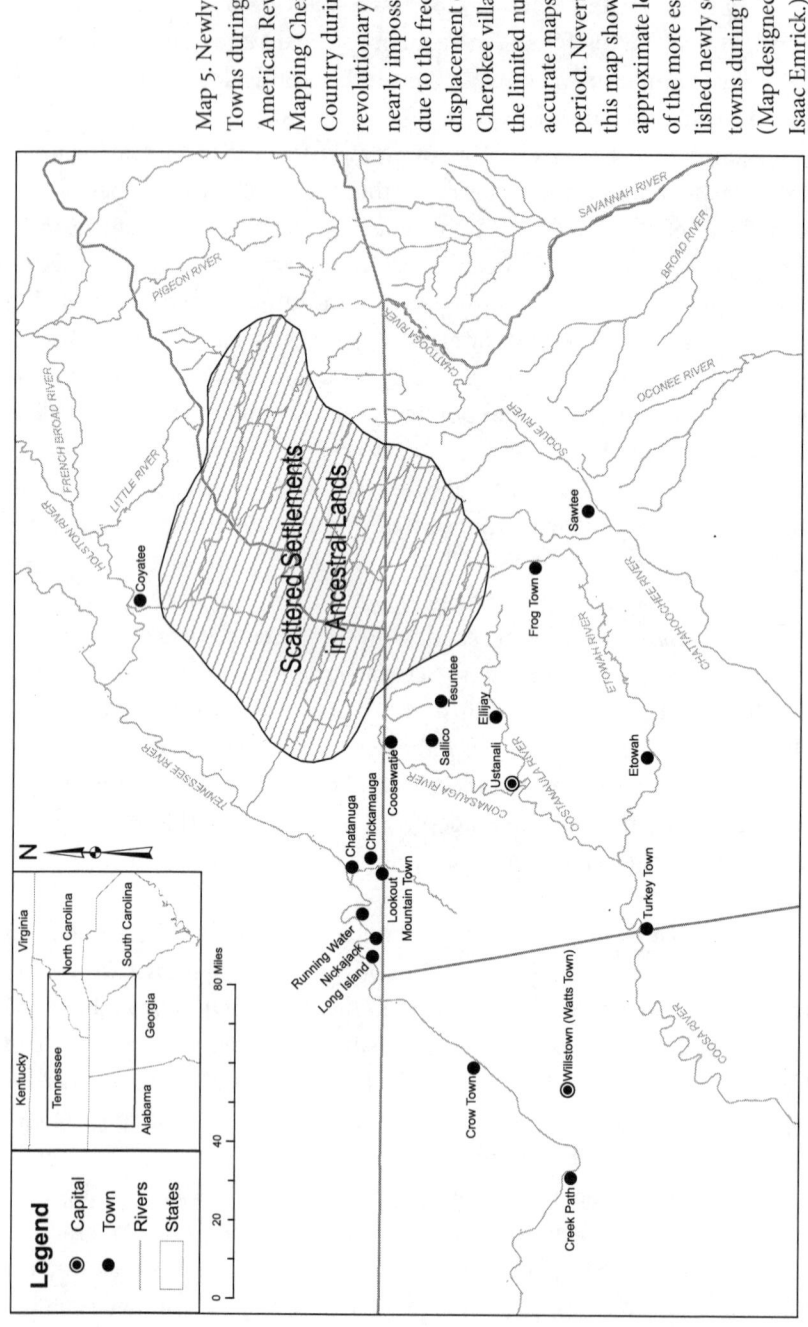

Map 5. Newly Settled Towns during the American Revolution. Mapping Cherokee Country during the revolutionary era is a nearly impossible task due to the frequent displacement of Cherokee villages and the limited number of accurate maps for the period. Nevertheless, this map shows the approximate location of the more established newly settled towns during the war. (Map designed by Isaac Emrick.)

Willstown (Watts Town). Townspeople remaining in the Overhill, Middle, and Valley Settlements, on the other hand, joined with displaced villagers in northern Georgia to become the Upper Cherokees. They shifted their regional council seat during the war from the beloved town of Chota to Ustanali, near present-day Calhoun, Georgia. Together, these Lower and Upper Cherokees carried the basic framework of town and regional identities and structures into the next century.

As Americans protested against British policies after 1763, the worsening political crisis did little to hinder their expansion into Indian country. Backcountry settlements grew exponentially following the Peace of Paris, with the Cherokees alone involved in five different land cessions prior to the Revolution. Many of the thousands of migrants who settled near Cherokee lands traveled south from Pennsylvania and Virginia. This new demographic surge, combined with Williamsburg's aggressive support for territorial expansion, prompted Native Americans throughout the region to identify the newcomers as "Virginians." Also referred to as "crackers," the proliferation of these Virginians ushered in a new age of Anglo-Indian relations in the southeastern borderlands.[2]

Cherokees frequently complained to British authorities about the Virginians who illegally hunted and settled in their territory, stole their horses, and sometimes killed their people. Such hostile acts predated the Revolution, but the interwar years marked a new epoch in settler-Indian relations as cultural and racial attitudes hardened for both sides. The rise in Indian-hating among whites has been well documented, but similar developments occurred among native populations. John Stuart observed that the Indians "Detest the back Inhabitants of these provinces," which accounted "for the Reluctancy with which they give up any part of their Lands being Anxious to keep such Neighbors at a Distance." Oconastota agreed that his people wished "to keep the Virginians at as great a distance as possible, as they are generally bad Men." Such attitudes reflected a growing tendency among Cherokees and other Indians to dismiss ethnic differences and political affiliation by lumping diverse immigrants into a single category.[3]

This is not to say, however, that Native Americans suddenly ignored geopolitical dynamics within the region. They could and did recognize differences between the British and their colonists when it suited them. The Creeks, who likewise faced the new settler invasion in Georgia, assured the British in 1768 that "the English and Scotch are good, but the Virginians they can not be reconciled to." Other Creek leaders later agreed they did "not want to kill any of the English. They are only for Cutting off all the Virginians, who steal their Horses & Settle upon their Land." When the British remained unsure of Creek intentions, a Coweta man living in Tugaloo clarified the matter for Indian agent Alexander Cameron. Creek Pigeon of Coweta told Cameron that backcountry settlers and Creeks had threatened each other for a long time. The Creeks therefore "wanted to have a Ball Play [war] or two with the Virginians," for they "did not doubt of driving the Virginians as far as the English down to the Sea Side."[4]

Recent experiences did not give Cherokees a similar confidence in driving colonists to the coast, but they too were keenly aware of colonial unrest and attempted to take advantage of the widening political rupture. Settler encroachment generated great discontent among the Cherokees, but townspeople recognized they could not attack the intruders without offending Britain. Interregional cooperation over land cessions during the 1760s and early 1770s largely stemmed from the need to preserve the Anglo-Cherokee alliance, which limited options for those Cherokees wishing to challenge British hegemony. The imperial crisis, however, presented Cherokees and other disgruntled Indians with the political rationale needed to distinguish the British from their aggressively expanding and seceding American subjects. It is therefore little wonder that pan-Indian militancy surged throughout America as the Revolution commenced. Earlier setbacks in forming a general Indian confederacy resulted in part from a similar reticence among native leaders to break with the British and their trade. The colonial rebellion changed this. As Gregory Evans Dowd argues, the Revolution gave pan-Indian militants an opportunity to cooperate with pro-British headmen to forcibly challenge American expansion. The result was "the largest, most unified Native American effort" at pan-Indian militancy that "the continent would ever see."[5]

Cherokee connections to the militants proved ambiguous before 1776. Frequent intertribal meetings were held at the Chota townhouse, but closed-door sessions and mysterious looking wampum plagued outsiders' efforts to translate Indian messages. No experienced interpreter was needed, however, to decipher the belts brought to Chota in the summer of 1776. Reports indicated the delegation consisted of Shawnees, Delawares, Mohawks, Mingos, and Ottawas representing all northern and western Indians in the confederacy. The belt they carried was an impressive nine feet long by six inches wide, and the red and black paint liberally applied to both the belt and messengers openly told of their mission. Addressing the younger warriors and hunters with language they could readily understand, the emissaries lamented that they "used to see nothing but deer Bear & Buffaloe" between their towns and Chota, but now "they found the Country thickly Inhabited and the people all in Arms." Complaining "particularly of the Virginians," the diplomats declared the confederacy had settled upon war. To further encourage Cherokees to join, they avowed that any natives refusing to unite with the pan-Indian militants would "forever hereafter be Considered as their Common Enemy and that they would all fall on them when Affairs with the White People should be settled." After years of debilitating warfare with northern and western Indians, the Cherokees could not fail to appreciate this threat.[6]

Dragging Canoe of Mialoquo (Great Island) readily accepted the war belt. He was soon followed by a Chilhowee headman and then by warriors from nearly every town who had painted themselves black. Realizing their influence could not dissuade the militants, older headmen "Sat down dejected & silent," perhaps reflecting a tacit endorsement of Cherokee militancy rather than outright disapproval of the warriors' conduct. Dragging Canoe and other warriors had good reason to receive the war belt. At the Treaty of Sycamore Shoals in 1775, Richard Henderson and his company of land speculators acquired more than 27,000 square miles of Cherokee hunting territory between the Kentucky and Cumberland Rivers. This land grant was larger than all other previous cessions combined, and it seemingly brought settlers to the very doorstep of the Overhill Towns. Dragging Canoe denounced the older headmen for signing the treaty and warned of the young warriors' resolve to recover their lands.[7]

While the Overhill people seemed most disconcerted by the Henderson purchase, reports indicated that the Lower Cherokees first broke out to war with the Americans. This was all the more surprising to Carolinians who recently had negotiated with six hundred Lower, Valley, and Middle Cherokees at Fort Charlotte along the Savannah River. Led by Ecuy of Seneca, headmen from these regions assured the commissioners that if the Overhills were for war, "the great ridge of mountains shall divide them, for they will have no hand in it." Cherokee policies, however, were not simply dictated by geography and regionalism; for the approaching war fractured Cherokee political responses both within and between towns and regions. Just as Ecuy promised Cherokee neutrality at Fort Charlotte, other Lower Town leaders met Henry Stuart at Toqua with pledges of military support for Britain. This latter faction acted in the summer of 1776, as cross-regional war parties mounted substantial attacks throughout the southern backcountry.[8]

Many Whig supporters believed Cherokee disaffection stemmed mainly from the nefarious influence of Britain's Southern Indian agents, namely John Stuart, his brother Henry, and Alexander Cameron. As the imperial crisis turned to military confrontation, rumors abounded that these agents actively recruited Cherokees to "massacre all the back settlers of Carolina and Georgia, without distinction of age or sex." For those Americans who believed such reports, British policies seemed strikingly similar to France's utilization of Indian allies against English settlers throughout the eighteenth century. Whig leaders accordingly tapped into frontier insecurity by instigating a relentless propaganda campaign to expose British and Native American associations. They thereby established themselves as the party that opposed Indian "savages." These anti-Indian policies found fertile ground among many backcountry settlers who believed Stuart was "Nothing but an old Cherokee Agent" who gave presents "to the damn'd Indians to kill the Back Woods people." Such opposition to the British and their Indian allies ultimately proved a decisive factor in securing the allegiance of many Americans whose loyalties were far from certain at the onset of the Revolution. Once Cherokee warriors initiated their attacks, the response of these border inhabitants would forever alter Cherokee country.[9]

Although the Revolution would later become "an uncivil war" in the southern backcountry, the year 1776 witnessed a remarkable unity of purpose among frontier inhabitants against Indians. Southern militia responses to Cherokee raids were both swift and harsh. Unlike the Anglo-Cherokee War, wherein the southern colonies failed to effectively coordinate their campaigns and only penetrated the Lower, Out, and Middle Settlements (as part of the British-led invasions), armies numbering into the thousands from Georgia, the Carolinas, and Virginia now cooperated to ravage nearly every Cherokee town. Like the Anglo-Cherokee War, militiamen burned houses, razed cornfields and orchards, plundered household property and livestock, and killed or captured unfortunate Cherokees. The "Whig Indian War of 1776," as it has been termed, was in essence a "conjunct attack" by the southern states that Dowd accurately describes as "remarkable in the record of Anglo-American irregular war during the Revolution."[10]

Cherokee defensive strategies at first seemed to emulate those of the previous generation. Village populations dispersed at the enemy's approach, while warriors from different towns and regions assembled to repel the invaders. Nearly three hundred Cherokees attacked South Carolina's army under Major Andrew Williamson near the town of Seneca. The defenders quickly gave way as Williamson's army burned the Lower Towns and then marched toward the Valley. A cross-regional force of nine hundred Cherokees, reportedly three hundred warriors "from the Overhills, and as many from the middle settlements and vallies," engaged the intruders at a place called the "Black Hole." They failed, just as Cherokee warriors failed to prevent General Griffith Rutherford's army of North Carolinians from razing the Middle Settlements, which also included those towns on the Tuckasegee River (former Out Towns). These two Carolina armies met at Hiwassee and eventually leveled more than thirty-six towns in the Lower, Middle, and Valley regions.[11]

Overhill warriors proved central to these cross-regional defensive stands, as witnessed at the Black Hole. Alexander Cameron confirmed that less than 150 men remained in the Overhill Towns during the invasions, which left their own homes especially vulnerable to Colonel William Christian's army of Virginians making its way toward the Little Tennessee River. Although Christian's spies reported "the whole force of the nation" prepared to resist his attack, the sporadic appearance of Cherokee defenders was most likely a bluff, as near-simultaneous attacks by southern militiamen stretched Cherokee forces to all corners of their mountain homeland. Unable to mount a proper defense, the Overhill people performed a limited scorched earth policy, as they "burnt many of their houses and destroyed a great part of their Corn that it might not fall into the hands of the Virginians." Christian's army added to the dislocation by burning four Overhill towns that had followed Dragging Canoe's lead in openly siding with the British.[12]

The conjunct attacks by the Americans also complicated Cherokee strategies of village retreat. Whereas during the Anglo-Cherokee War many villagers found shelter in less exposed regions, concurrent invasions during the Whig Indian War limited this option. Many Cherokees fled to remote mountain areas, while others sought refuge among neighboring indigenous peoples. John Stuart reported that the Cherokees were "distressed disarmed and flying into every nation for protection." Lower and Valley Cherokees in particular fled to the Creeks. British agents in Creek country informed Stuart that women and children from the Lower Towns arrived at Coweta with vivid accounts of the invasions. These and other refugees had a profound impact on Creek policy. "The fate of the Cherokees," British commissary David Taitt wrote, "has struck the People of this Nation with such a Panic, that although they have a very great aversion to the Rebels yet they are afraid to go against them until they hear of His Majestys Troops being at Charles Town or Savannah." Cameron likewise believed the Creeks were "intimidated from raising the hatchet by the example of the Cherokees," an effect originally intended by Whig leaders in their rationale for invading Cherokee country.[13]

Cross-regional defensive efforts and shared refugee experiences in 1776, however, should not obscure the factionalism within Cherokee country that worsened with the escalation of war. Cameron observed in the midst of the invasions that the Cherokees "are so divided at present that their resistance will not avail." The Valley people, he continued, do "not incline to assist in the Defence of their Country but seem more inclined to treat for peace." A Valley woman agreed, telling her Carolina captors that "the Indians of the Valleys had no notion of war, but the Over Hills came to them & encouraged them." A strong peace platform seemingly ran throughout the Valley even before the war commenced, according to Henry Stuart, who believed American presents had secured these villagers' neutrality.[14]

Access to a reliable trade encouraged other Cherokees to decide upon war or peace. British goods normally sent from Charlestown, Augusta, and Williamsburg became scarce as the poorly supplied Americans prevented shipments to hostile Cherokees. Many Cherokees thereafter looked to Florida, specifically Pensacola, to acquire British goods. This placed the Cherokees at a decided disadvantage, because the new trade routes were not only longer but also more precarious as they wound through Creek country. The Creeks seemed willing to allow this new trading path to their former enemies, partly because many Creeks favored war against the "Virginians," but also because they could use the power of trade against the Cherokees. When neutral Creeks received a Cherokee war delegation, for instance, they quickly reminded their guests "they had no door open for a Supply" except through Creek towns.[15]

A few goods did arrive from Pensacola, but the waning months of 1776 demonstrated Britain's inability to properly supply or militarily assist the Cherokees. David Taitt recognized by the spring of 1777 that militant Cherokees "cannot do any service for want of Provisions." The burning of Cherokee towns, accompanied by wartime disruptions to economic exchange and annual hunting and farming cycles, prompted mountain villagers to negotiate with the Americans for peace. In May 1777, Lower, Middle, and Valley Cherokees met with representatives from South Carolina and Georgia to sign the Treaty of DeWitt's Corner. Overhill leaders brokered a peace with Virginia and North Carolina at the Long Island of Holston two months later. These conferences reflected a regional approach to peace, as Cherokees from different settlements negotiated an end to the war. Headmen also sought to reestablish trade connections with the Americans to acquire supplies for their respective peoples. The cost of peace in terms of land was high. Although headmen adamantly denied American claims to Cherokee lands by right of conquest, they ceded large tracts of territory to end hostilities.[16]

The Treaties of DeWitt's Corner and Long Island of Holston officially brought the Whig Indian War of 1776 to a close. The following two years appeared on the surface to have been rather uneventful for the Cherokees. The southern theater of war abated as the British redoubled their efforts in the north, and no American militia ventured toward the mountain villages. Yet Cherokee country was in a state of flux. The 1777 land cessions for the first time included ancestral village sites, which permanently displaced certain townspeople. The Lower Cherokees in northwestern South Carolina, who had figured so prominently in Anglo-Cherokee exchanges throughout the colonial era, were the first to experience dislocation on a regional scale. While some villagers remained in the area, most Lower Towns people moved west toward the Creek borderlands above Georgia. Here they reestablished their towns along the upper reaches of the Chattahoochee and Coosa Rivers.[17]

The movement of Lower Cherokees to the north Georgia mountains was matched by an equally substantial exodus of Overhill people down the Tennessee River. Many Overhill Cherokees left their homeland for political reasons. Generally, those who withdrew wished to fight the Americans, a policy often challenged by the remaining Overhill people. This political split had sharpened during Colonel Christian's Overhill campaign in 1776. The Raven of Chota at the head of three towns treated with the Virginians, while Dragging Canoe and his adherents opposed the peace faction. Christian worried that this growing divide would prevent Overhill delegates from attending peace talks in Virginia. "If any of your Towns break off and are troublesome," Christian told the Raven, "don't lett that hinder those that are friends from sending in warriors to go to Williamsburg." The colonel's remarks foreshadowed the beginnings of the Chickamauga Cherokees, for in the spring of 1777, the first reports arrived which told of large numbers of Cherokees having "run off and settled down the River."[18]

The movement of Cherokees away from ancestral lands was a town-driven process. Refugees asserted town identities by renaming new settlements after former villages. Lower Cherokees from Seneca established New Seneca in the upper Coosa watershed, also known as Turkey's Town after its influential beloved man Little Turkey. Overhill people from Great Island, Tellico, Toqua, Settico, and Chilhowee likewise built new towns with the same names along the Tennessee River. Displaced villagers accordingly maintained separate town affiliations, but regional identities and structures proved harder to reengineer. Cherokees from all regions settled in relative proximity to one other and even intermixed in these new locations. Nevertheless, those led by Dragging Canoe in the environs of Chickamauga Creek became known as the Lower Towns or Chickamauga Cherokees. The Lower Cherokees in northern Georgia, on the other hand, affiliated with the Chickamauga Towns but did not initially fall under that appellation. Eventually, they would associate more closely with villagers remaining on ancestral lands to become the Upper Cherokees.[19]

These vaguely defined regional assemblages were further unsettled as the war progressed. Aside from the Whig Indian War of 1776, the most destructive invasions of Cherokee country occurred during a three-year period that coincided with British incursions into the Lower South (see table 1). Between 1779 and 1782, southern militia carried out eight campaigns against the Cherokees. In 1779 Carolinians burnt seven towns in the Valley, while Evan Shelby's Virginia troops razed all eleven Chickamauga Towns. John Sevier and backcountry militiamen destroyed twenty-three towns in 1780 and fifteen more the following year, primarily in the Valley, Overhill, and Middle regions. Carolinians and Georgians added to the destruction by again attacking the Valley Towns and the recently established north Georgia settlements in 1781 and 1782.[20]

The campaigns proved especially disruptive to the Chickamauga Towns. Cherokees in these eleven towns, which included an estimated

Table 1. Reported American Invasions of Cherokee Country, 1776–1794

Date	Commander	Place of Attack
1776	Samuel Jack	Estatoe and Tugaloo
1776	Williamson	Lower, Valley, Middle (36 towns)
1776	Rutherford	Middle, Valley (36 towns)
1776	Christian	Overhill
1776	Moore	Tuckasegee River
1779	Evan Shelby	Chickamauga (11 towns)
1779	Williamson	most likely Valley (7 towns)
1780	Campbell/Sevier	Valley and Overhill (23 towns)
1781	Sevier	primarily Middle (15 towns)
1781	Pickens	Valley and Upper Cherokees (13 towns)
1781	Clarke	most likely northern Georgia (7 towns)
1782	Pickens/Clarke	Cheowee and neighboring towns
1782	Sevier/McDowell	Upper Coosa River
1786	Sevier	Valley (3 towns)
1787	Unspecified	Upper Cherokees
1787	Robertson	Cold Water (Chickamauga)
1788	Sevier	Valley and Overhill
1789	Sevier	most likely Chickamauga
1792	McCloskey	Cherokee Town near Franklin County, Georgia
1793	Beard	Coyatee, Hiwassee
1793	Wear	Tallassee
1793	Sevier/Evans	Upper Coosa River and Upper Creek
1794	Ore	Nickajack, Running Water (Chickamauga)

1,000 warriors prior to Shelby's attack, uprooted once again. Some returned to the Overhill country, while others relocated to Hiwassee River among the Valley people. The most important resettlement, in terms of regionalization, was that which Dragging Canoe initiated. The war leader conducted the remaining Chickamauga Cherokees even farther down the Tennessee River. They established five primary towns—Running Water, Nickajack, Long Island, Crow, and Lookout Mountain—which were thereafter identified as the Five Lower Towns. Thus, although the militia invasions of 1779–82 greatly destabilized Cherokee country, they correspondingly provided the impetus for a more clearly defined Cherokee regional framework. As will be seen, the Five Lower Towns would ultimately play a central role in the coalescence of the Cherokees into the Upper and Lower Towns by the end of the revolutionary era.[21]

In 1782, however, the precise nature of Cherokee regionalism remained less structured. Remnants of the Overhill, Valley, and Middle Cherokees endured, joined now by the Five Lower Towns (Chickamaugas) and the less regionally cohesive upper Coosa River towns. The shifting regional dynamic of Cherokee country failed to achieve stability with the conclusion of the Anglo-American war the following year. The Treaty of Paris excluded Native Americans, which forced Indian peoples to make separate peace agreements with the United States. Cherokees subsequently conducted negotiations with the Americans, which culminated in the Treaty of Hopewell in 1785. The treaty accomplished little in terms of bringing stability to the contentious southeastern borderlands. While the Overhill and Middle Towns seemed predisposed toward peace, the Valley and Chickamauga Towns continued their hostility, which elicited renewed invasions from the Americans after a four-year hiatus. In 1786 Sevier and his men attacked the Valley people, reappearing in 1788 and again in 1789 to burn both the Valley and Overhill Settlements, including the beloved town of Chota. Two other expeditions in 1787 likewise brought total war to Cherokee country. These post-Hopewell campaigns, coupled with prior attacks between 1776 and 1782, further unsettled the Overhill, Middle, and Valley Cherokees.[22]

A Creek headman in 1788, for instance, described the Cherokees as "a broken people, scattered, and divided amongst themselves." The Overhill Settlements and its beloved town of Chota provide a case in point. One Overhill headman lamented after the 1788 Sevier campaign that his people were "now like wolves, ranging about the woods to get something to eat. Nothing to be seen in our towns but bones, weeds, and grass." A Chota resident agreed that his town was once "a pretty and flourishing place," but the attacks had driven them "from our homes, and our lands, and obliged [us] to seek new habitations." The declining influence of the Overhill Towns was most clearly evinced in the relocation of the Cherokee council seat in 1788 from Chota to Ustanali in northern Georgia. Although Chota continued to host councils thereafter, the one-time epicenter of both regional and national power had been reduced to a few scattered homes.[23]

The decline of the Overhill Towns begs the question: Why did southern militia attack neutral and more peace-minded Cherokees? The answer typically given is that indiscriminate settlers showed little interest—and perhaps even an incapability—in distinguishing Chickamauga militants from Overhill accommodationists. Indeed, throughout the revolutionary border wars between Cherokees and Americans, it seemed as if the militia targeted peace towns as often as hostile towns. Though true to a certain extent, the above explanation does not adequately address the complexities of the struggle. The most glaring oversight involves the imprecise boundaries separating peace and war towns. The Chickamaugas may have formed the core of anti-American hostility, but Cherokees from other regions regularly attacked and plundered backcountry settlers, sheltered war parties, and provided intelligence to militant towns. The simple, clear-cut formula of pro-war Chickamaugas and peace-minded Overhill Cherokees, which scholars often use to explain the American Revolution in Cherokee country, does not reflect the realities of war in the southeastern borderlands.[24]

This was particularly evident in 1788, when a series of incidents spurred Cherokees from peace towns to attack the Americans. A small party of settlers under a flag of truce entered the town of Chilhowee and unceremoniously killed several Overhill headmen, including the prominent Old (Corn) Tassel. The death of Old Tassel, according to his executioner, resulted from the murder of his own family by a gang of Settico people. John Kirk Jr. claimed the Settico attack "begun the war," which caused him to take "ample satisfaction" by killing Old Tassel and other elders in the Chilhowee townhouse. The Cherokees, in turn, blamed the Americans. Settlers had continued to populate Cherokee lands "with amazing rapidity" after Hopewell, a violation that prompted "a few of the young warriors" to kill "a family of white people within those boundaries." Individual reprisals were further compounded by John Sevier and Alexander Outlaw, who led two subsequent attacks against the Overhill Towns. These border raids, coupled with the massacre "in cold blood" of Old Tassel, widened hostilities. "The Overhills," wrote one eyewitness, "seem determined for war." Another account held that Little Turkey, usually a reliable proponent of peace, circulated a "virulent talk from the northward Indians," urging them and the Chickamaugas "to strike hard." Later reports indicated over 1,200 Cherokees "had marched against the frontiers," many of whom lived in supposed peace towns. Fighting in the winter of 1788-89, in fact, proved to be the bloodiest and most unified engagements for the Cherokees of the entire war.[25]

Cross-regional participation in war continued into the next decade. In the early 1790s, the Five Lower Towns were openly at war with the Americans, but reports indicated other Cherokees also took "hair and horses from the frontiers." Scalping and horse stealing parties frequently originated from the peace towns. In 1792 interpreter James Carey passed through the Overhill Towns and encountered Coyatee warriors returning from a raid. Five Chilhowee people soon proudly displayed a white scalp to Carey and asked, "Don't you think it pretty hair?" Likewise, Governor William Blount of the Southwest Territory found that one Chickamauga headman raised a party of fifty warriors "generally from the Upper towns, and some of them from near the borders of South Carolina." At least sixteen Hiwassee warriors joined in other raids that year, while Cherokees from the upper Coosa River towns also attacked American settlers. When Sevier invaded Cherokee country the following year, it was no coincidence he specifically targeted the latter settlements. Upon arriving at Ustanali, he learned of a Cherokee army then on the frontiers that was "composed of Indians, more or less from every town in the Cherokee nation." At other upper Coosa River towns, such as Turkey's Town, Sallico, and Coosawatie, Sevier found "almost to a man was out" against the Americans. These wartime connections between Cherokees from different towns and regions were so well known to Sevier that he detached troops to the mouth of the Clinch River, hoping it would "cut off all communication by water, between the Upper and Lower Cherokees."[26]

Nowhere was the connection between Cherokees and Chickamaugas during war more evident than in the selection of Dragging Canoe's successor upon his death in 1792. When Chickamauga headmen sent an invitation to John Watts "to offer him the place of Dragging Canoe," they strategically chose a leader with political and kinship ties that crossed regional lines. The Cherokee son of a British trader, Watts resided in the Upper Towns. Although he had previously led Chickamauga war parties against backcountry settlers, Watts had returned to Chota alongside Hanging Maw by the spring of 1792. For this reason, American officials thought Watts would decline the Chickamaugas' offer, believing he had "a dislike to living in that part of the nation, and a strong desire for peace." They were soon dissuaded of this notion when Watts relocated to Willstown and declared the time had arrived "when I must bloody my hands again." War parties subsequently attacked Americans throughout the Southwest Territory.[27]

Watts maintained political connections to the Upper and Lower Cherokees throughout the war, and these connections were further strengthened through kinship. Watts was the nephew of Old Tassel of Chota. He was also related to other Upper Cherokee leaders, among them Noonday of Toqua, whom Watts called "my brother in our way of kindred." These networks likewise extended to the Lower Towns. Watts was "a near relation of [the] Bench," a noted militant, and a brother of Unacata, "or White-Man Killer." Perhaps his most intimate relation among the militants was his uncle Taloteeskie, who was also a nephew of Old Tassel. Watts and Taloteeskie worked closely to formulate policy, conduct negotiations with foreign powers, and organize and lead war parties. These familial ties at times actuated the two headmen to war. When hostile Americans killed Old Tassel, for instance, Taloteeskie "ever breathed resentment for his death," just as Watts indicated "the death of his uncle so affected him, that he could not speak anymore" of peace even three years after the murder. Later, after news reached Taloteeskie that Watts had died during battle in 1792, his uncle "cried bitterly" and clamored "for [the] vengeance he would have for Watts." Watts had only been injured in the engagement, and the wartime raids involving both Upper and Lower Cherokees continued for another two years.[28]

Americans found that Cherokees from neutral towns supported the Chickamaugas in other ways. One observer believed that Upper Cherokees professed peace to "serve as a barrier" between the Americans and Chickamaugas, whereby they provided intelligence "to such as are in arms against us." The male population of these peace towns, he continued, consisted only of those who were not warriors: "The infirm, aged, and such as the Indians called mush men resort to the upper towns, where they are suffered to remain in peace to make provisions for their army." The assumption that only older or emasculated men resided in peace towns is inaccurate, but the above observation speaks to the generational aspect of the conflict, which made it a cross-regional affair. Large numbers of young Cherokees who favored war had congregated in the Five Lower Towns. Governor Blount found the Chickamaugas attracted young warriors "from every town in the nation," while Sevier likewise noted that Cherokees "from other parts of the nation have also settled in these five towns." Thus when John Watts assumed command of Chickamauga operations in 1792, the forty-year-old warrior, who was relatively young according to Cherokee leadership standards, became "the life and spirit of the junior part of the Cherokee nation."[29]

Younger warriors who did not relocate to the Five Lower Towns also participated in border raids, thereby complicating the peace and war town dichotomy. American settlers found "the young men of every part of the nation" inclined "to join the war party of the Lower towns," as seen with the scalping and horse stealing parties that plagued the Southwest Territory. Backcountry settlers therefore believed the peace and war factions cooperated closely to concert their policies. Governor Blount, for instance, mistakenly held that no Chickamauga representatives attended either the Treaty of Hopewell (1785) or the Treaty of Holston (1791). In the governor's view, this "afforded a pretext" for those Cherokees who did attend to say, whenever hostilities had been committed, "that it was the Chickamaugas, and would often add, as a proof of their sincerity, why did not the white people cut them off? they were murderers and thieves, and they who treated had nothing to do with them." Others agreed the Upper Cherokees "pretended to be adverse" to war to protect their villages, but secretly encouraged their own people to join the war effort.[30]

Americans accordingly viewed those Cherokees outside the Five Lower Towns as equally culpable in the deaths of their countrymen and the loss of their property. Still, the widening of hostilities should not obscure the significant and sustained efforts by both Cherokees and Americans to highlight Cherokee political and regional divisions throughout the revolutionary era. Peace leaders worked especially hard to connect politics to place; meaning, in short, they aimed to convince Americans that the Chickamaugas were for war while Cherokees in other towns favored peace. This was particularly evident when the Five Lower Towns openly declared war against the Americans in 1792. Upper Cherokee leaders maintained that only the Chickamaugas were hostile and "every other part of the nation [was] for peace with the United States." Cherokees in the upper Coosa River towns, in proximity to the Five Lower Towns and often their affiliates, proved especially adamant in distancing themselves from the Chickamaugas as the war progressed. Their most influential spokesman, Little Turkey, became "incensed at the conduct of these five towns," and publicly forbid "all intercourse between them." Little Turkey then sent an express to Chickamauga leaders, a copy of which he forwarded to the Overhill, Valley, and Middle Cherokees, wherein he declared that he was "tired of talking" to the Chickamaugas and "did not intend to travel the path to them anymore to hold talks." If the Chickamaugas "wanted to go to war," he added, then "he would sit still and look at them," additionally warning them to "stay on their own side of the mountain [Chatanuga], and not mix with the other parts of the nation."[31]

Little Turkey sent similar messages to American officials announcing that the Five Lower Towns "make war by themselves." The beloved man informed Blount, "Now you may know where the bad people lives; both you and your people may now know where the good and bad lives." Neither Blount nor American settlers were ultimately convinced, but Little Turkey was one of many leaders who sought to establish a clear regional demarcation between those for war and those for peace. This connection between place and politics was further influenced by internal Cherokee migration. It was well understood among Cherokees, one observer noted, "that such inhabitants of the five Lower towns as did not want war, had best leave them; and that such of the other towns as did want war had best move to them." Subsequent reports indicated "some of both parties were moving, so as to take the situation which best suited their wishes and disposition for war or peace."[32]

Although political lines were not absolute, Americans typically identified the Five Lower Towns as the militant region. The problem for the Americans, however, was that even if they singled out the Chickamaugas or other known hostiles, this did little to protect their settlements. Backcountry settlers vented their frustrations in trying to conduct a limited border war, or what many termed "half war half peace." The idea of "half war half peace," wrote one American, "was a novelty until the year 1776; then introduced by the Cherokees, and ever since suffered to be carried on by that people." The writer described it as "the worst of wars that ever had an existence," in large part because settlers found it nearly impossible to distinguish between friend and foe. In a letter addressed to Cherokee headmen, a militia captain assured peaceable leaders that a recent expedition had not been "sent out with any hostile intentions against the Upper Towns, but against the Chickamaugies." Despite efforts to target the guilty towns, militiamen attacked peaceful Cherokees, finding they "could not possibly distinguish them from that of the Chickamaugies." This restricted war exasperated settlers who wanted to easily identify the enemy. Americans thus grew increasingly impatient with such ambiguities. "The situation of this country is very critical at present," wrote one resident of the newly established town of Knoxville, for "we have neither peace nor open war; what will be the event we know not."[33]

Other border citizens believed they had the answers, which often fell within two intersecting lines of thought. The first was to establish an open and declared war against all Cherokees, with some even advocating war with all Indians. "The reason is obvious," noted one settler, "a man would then know, when he saw an Indian he saw an enemy, and be prepared and act accordingly." The second strategy was to treat the Cherokees "as a nation," whereby all Cherokees "must be accountable for the depredations committed by their people." For this policy to work for the Americans, the Chickamaugas had to be identified and treated as Cherokees. Wartime reports employed an array of terms to define the Chickamaugas. Labels included "the seceding Cherokees," "outlying Cherokees," "a banditti of that nation," and, more frequently, "that part of the Cherokees distinguished as Chickamaugas." Despite these many labels, the above phraseology projected a similar message: the Chickamaugas were Cherokees, and they were accordingly identified and treated as a regional extension of the Cherokee nation. Thus, although Americans acknowledged "the Separation of the Chikamakas," they nonetheless considered them "lower Cherokees, which are properly one Nation with the upper Cherokees."[34]

Outsiders' views of Cherokee sociopolitical organization are relevant because ethnic identity consists of self-identification and social assignment. In other words, both internal and external forces influence the construction of identity. Americans considered the Chickamaugas to be Cherokees, and the Cherokees, including the Chickamaugas, likewise envisioned no sharp break in identity through the relocation of towns. Dragging Canoe and his followers referred to themselves as Ani-Yun-wiya, or "the Real People," while they insultingly labeled neutral Cherokees "Virginians" because they were willing to sell Cherokee lands to make peace. Furthermore, Cherokees had long abandoned familiar village sites during stressful times, as seen in the Cherokee-Creek War and the Anglo-Cherokee War. Although townspeople in these earlier conflicts returned to rebuild their homes once the fighting ended, permanent dislocation during the revolutionary era did not initiate ethnogenesis among the Chickamaugas. As the Cherokee experience in the aftermath of the Trail of Tears demonstrated nearly two generations later, distance from ancestral lands, no matter how great, meant little in terms of ethnic identity.[35]

American understandings of Cherokee collectivity are additionally significant because such views directly affected all Cherokees. This was especially evident in wartime retribution. The Chickamaugas as Cherokees presented a particular dilemma for the peace proponents in that Americans intensified their calls for war and not just against the Five Lower Towns. Backcountry settlers believed only "a sudden, indiscriminate, well-directed attack" on all Cherokees would procure peace. "If we attack the upper towns," one citizen argued, "they will find that we are determined no longer to stand by as idle spectators." Another frustrated observer proposed to march an army "through the peaceable towns, and into the disaffected towns of the Cherokees." Others wanted to go much further. A letter from the Southwest Territory insisted that the Chickamaugas and their Upper Creek allies "must be scourged without mercy." If Congress failed to act, then "the frontier people" would "destroy the whole of the Cherokees and Creeks, the friendly as well as the hostile parts."[36]

Such bold challenges to the federal government were indicative of a growing rift between U.S. Indian policy and backcountry strategies. Although Blount agreed it was "good policy" to use peaceful Cherokees as "instruments to punish the revolted towns," the governor nevertheless ordered border citizens to exercise restraint when responding to Cherokee raids. After the Chickamaugas declared war in 1792, Blount wrote to frontier inhabitants, advising them to treat peaceable Cherokees "in the same friendly manner as if no part had declared for war." He also directed militia patrols to "only be of the defensive sort" and prohibited troops or private settlers from pursuing raiding parties into Cherokee towns. Some Americans balked at these constraints. Border hostilities intensified, and settlers grew less tolerant both of "the inefficiency of the Federal Administration" to protect them and the Cherokees' "partial disposition for war." The "people in general are so prejudiced," Blount admitted, "they believe every murder is committed by Cherokees, commit it who will." Such attitudes led to increased calls for "open war," causing Blount to encounter "the utmost difficulty" in restraining settlers "from embodying, [and] going and destroying the Cherokee towns."[37]

Between 1792 and 1794, unauthorized gangs of settlers and border militia retaliated against professed peace and war towns. In June 1793, a party of militia under Captain John Beard followed horse thieves to Coyatee. Despite evidence that the guilty individuals were Chickamaugas or Creeks, Beard attacked the household of the most prominent Upper Cherokee headman, Hanging Maw. Hanging Maw escaped with minor injuries, but nine people fell in the assault, including, according to one Lower Town leader, "some of the first and principal head-men of our nation." In the fall of 1793 and 1794, border militia also launched two incursions into Cherokee country. Sevier, whose name many believed "carries terror to the Indians," led the first expedition against the Cherokees of northern Georgia. His men destroyed several Cherokee and Creek towns on the upper reaches of the Coosa River. The following year Major James

Ore targeted the Chickamaugas and burned Running Water and Nickajack, two towns known to be the most "hostile" and most frequented by anti-American Creeks. When Cherokees questioned these seemingly indiscriminate attacks, one militia officer spoke for all his fellow border citizens: "We will not listen to half-way peace, that we are tired of; our ears are shut to such talks."[38]

Cherokees from every region participated in war and subsequently experienced the pangs of war when border militia targeted their towns. As a result, peace efforts among all Cherokees, including those of the Five Lower Towns, intensified. Cross-regional participation in peace—as in war—was not new in 1794. The Treaty of Hopewell in 1785, for instance, was the first official peace agreement between the United States and the Cherokees. Contrary to some scholarly assumptions, which mistakenly assert only representatives from the Upper Towns signed the treaty, Chickamaugas and their neighbors from the north Georgia towns also partook in the Hopewell proceedings, albeit on a limited basis. Representatives from Chickamauga, Frog Town, Hightower (Etowah), Pine Log, and Lookout Mountain Town attached their marks to the agreement along with leaders from the Overhill, Valley, and Middle Towns. This cross-regional participation widened with the Treaty of Holston in 1791. One American recognized prior to the conference that, "Should it take place," it would be "the largest and most general treaty" held with the Cherokees since the revolution began, "as the heads of the whole nation have promised to attend." As it turned out, such notable Chickamauga headmen as Doublehead and Bloody Fellow joined Hanging Maw and thirty-six other Cherokee leaders to renew peace with the Americans.[39]

Public affirmation of the Holston treaty the following summer proved even more inclusive. Over 2,000 townspeople received Governor Blount at Coyatee among the Upper Cherokees. Hanging Maw and Upper Cherokee leaders ate, drank, and smoked with Bloody Fellow and other prominent headmen of the Five Lower Towns. Months later even more townspeople attended a "Grand Cherokee National Council at Estanaula" to discuss peace. Hanging Maw had earlier required all headmen to attend "and not be absent, under any pretence whatever." The Overhill beloved man was not disappointed. At this meeting were the most notable headmen from all corners of Cherokee country. The peace did not last long, of course, since warfare erupted almost immediately after these councils, but the above examples demonstrate the connectedness of Cherokee peoples across town and regional boundaries, thereby calling into question the assumption of seceding Chickamaugas.[40]

Peace efforts in 1794, which eventually ended the near twenty-year war between the Cherokees and Americans, likewise involved townspeople and headmen from every region. John Watts, Bloody Fellow, and the Glass, "the three greatest chiefs of the Lower towns," brought a string of white beads as "a public talk" from the Chickamaugas. They implored Hanging Maw "not to throw them away . . . and present this talk in their behalf." Since Cherokee leaders outside the Lower Towns had fashioned themselves as the peace proponents, it was they who served as intermediaries when the warring parties sought to end hostilities. Hanging Maw initially proved reticent, telling the Chickamauga headmen he had often sent them peace talks but to no avail. The Overhill headman then chastised the militant faction, observing that not only had "their own conduct brought destruction upon them," it also "drew the white people on me, who injured me nearly unto death." Hanging Maw nevertheless granted their request but with a condition: "If they do not now desist from war, and live at peace, I will give them up to the United States, to deal with as they shall judge proper."[41]

Hanging Maw's warning to the Chickamauga headmen represented the culmination of a long struggle by peace leaders to both project their own authority over all Cherokee peoples, including hostile Chickamaugas, and to politically distance themselves from the Five Lower Towns. They were successful in these endeavors primarily because most Chickamaugas viewed the war as unwinnable by 1794. No European power had effectively provided supplies and military assistance, and the Chickamaugas' pan-Indian allies had been thoroughly routed at the Battle of Fallen Timbers. Major Ore's expedition against Running Water and Nickajack also demonstrated the more distant Five Lower Towns did not enjoy the same protection in 1794 as they had earlier in the war. When rumors surfaced in the fall of another militia invasion, the Five Lower Towns people listened more intently to Governor Blount's forewarning: "War will cost the United States much money, and some lives, but it will destroy the existence of your people, as a nation, forever." Equally important, Blount believed this unauthorized expedition would attack the Upper Cherokees once they destroyed the Chickamaugas.[42]

The war also drew to a close because Cherokees from all regions, especially those in the Upper Towns, recognized the failure of "half war half peace." This policy both harmed and helped Cherokees during their struggles, but by 1794, it had run its course. A central reason for its failure was that Cherokees beyond the Five Lower Towns were no longer willing to tolerate its consequences. The conduct of the militants brought retribution upon the neutralists, prompting leaders such as Hanging Maw to increasingly profess that "the enemies of the United States are his enemies, and that he shall view the Lower towns as other enemies of the United States" if they did not cease hostilities. Peaceable Cherokees backed this strong talk with more open displays against the militants, such as exerting greater control over younger warriors by limiting scalping and horse-stealing raids. They also assisted the Americans by providing intelligence of Lower Town schemes and maneuvers, even though a "law" had been established that "any native of the Cherokees, who should give intelligence to the whites of any orders which the nation took in council, or otherwise, he should forfeit his property, and be banished [from] the country." Some headmen not only provided intelligence but also promised the Americans "provisions as you pass" if they attacked the Lower Towns.[43]

Peace leaders also disrupted the militants by enacting stronger measures against the Upper Creeks. Throughout the revolutionary era, the Chickamaugas often undertook joint operations with Creek and Shawnee warriors against the Americans. A detailed discussion of these connections is beyond the scope of this work; for such discussion, see Gregory Evans Dowd's book *A Spirited Resistance*. It should be noted nonetheless that the Chickamauga-Creek alliance complicated efforts by peace leaders to protect their own villages and end the war. "The root of the evil is the numerous and insolent Creeks," wrote Governor Blount, who "encourage and lead forward the too willing young Cherokees to murder and rob." Some Americans, as previously noted, proposed to "carry a vigorous campaign into the Creek country," which actually occurred during John Sevier's 1793 expedition against Cherokee and Creek towns along the upper reaches of the Coosa River. More often than not, however, Americans effected their policies by pressing Cherokees to distance themselves from hostile Creeks, either through providing intelligence of Creek movements or by preventing Creek warriors from passing through Cherokee towns.[44]

Peace leaders at first remained hesitant because of Creek power. John Watts called the Creeks "a great and powerful nation" who could not be prevented from "passing through their lands, when they please, to war," adding that "on their passage they kill our hogs and cattle, and steal our horses, which we dare not resent." The Cherokees, however, ultimately came to respect American power more and took steps to thwart Creek hostiles. Sometimes this resistance took subtle forms. In one instance, Hanging Maw refused to provision Creek warriors on their return from attacking backcountry settlers, "upon which they shot his dog and went off." Other actions were more confrontational, as when Cherokees began to range near American settlements to "serve as a guard against the hostile Creeks." In the fall of 1794, Hanging Maw sent warriors toward Holston River "to intercept the party of Creeks" in that area. Cherokee rangers also joined American militia and federal troops during scouting expeditions. Fifty Cherokees and seven federal troops pursued Creek warriors toward the Tennessee River during one encounter, whereupon they killed and scalped one of them and wounded another. An American agent residing among the Upper Cherokees believed those people were sincere in their friendship toward the United States "and determined for war with the Creeks." They had "stepped too far in Creek blood to look back," he declared, as "they have passed the Rubicon."[45]

Peace leaders intensified their efforts against the Creeks to unsettle the Chickamauga-Creek alliance. In so doing, they projected their authority upon their removed kinsmen by forcing the Chickamaugas to side either with hostile Creeks or the Cherokee peace faction. By 1794, Cherokees in the Five Lower Towns chose peace. Chickamauga headmen traveled to Creek country with requests that they no longer pass through Cherokee towns to war against the Americans. They also prevented their own warriors from attacking the frontier, and likewise sent peace representatives to the Americans to formally end hostilities.[46]

The American Revolution proved the most comprehensive and destructive border war for Cherokee peoples during the eighteenth century. Seemingly unending militia invasions and land encroachments displaced thousands of Cherokees from their original homeland. The center of Cherokee population shifted south and west to the environs of the Chattahoochee, Coosa, and Tennessee Rivers. Equally significant, the war divided the Cherokees as never before. Some looked to treaties while others took to their guns. Disagreements over how to engage the conflict exacerbated tensions both within and between towns and regions. Political factionalism therefore permeated and challenged long-entrenched community boundaries and identities, which subsequently shaped Cherokee responses to the crisis.[47]

Despite this factionalism, Cherokees maintained their political connections and sense of identity in both war and peace. No civil war occurred and no new tribe formed. When scholars assert that the year 1794 witnessed "the return of the splinter Chickamauga tribe to the Cherokee Nation," they mistakenly project a secessionist divide that simply does not fit the reality of Cherokee experiences during the revolutionary era. Instead, the migration and forced removal of townspeople reshaped the parameters of Cherokee regionalism. The once-formidable Lower, Middle, Valley, and Overhill regions had been either dismantled or restructured, with new centers of power established on lands once considered the periphery of Cherokee country. The Chickamauga, or Five Lower Towns, emerged as a new region whose townspeople generally favored war with the Americans. Cherokees in other parts of the nation, namely the Upper Cherokees, cast themselves as the proponents of peace. Place and politics thus became more visibly connected for the Cherokees by the end of the war.[48]

The coalescence of peace and war factions according to location, while not absolute, helped to crystallize Cherokee regionalism even further as a new century neared. The Cherokees became more clearly demarcated as the Lower and Upper Towns (see map 6), with their respective regional council seats at Willstown and Ustanali (Estanaula). The former label applied to the Five Lower Towns as well as those neighboring villages established by Chickamauga settlers. The Upper Cherokees, on the other hand, consisted of the remaining towns in the upper Coosa River watershed and those along the headwaters of the Hiwassee and Little Tennessee Rivers. Subregions within these larger political structures endured, especially among the Upper Cherokees, where the Overhill, Valley, and Middle Cherokees maintained separate councils, even as they participated in broader regional and national debates. Nevertheless, the Revolution played a key role in the transition from four primary regions to two, as the Upper and Lower Cherokees became the dominant regional powers which sought to protect Cherokee lands and peoples in a new era of peace.[49]

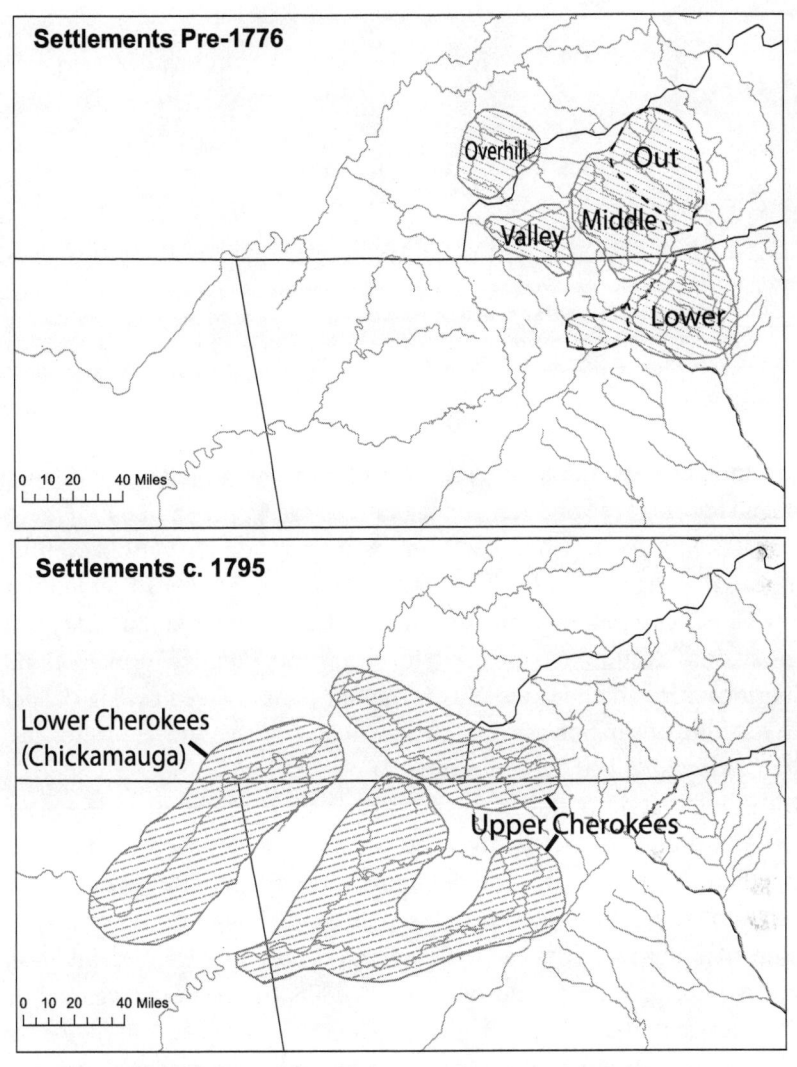

Map 6. Cherokee Regions before 1776 and c.1795. Although Cherokee towns remained on ancestral lands following the American Revolution, particularly along the Hiwassee River watershed, the bulk of the Cherokee population had relocated southwest to the upper Coosa River basin and eastern Tennessee River valley. The two major divisions to emerge after the war were the Lower and Upper Cherokees. (Map designed by Isaac Emrick.)

Epilogue

Toward the Cherokee Nation

The military phase of the American Revolution ended, and many villagers looked to bridge the political divide between the Upper and Lower Cherokees. One visitor to Cherokee country in 1799 found that old wounds appeared to have been healed. Brother Abraham Steiner observed that "the Upper and Lower Cherokees were entirely at peace and in unity, and one nation." Not quite convinced, however, and attentive to the regional divisions that had flourished during the war, Steiner asked a village leader, "What kind of a nation are the Chickamaugas?" "They are all Cherokees," the headman replied, "and we know of no difference. There is, indeed, a town here that bears this name, but that is all the difference." The headman's response was not entirely forthcoming, for it belied the long-entrenched regional divisions that continued to plague Cherokee peoples well into the nineteenth century. As William McLoughlin rightly asserts, "Regional divisions between the Upper and Lower Towns became more pronounced" during the postwar era. In 1808, for example, regional divisiveness became so acute that some Cherokees proposed to divide the nation with a fixed boundary and to place themselves "under the government of the United States, [and] become citizens thereof."[1]

Through this regional persistence, the Cherokees demonstrated a cultural continuity that, ironically, McLoughlin readily dismisses. He instead puts forward the idea of "anomie," which theorists describe as the point at which "traditional values break down" and "a normlessness results." The "anomic gap" is more specifically "the period between the abandonment of a traditional value system and its replacement with other values." For the Cherokees in particular, McLoughlin utilizes the concept to explain the collapse and eventual rebirth of Cherokee culture and identity during and after the revolutionary era. Some have challenged his assertions. In her study of Cherokee women, Theda Perdue finds "the story of most Cherokee women is not cultural transformation, as McLoughlin describes it, but remarkable cultural persistence." If one inserts Cherokee regionalism into this debate, then Perdue's perspective holds more value. Although the American Revolution fractured and geographically resituated Cherokee country, regionalism remained a defining feature of Cherokee sociopolitical organization after the revolutionary era. McLoughlin's *Cherokee Renascence in the New Republic*, in fact, serves as an excellent example of Cherokee regional and national history during the early nineteenth century.[2]

McLoughlin's emphasis on cultural change is not without merit, however. The Cherokees faced new challenges to their homeland and sense of peoplehood. "Civilizing" programs, missionary efforts, the rise of capitalistic elites, and the introduction of African slavery—all of which have been well explored in the literature—were recent developments with which Cherokees had little experience during the eighteenth century. More relevant to this discussion are changes in town and clan structures. Wartime disruptions significantly undermined Cherokee localism, as widespread displacement forced Cherokees from different towns and regions into new interactions that challenged local insularities. Equally important, repeated militia invasions prompted Cherokees to recognize that towns made easy targets. The result was the dispersal of many villagers to isolated farmsteads. Individual and family choices relating to these new settlement patterns were bolstered by council policy. Cherokee leaders encouraged dispersed agricultural tracts by directing that Cherokee farms could not be within a quarter mile of each other. In his travels through Cherokee country, Steiner noted that houses at Chota "were well scattered over the plain," while at Toqua he found "only two houses were close to each other." His description of Great Tellico revealed much the same: "In this town, as in all that we saw, the houses were scattered, so that a large town may be several miles long and broad. A few houses are close together, at some distance there are a few more, further off only isolated houses."[3]

The demise of the town—at least as it was known among prior generations—was evinced in Cherokee treaties with the United States. In the 1785 Treaty of Hopewell, American commissioners recognized and referenced internal divisions among the Cherokees. The treaty forged a peace with "their respective tribes and towns," even as the Americans attempted to centralize their dealings with the Cherokees. More revealing, especially when compared to later treaties, is the list of signers at the end of the document. In 1785 there appeared a lengthy register of Cherokee towns represented by the signers. In subsequent treaties with the United States, however, mention of towns was nowhere to be found, replaced instead with the names of individual leading men who represented the "Cherokee Nation of Indians."[4]

Despite their absence in treaties, towns continued to play an important but limited role in Cherokee sociopolitical organization and collective identities. Town-centered rituals and community ethos did not suddenly disappear, but they were noticeably less relevant to Cherokee daily interactions. So, too, were town governments. The influence of local councils suffered as a result of more diffused settlement patterns. "Local government disintegrated," notes McLoughlin, as villagers moved to distant farms. Into this political vacuum stepped vocal and aggressive regional leaders, but even more significant was the rise of the national council and an institutionally based centralized government that increasingly came to dominate Cherokee affairs.[5]

The national council also grew at the expense (and, at times, the support) of Cherokee clans. This in large part stemmed from Cherokee experiences during the eighteenth-century border wars. The law of revenge meant that clan members were obligated to mollify the spirits of the deceased. Often this was accomplished by killing an equal number of the offending party. Problems arose, however, when clan retaliation conflicted with the expressed wishes of local, regional, and national councils. Headmen prior to the Anglo-Cherokee War, for example, denounced the killing of English settlers, avowing they were instead done by the young warriors who sought revenge for the murders committed "on their Relations in Bedfored [County]." Likewise, those who "can't quite forget their relations and friends" conducted border raids during the revolutionary era. British and Americans responded with forceful determination. "This practice must be put an end to soon," declared one American who threateningly sent his "Talk as a Virginian," or "certain destruction will before many years befall the whole Cherokee nation." As has been shown, British and Americans countered Cherokee raids by dispensing retribution not against any particular town or clan but against all Cherokees. The action of one thus affected all, which made many Cherokees desirous of implementing new laws and developing new institutions that could safeguard their physical security and their ever-decreasing territory.[6]

Not only did town leaders and clan members fail to prevent British and American punitive expeditions, they also failed to protect Cherokee lands. The thirst for Cherokee lands intensified after the Revolution as settlers arrived by the thousands. Even those American officials sensitive to Cherokee rights and claims realized that border citizens could not be stopped, only restrained and regulated. Twelve treaties between 1785 and 1819 appropriated familiar village sites and hunting grounds, prompting many Cherokees to fear for their future. One villager warned his people that if they did not change, "they would deteriorate and would be despised, as is now the case with the Catawbas, who formerly were, also, numerous but were now a very small and despised nation." Such feelings were widespread. Since Cherokees communally owned the land, territorial loss affected all Cherokees and awakened a more collective spirit and national consciousness. The rapid erosion of territory, in short, encouraged stronger attachment to a more clearly defined and smaller Cherokee homeland.[7]

A centralized and institutionally based government accordingly emerged to meet these threats. In the nineteenth century, Cherokees strengthened the national council, established a National Committee, and elected a principal chief of the Cherokee Nation. They abolished the law of clan revenge and created a national police force. Cherokees established a Republic with written laws, courts, a bicameral legislature, and a constitution. In the end, the once formidable political authority of town governments and regional associations gave way to a more centralized national polity. While town, region, and clan remained important to Cherokee collectivity, a more coherent national identity and government crystallized in response to the border wars and land encroachments of the late eighteenth and early nineteenth centuries.[8]

The argument herein, which underscores some of the more substantial challenges posed to Cherokee collective identities during the eighteenth century, should not be taken to mean that Cherokees emerged from these crises as a united people. The emergence of a sovereign Cherokee Nation had its domestic opponents. Tensions were ever-present between Upper and Lower Cherokees, between nationalist leaders and those wishing to safeguard town autonomy, and between capitalist-minded and more culturally conservative villagers. Many Cherokees, in fact, removed themselves entirely from Cherokee country during and after the Revolution. A few traveled north of the Ohio River to live among the Shawnees. Others relocated west of the Mississippi River even before American bayonets forced Cherokees off their lands during the era of removal. But nationhood was centered not so much on unity as identity. Political factionalism is an inherent part of all nations, and the early Cherokees were no different. Those who disapproved of the direction that Cherokee culture and foreign policies were taking distanced themselves even as they maintained their Cherokee ethnic identity, albeit in separate political bodies. For the majority of Cherokees who stayed in the east, however, the attachment to their home—their sense of place—only intensified. Their "strong mountainous territory, cut with deep, and wide rivers" had sustained them for generations, even as Creek, "Northward," British, and American armies unsettled the land and penetrated deep into Cherokee country. A more clearly defined national identity and sovereign Cherokee Nation accordingly emerged from these long and disruptive wars. Answering that elusive question "Who were [and are] the Cherokees?" therefore begins with understanding Cherokee internal responses to their borderland experiences in the era before removal.[9]

Notes

Abbreviations

ASP *American State Papers: Indian Affairs*, vol. 1. Washington, D.C.: Gales and Seaton, 1832.
CO British Public Record Office, Colonial Office. Microfilm at Hunter Library, Western Carolina University, Cullowhee, N.C.
DRIA William L. McDowell Jr., ed. *Documents Relating to Indian Affairs*. 2 vols. Columbia: South Carolina Archives Department, 1958, 1970.
GW George Washington Papers at the Library of Congress, 1741–1799: Series 2 Letterbooks.
JCIT William L. McDowell Jr., ed. *Journals of the Commissioners of the Indian Trade, September 20, 1710–August 29, 1718*. Columbia: South Carolina Archives Department, 1955.
JGBP James Grant of Ballindalloch Papers. National Archives of Scotland, Edinburgh. Microfilm at the David Library of the American Revolution, Washington Crossing, Pa.
SWJP James Sullivan et al., eds. *The Papers of Sir William Johnson*. 14 vols. Albany: University of the State of New York, 1921–65.
SCCJ South Carolina Council Journals. Microfilm at South Carolina Department of Archives and History, Columbia, S.C.
WLP William Lyttelton Papers. William L. Clements Library, University of Michigan, Ann Arbor.

Introduction

1. Mooney, *Myths of the Cherokee*, 375–77.
2. Reid, *A Law of Blood*. Such fratricidal infighting among the Cherokees as depicted in "The False Warriors of Chilhowee" is rarely noted in the historical record. The trader James Adair did observe "that sometimes a small party of warriors, on failing of success in their campaign, have been detected in murdering some of their

own people, for the sake of their scalps," but the law of clan revenge ensured that Cherokees did not war among themselves. Adair, *American Indians*, 258–59.

3. Brown, *Old Frontiers*, 14; Hoig, *The Cherokees and Their Chiefs*; Mooney, *Historical Sketch of the Cherokee*; Starkey, *The Cherokee Nation*; Corkran, *The Carolina Indian Frontier*; Woodward, *The Cherokees*; King, ed., *The Cherokee Indian Nation*; Conley, *The Cherokee Nation*.

4. Hatley, *The Dividing Paths*; Perdue, *Cherokee Women*; McLoughlin, *Cherokee Renascence*; Reid, *A Law of Blood*; Oliphant, *Peace and War*; Thornton, *A Population History*; Corkran, *The Carolina Indian Frontier*; Horr, *Cherokee and Creek Indians*.

5. Piker, *Okfuskee*, 1, 9–10; Calloway, *The American Revolution in Indian Country*, chapter 7; Hatley, "The Three Lives of Keowee," 241–60.

6. Perdue, "Race and Culture," 704.

7. Perdue, *Cherokee Women*, 41–42, 49; Fogelson, "Perspectives on Native American Identity," 44; DeMallie, "Kinship," 306, 345; Reid, *A Better Kind of Hatchet*, 6, 38; McLoughlin, *Cherokee Renascence*, 10–11. Josh Piker's argument in *Okfuskee* deserves repeating here: "When we examine the logic and practice of Creek life, however, the clan's importance diminishes, although it does not disappear, and towns return to center stage. Without the town, in fact, Creek society would not have existed. At the town level, the factions and centripetal forces unleashed by individual and clan interests were harnessed to whatever degree possible. Town-based networks, events, and rituals called on townspeople to transcend—although not forsake—personal and familial agendas and loyalties." Piker, *Okfuskee*, 9–10.

8. Hudson, *The Southeastern Indians*, 184–85.

9. Since Charlestown did not become Charleston until the end of the Revolution, I use the colonial spelling throughout the book.

Chapter 1. Town, Region, and Nation

1. Hatley, *The Dividing Paths*, 8; King, ed., *The Memoirs of Lt. Henry Timberlake*, 14; Talk of Twelve Cherokees to Governor Glen, April 1, 1752, *DRIA*, 1:227; Three Nations to the Catawbas, November 23, 1751, *DRIA*, 1:203–204; Bohaker, "Nindoodemag."

2. Hudson, *The Southeastern Indians*, 77–97; Hally, "The Nature of Mississippian Regional Systems"; Booker, Hudson, and Rankin, "Place-Name Identification and Multilingualism in the Sixteenth-Century Southeast," 425–26; Lewis, ed., "The Narrative of the Expedition of Hernando de Soto," 178–80; Speck, Juan Pardo's Letter (1566).

3. Adair, *American Indians*, 428–29; Stuart to Board of Trade, March 9, 1764, CO 323/17/240; Journals of His Majesty's Council in South Carolina, August 10, 1726, CO 5/429; Reid, *A Law of Blood*, 29; Hatley, *The Dividing Paths*, 12.

4. Stuart to Board of Trade, March 9, 1764, CO 323/17/240; "Journal of Sir Alexander Cuming," 122–23; Stuart to Lyttelton, June 12, 1757, WLP; Proceedings of the Council Concerning Indian Affairs, *DRIA*, 1:440.

5. Gearing, *Priests and Warriors*, 65, 108; Hoig, *The Cherokees and Their Chiefs*,

12–15; Fogelson, "The Cherokee Ball Game," 211–12. Gearing's work is difficult to evaluate. In some instances, he brilliantly interprets political structures and developments for the eighteenth-century Cherokees. To a large degree, however, his work—by his own admission—infers, speculates, and theorizes to an extent which often makes *Priests and Warriors* incompatible to what is found in the documentary record.

6. "Journal of Sir Alexander Cuming," 122–23, 137; Journals of His Majesty's Council in South Carolina, August 10, 1726, CO 5/429; Proceedings of the Council Concerning Indian Affairs, *DRIA*, 1:452–53; Demere to Lyttelton, July 30, 1757, *DRIA*, 2:393.

7. Brown, *Old Frontiers*, 30; Hatley, *The Dividing Paths*, 12; "Journal of Sir Alexander Cuming," 123; Gearing, *Priests and Warriors*, 81; Miln to Lyttelton, February 28, 1760, WLP.

8. The Head Men and Warriors of the Lower Cherokees to Glen, May 10, 1751, *DRIA*, 1:63; Salley, ed., *Journal of Colonel John Herbert*, 21; Stuart to Lyttelton, June 12, 1757, WLP; Lud. Grant to Glen, March 5, 1752, *DRIA*, 1:224; Paul Demere to Lyttelton, November 23, 1759, WLP; Arthur Kelly to Dr. Speck, August 9, 1929, Correspondence with informants on Cherokee, Speck Cherokee Collection, APS; Klinck and Talman, eds., *Journal of Major John Norton*, 135.

9. *General Evening Post*, London, August 17, 1745; "Journal of Colonel George Chicken's Mission," 136; Glen to Old Hop, December 12, 1754, *DRIA*, 2:24; Richard Smith to Glen, March 23, 1755, *DRIA*, 2:38; Stuart to Board of Trade, March 9, 1764, CO 323/17/240; Hatley, *The Dividing Paths*, 11.

10. "Journal of Colonel George Chicken's Mission," 108, 116–17, 135; Talk of the Cherokee Indians to Glen, November 15, 1751, *DRIA*, 1:180–83.

11. Hudson, *The Southeastern Indians*, 78; Adair, *American Indians*, 421–22, 428–29; Jacobs, ed., *Appalachian Indian Frontier*, 10; Mooney, *Myths of the Cherokee*, 395–97; Mooney, "The Sacred Formula of the Cherokees," 335–36; *South-Carolina Gazette*, Charleston, S.C., June 28–July 5, 1760.

12. "Bro. Schneider's Journey to the Cherokee Country," 261; Perdue, *Cherokee Women*, 17–18, 24; Adair, *American Indians*, 406–407; Stuart to Board of Trade, March 9, 1764, CO 323/17/240; Hudson, *The Southeastern Indians*, 313.

13. "Bro. Schneider's Journey to the Cherokee Country," 261. Adair also noted that the nearest relations in neighboring towns sometimes assisted in building new houses. Adair, *American Indians*, 417; Paul Demere to Lyttelton, October 11, 1757, WLP; Hicks, "Manners, Customs, &c., of Cherokees in 1818"; Perdue, *Cherokee Women*, 25–27; Cherokee music, dances, and recordings, Speck Cherokee Collection, APS.

14. Bartram, *Travels*, 369–71, 508; Adair, *American Indians*, 399–400; Mooney, "The Cherokee Ball Play," 105–32; Fogelson, "Report on a Summer's Field Work among the Cherokee"; Vennum, *American Indian Lacrosse*, 36–37; Fogelson, "The Cherokee Ballgame Cycle," 333, 337; Herndon, "The Cherokee Ballgame Cycle," 345–49; Fogelson, "The Cherokee Ball Game," 74–78, 95; Hudson, *The Southeastern*

Indians, 191–92. The limitations of clan supremacy have been suggested by other scholars who see clan loyalties and obligations not as formal laws but rather as descriptions of behavior. Saunt et al., "Rethinking Race and Culture in the Early South," 401. For more on the Cherokee ball play, see Zogry, *Anetso*.

15. Hatley, "The Three Lives of Keowee," 246; Booker, Hudson, and Rankin, "Place-Name Identification and Multilingualism in the Sixteenth-Century Southeast," 415; Hudson, *The Southeastern Indians*, 270; Mooney, "The Sacred Formula of the Cherokees," 342.

16. Mooney, *Myths of the Cherokee*, 329–30, 336–37, 343–45, 407–408.

17. Reid, *A Better Kind of Hatchet*, 149; Reid, *A Law of Blood*, 11. John Oliphant also displays a fair sensitivity to Cherokee regionalism throughout his work. Oliphant, *Peace and War*.

18. Journal of the Commissioners of the Indian Trade, 1716–1718, *JCIT*, 84, 123–26; "Journal of Colonel George Chicken's Mission," 110–12; Journals of the South Carolina Upper House of Assembly, November 15, 1726, CO 5/429; Jacobs, ed., *Appalachian Indian Frontier*, 48; Adair, *American Indians*, 226. Adair's description of how Cherokees defined their settlement groupings (Ayrate and Ottare) does not correspond to their regional linguistic, cultural, geographic, and historical differences. While Lower, Middle, Valley, and Overhill may have British origins, the Cherokees and British increasingly relied on the above designations after midcentury and until the Revolution. In other words, although these regional descriptors may not have indigenous origins, the Cherokees frequently asserted these regional identities to outsiders. Mooney, *Historical Sketch of the Cherokees*, 4.

19. Tom Hatley recognizes four divisions among the Cherokees: the Overhill, Lower, Middle, and Valley Towns. David Corkran and Charles Hudson find only three regions, the Lower, Middle, and Upper Towns, since they argue that the Valley Settlements should be included with the Overhills to form the Upper Towns. The archaeologist Roy Dickens Jr. also compartmentalizes the Cherokees into three regions, but he lumps the Valley, Out, and Middle Towns into a single region alongside the Lower and Overhill Settlements. William McLoughlin and John Oliphant, on the other hand, identify five regions (Lower, Middle, Valley, Out, and Overhill). The Cherokee Nation Web site based in Oklahoma recognizes only three regions (Overhill, Middle, and Lower), whereas another Cherokee Web site lists as many as six regions (Overhill, Valley, Middle, Out, Keowee, and Lower). Hatley, *The Dividing Paths*, 6; Corkran, *The Carolina Indian Frontier*, 13–14; Hudson, *The Southeastern Indians*, 5; Dickens, "The Origins and Development of Cherokee Culture," 24–28; McLoughlin, *Cherokee Renascence*, 9; Oliphant, *Peace and War*, 2; www.cherokee.org; www.tngenweb.org/cessions/cherokee-towns.html; Zuckerman, "Regionalism," 326–27.

20. Bartram, *Travels*, 363; Jacobs, ed., *Appalachian Indian Frontier*, 49; French, "Journal of an Expedition to South Carolina," 284–88; *Pennsylvania Gazette*, Philadelphia, August 7, 1760; "Journal of Sir Alexander Cuming," 125, 137.

21. Stuart to Board of Trade, March 9, 1764, CO 323/17/240; Williams, ed., *Lieutenant Henry Timberlake's Memoirs*, 98; Gadsden, *Some Observations on the Two*

Campaigns against the Cherokee Indians, 51–52. The anthropologists Ted Gragson and Paul Bolstad find that most Cherokee towns in 1721 were situated within one to two hours' walking distance from a neighboring town or towns. For this reason, they believe the regional classification of Lower, Middle, Valley, and Overhill is somewhat problematic. They argue that "the neighborhood of Cherokee towns was much tighter and more selective in terms of membership," and thus Cherokee town clustering "was more nuanced than the literature suggests." This assessment perhaps carries more weight for the early Cherokees, as Gragson and Bolstad argue, but less so as the eighteenth century progressed. As John Oliphant correctly notes, the names of Cherokee regions "may well be of European origin, reflecting as they do the geographical view from South Carolina. Yet the European classifications were based at least to some extent on Cherokee reality, for in diplomacy and war each tended to follow its own interests." Gragson and Bolstad, "A Local Analysis of Early-Eighteenth-Century Cherokee Settlement," 453–56; Oliphant, *Peace and War*, 2.

22. Jacobs, ed., *Appalachian Indian Frontier*, 49; Dickens, "The Origins and Development of Cherokee Culture," 3–32.

23. Mooney noted that other lesser dialects also existed. Mooney, *Myths of the Cherokee*, 16–17; Horr, *Cherokee and Creek Indians*, 68, 126; Hatley, *The Dividing Paths*, 6–9, 57; Reid, *A Law of Blood*, 9; Vorsey, ed., *De Brahm's Report*, 131; Mooney, "Sacred Formula of the Cherokees," 343; Talk of the Raven, May 14, 1751, DRIA, 1:76; Journal of John Stuart regarding Cherokee and Creek land cessions and boundary line, October 8–17, 1768, CO 5/70/76. Beamer was a licensed trader in the Lower Cherokee Towns, while Robert Bunning was a longtime trader in the Valley Settlements.

24. Bolstad and Gragson, "Resource Abundance Constraints on the Early Post-Contact Cherokee Population." Some towns did move, but they typically relocated to other areas within their own region.

25. Stuart to Board of Trade, March 9, 1764, CO 323/17/240; Atkin to Lyttelton, April 30, 1757, WLP; Mackintosh to Lyttelton, November 29, 1757, DRIA, 2:420; July 12, 1748, SCCJ; Talk of the Cherokee Indians to Glen, November 14, 1751, DRIA, 1:175; Talk of Governor Glen to the Cherokees Concerning Their Treaty, November 26, 1751, DRIA, 1:188.

26. Gadsden, *Some Observations*, 22, 58; *Pennsylvania Gazette*, January 24, 1760; Stuart to Lyttelton, January 29, 1760, WLP.

27. Noyowee may also have been a mother town in the Valley. Cuming, for instance, identifies Noyohee as a beloved town, but it is unclear whether he meant Noyowee in the Valley or Noyowee in the Lower Towns. "Journal of Sir Alexander Cuming," 122; Corkran, *The Carolina Indian Frontier*, 14; Reid, *A Law of Blood*, 14; Talk of the Raven, May 14, 1751, DRIA, 1:74; Oliphant, *Peace and War*, 6; Zuckerman, "Regionalism," 326–27.

28. "Journal of Sir Alexander Cuming," 122; Corkran, *The Carolina Indian Frontier*, 14; Oliphant, *Peace and War*, 6; Talk of the Raven, May 14, 1751, DRIA, 1:74.

29. Ramsay, *History of the Revolution of South-Carolina*, 346–49; *Pennsylvania*

Gazette, November 13, 1760; Perdue, *Cherokee Women*, 41, 46–47; Shoemaker, "An Alliance between Men," 250–51.

30. Corkran, *The Carolina Indian Frontier*, 14; Harmon, "Eighteenth-Century Lower Cherokee Adaptation and Use of European Material Culture," 26–27; Reid, *A Better Kind of Hatchet*, 4; "Journal of Colonel George Chicken's Mission," 145.

31. Mooney, *Myths of the Cherokee*, 15, 395–97; Fogelson, "The Cherokee Ball Game," 199. The Mohawk leader John Norton found that "the Cherokees are sometimes called, and generally known to the Chippawa Race, by the name of Kittoghwague or Kittowaki." Klinck and Talman, eds., *Journal of Major John Norton*, 62, 198.

32. "Journal of Colonel George Chicken's Mission," 140–42; Paul Demere to Lyttelton, September 13, 1759, WLP; McIntosh to Lyttelton, August 8, 1758, WLP; "Report of the Journey of the Brethren Abraham Steiner and Frederick C. DeSchweinitz," 474.

33. "Journal of Colonel George Chicken's Mission," 155; Coytmore to Lyttelton, July 23, 1759, WLP; Beamer to Lyttelton, September 10, 1759, WLP.

34. Dean to Bunning, August 12, 1751, *DRIA*, 1:116; Cherokee Warriours to Lyttelton, April 13, 1758, *DRIA*, 2:452; Otacite, commonly called Judges Friend, to Connecotte, called Old Hop, May 26, 1757, enclosed within Demere to Lyttelton, July 4, 1757, WLP; King, ed., *The Memoirs of Lt. Henry Timberlake*, 17; Demere to Lyttelton, July 20, 1757, WLP.

35. Demere to Lyttelton, July 20, 1757, WLP; Stuart to Board of Trade, March 9, 1764, CO 323/17/240; Demere to Lyttelton, July 9, 1757, WLP.

36. John Reid supports this view. He writes, "We cannot conclude that there was no national government. When the headmen of certain towns furnished a leadership that others would follow, the nation became a functioning reality, and this occurred as often as not." Reid, *A Law of Blood*, 33.

37. Reid, *A Law of Blood*, 35–37; Perdue, *Cherokee Women*, 41–42, 59. Adair further observed that when a traveler's "lineage is known to the people . . . his relation, if he has any there, addresses him in a familiar way, invites him home, and treats him as his kinsman." His clan relations would then be "very kind and liberal . . . even to the last morsel of food they enjoy." This often-used quote by Adair should be read with some caution. A British officer serving in Cherokee country observed that Attakullakulla of the Overhills frequently visited the Lower Towns where his brother Tistoe of Keowee lived. Tistoe and other Lower Town headmen, however, "complained much of the Little Carpenter's [Attakullakulla] People eating all their corn while at Keowee." Such statements should remind us once again of the social realities of clan loyalties. Adair, *The History of the American Indians*, 15, 17–18, 431; Tistoe of Keowee and the Wolf to Lyttelton, July 12, 1758, enclosed within McIntosh to Lyttelton, July 21, 1758, WLP; *Pennsylvania Gazette*, April 23, 1761.

38. Perdue, *Cherokee Women*, 46; McLoughlin, *Cherokee Renascence*, 11; Reid, *A Law of Blood*, 37; Reid, *A Better Kind of Hatchet*, 7.

39. Hudson, *The Southeastern Indians*, 111–12; Booker, Hudson, and Rankin, "Place-Name Identification and Multilingualism in the Sixteenth-Century Southeast," 434; Mooney, *Historical Sketch of the Cherokees*, 4.

40. Mooney, *Myths of the Cherokee*, 239.

41. Hewat, *An Historical Account of the Rise and Progress of the Colonies of South Carolina and Georgia*, 1:9; *South-Carolina Gazette*, Charleston, S.C., May 6, May 18, 1745; Glen to Old Hop, December 12, 1754, DRIA, 2:25; McIntosh to Glen, July 24, 1753, DRIA, 1:381; McIntosh to Glen, November 2, 1753, DRIA, 1:465. The linguists Michael Montgomery and Joseph Hall define "mounting" as a variant form of "mountain" used by settlers of the southern Appalachian Mountains, although they fail to cite earlier instances of the word's usage. Montgomery and Hall, *Dictionary of Smoky Mountain English*, 397–98; *London Magazine, or Gentleman's Monthly Intelligencer, for the year 1755*, 498.

42. White, "Using the Past," 237; Fogelson, "Perspectives on Native American Identity," 40.

Chapter 2. "the antient Friendship and Union"

1. Gallay, *Indian Slave Trade*.

2. The trade in deerskins was voluminous. Charlestown alone exported anywhere from 130,000 to 355,000 pounds of deerskins annually between 1740 and 1762. Stuart to Board of Trade, March 9, 1764, CO 323/17/240; "Journal of Colonel George Chicken's Mission," 12–13; Dougharty to Maxwell, April 28, 1751, DRIA, 1:83.

3. For a brief overview of scholarly interpretations of the fur trade and Native American dependency, see Greer, "Comparisons: New France," 473–74.

4. Bull to Grant, July 8, 1760, reel 31, JGBP. Edmond Atkin similarly styled the Yamasee War "the Indian War in 1715." Jacobs, ed., *Appalachian Indian Frontier*, 11, 44; Gallay, *Indian Slave Trade*, 338. South Carolina established Savannah Town on the eastern bank of the Savannah River near present-day Augusta, Ga. The Congaree factory was situated farther to the east near present-day Columbia, S.C. JCIT, ix.

5. The commissioners presented the Conjuror with gifts, including "a Gun, a Cutlash, and Belt, a Cag of Rum, a Bagg Sugar, a Blanket, a Piece Calicoe and some Strings of Beads" following a meeting in Charlestown. The Tugaloo townspeople also received the benefits of a gunsmith, which the Commissioners sent among them in July 1718. JCIT, 73, 84, 135, 152, 157–58, 296, 299; Reid, *A Better Kind of Hatchet*, 62.

6. JCIT, 75, 84, 123, 152, 157–58.

7. JCIT, 123.

8. JCIT, 123, 130, 154, 178, 214–15.

9. Reid, *A Better Kind of Hatchet*, 94–95.

10. Booker, Hudson, and Rankin, "Place-Name Identification and Multilingualism in the Sixteenth-Century Southeast," 410, 425–26, 432–33; "A Faithful Relation of My Westoe Voyage, by Henry Woodward," 132–33.

11. The British during these early years often used the term "Upper" to denote Cherokees from the Middle, Valley, and/or Overhill Towns. I likewise employ this terminology when the records fail to identify precise regional locations. Hatley, *The Dividing Paths*, 25–27; Reid, *A Better Kind of Hatchet*, 57–59, 65–70; Gallay, *Indian Slave Trade*, 335–38; Corkran, *The Carolina Indian Frontier*, 22.

12. Sources indicate more than one Ellijay existed in the eighteenth century. The most commonly referenced Ellijay was located in the Middle Towns (near present Franklin, North Carolina), but Chicken's travels suggest this Ellijay was in the Valley Settlements.

13. "Journal of Colonel George Chicken's Mission," 106, 112, 138.

14. Ibid., 141. Carolina's agent and principal trader Theophilus Hastings would later move to Keowee, but the Commissioners ordered him to return to the Tugaloo store and relinquish the Keowee factory to an assistant. Hastings shortly thereafter became a factor for the Creek trade. The "Principal Factor" for the Cherokee Trade reverted to William Hatton, who also took up residence at Tugaloo. *JCIT* 74, 190–91, 231, 241, 300; Corkran, *The Carolina Indian Frontier*, 26.

15. "Journal of Colonel George Chicken's Mission," 105, 109, 124, 151.

16. Ibid., 110–11.

17. Ibid., 122–26, 134, 140. Chicken at first related that only seven Lower Towns skipped the Ellijay council but later noted it was in fact ten towns.

18. Ibid., 146–47, 150–54; Lee, "Fortify, Fight, or Flee."

19. "Journal of Colonel George Chicken's Mission," 145, 148–49, 155–57, 161.

20. May 24, 1725, SCCJ; Journals of His Majesty's Council in South Carolina, August 10, 1726, CO 5/429; Journals of the South Carolina Upper House of Assembly, October 8, 1726, CO 5/429; August 4, 1725, SCCJ.

21. May 24, 1725, SCCJ; Journals of the South Carolina Upper House of Assembly, October 8, 1726, CO 5/429; Bull to Grant, July 8, 1760, reel 31, JGBP.

22. Journals of His Majesty's Council in South Carolina, August 10, 1726, CO 5/429; Journals of the South Carolina Upper House of Assembly, October 8, November 15, 1726, CO 5/429. The Chickasaws had a vested interest in promoting warfare between the Cherokees and Creeks, since the Creeks and Chickasaws were themselves at war during this time. If a Cherokee-Creek peace occurred, then the Creeks would be free to attack the Chickasaws with little distraction.

23. August 1, 1725, SCCJ; Journals of the South Carolina Commons House, August 31, 1727, CO 5/429; Journals of the South Carolina Upper House, February 1, 1727/28, CO 5/430; Salley, ed., *Journal of Colonel John Herbert*, 15–18.

24. Salley, ed., *Journal of Colonel John Herbert*, 13–19, 21, 26–27.

25. May 24, 1725, SCCJ; Journals of His Majesty's Council in South Carolina, September 3, 1726, CO 5/429; Journals of the South Carolina Upper House of Assembly, October 8, 1726, CO 5/429; Salley, ed., *Journal of Colonel John Herbert*, 11, 15–18, 22–23.

26. Journals of His Majesty's Council in South Carolina, August 10, September 2, 1726, CO 5/429; May 24, 1725, SCCJ.

27. Oliphant, *Peace and War*, 22; *General Evening Post*, London, August 17, 1745.

28. Persico, "Early Nineteenth-Century Cherokee Political Organization," 92–93; Perdue, "Cherokee Planters," 115–16; Hudson, *The Southeastern Indians*, 96.

29. Journals of His Majesty's Council in South Carolina, August 10, 1726, CO 5/429; "Journal of Sir Alexander Cuming," 123, 126, 132, 135. Following the council at Nequassee, for instance, Moytoy's emperorship exacerbated tensions between the two most potent political rivals within the Overhill Towns, one centered at Great Tellico and the other at Chota-Tenasee. The English had earlier contributed to this rivalry, first by recognizing the Long Warrior and King of Tenasee as the most consequential men in the Overhills, and then by shifting their diplomatic attention to Moytoy and Great Tellico. The Chota-Tenasee and Tellico rivalry surfaced repeatedly in the ensuing years, with Chota ultimately emerging as the recognized political center of the Overhill Towns by midcentury. King, ed., *The Cherokee Indian Nation*, xi.

30. "Journal of Colonel George Chicken's Mission," 111, 131, 136–38, 162–64; Salley, ed., *Journal of Colonel John Herbert*, 24–26.

31. *General Evening Post*, London, August 17, 1745; Hatley, *The Dividing Paths*, 27.

32. *Echo or Edinburgh Weekly Journal*, October 21, 1730; "Journal of Sir Alexander Cuming," 136; *London Evening Post*, September 6, October 16, 1755; *Gazetteer and London Daily Advertiser*, April 16, 1756. Italics mine.

33. *Echo or Edinburgh Weekly Journal*, October 21, 1730; Conley, *The Cherokee Nation*, 25–37.

34. Hatley, *The Dividing Paths*, 35.

35. Jacobs, ed., *Appalachian Indian Frontier*, 8, 28–29.

36. Byrd to Lyttelton, May 1, 1758, WLP; Tistoe of Keowee, the Wolf of Keowee to Lyttelton, March 5, 1759, WLP.

37. Dogharty to Glen, July 31, 1751, DRIA, 1:115; Warriors of Highwassee and Tommothy to Glen, April 15, 1754, DRIA, 1:505–506; Perdue, *Cherokee Women*, 106; Braund, *Deerskins & Duffels*, 87, 109; Jacobs, ed., *Appalachian Indian Frontier*, 29; Paul Demere to Lyttelton, April 2, 1758, DRIA, 2:456; Hatley, *The Dividing Paths*, 42–44.

38. Perdue, *Cherokee Women*, 42–43; Klinck and Talman, eds., *Journal of Major John Norton*, 49; "Brethren Steiner and DeSchweinitz," 490; Stuart to Board of Trade, March 9, 1764, CO 323/17/240; DeMallie, "Kinship," 327.

39. Fogelson, "Report on a Summer's Field Work among the Cherokee," 3, 52–54.

40. Talk from Saluy to Boone, January 26, 1764, CO 323/17/172; *Pennsylvania Gazette*, Philadelphia, December 17, 1767; Salley, ed., *Journal of Colonel John Herbert*, 12; July 18, 1748, SCCJ.

41. Harrison to Glen, March 27, 1754, DRIA, 1:485; Beamer to Glen, n.d., DRIA, 1:486.

42. Paul Demere to Lyttelton, August 31, 1757, WLP; Jacobs, ed., *Appalachian Indian Frontier*, 38–39.

43. Governor Glen's Talk to the Cherokees, DRIA, 1:43–45; Talk of the Over Hill Cherokees, April 9, 1751, DRIA, 1:63–64; Affidavit of Robert Gandey, June 5, 1751,

DRIA, 1:71–72; Glen to the Cherokee Emperor, June 8, 1751, DRIA, 1:173–74. For details about the crisis within the context of rumor analysis, see Dowd, "The Panic of 1751: The Significance of Rumors on the South Carolina–Cherokee Frontier."

44. Governor Glen's Talk to the Cherokees, n.d., DRIA, 1:43–45; Glen to the Town of Ketowaw, n.d., DRIA, 1:76; Glen to the Head Men of Tomasey, June 8, 1751, DRIA, 1:79; Glen to Tucosigia, n.d., DRIA, 1:79; Glen to the Head Men of Oustenalley, n.d., DRIA, 1:81; Glen to the Town of Kewochee, n.d., DRIA, 1:84.

45. Instructions from Governor Glen to Mr. Bunyon, n.d., DRIA, 1:66–67; Glen to Tacite of Hywasse, n.d., DRIA, 1:67–68. Glen's proposal to raise a colonial army had support from the council, but it met quick defeat in the money conscious Assembly. Dowd, "The Panic of 1751," 536.

46. Talk of the Raven, May 14, 1751, DRIA, 1:74–75; Talk of the Head Men of Chotee and Tanacy, August 9, 1751, DRIA, 1:100; Talk of Tasitte of Euphassee and Others, July 30, 1751, DRIA, 1:107; A Conference with the Indians, n.d., DRIA, 1:162.

47. Glen to the Committee on Indian Affairs, n.d., DRIA, 1:52–55.

48. Glen to the Traders of the Cherokee Nation, n.d., DRIA, 1:66–67; Glen to the President and Council of Georgia, June 15, 1751, DRIA, 1:171; Talk of the Cherokee Towns to Glen, May 6, 1751, DRIA, 1:172.

49. For the Charlestown conference between Governor Glen and the Cherokee delegation, see DRIA, 1:175–98.

Chapter 3. "in constant hostility with the Muskohge"

1. Jacobs, ed., *Appalachian Indian Frontier*, 49, 62; Adair, *American Indians*, 227–28; Mooney, *Myths of the Cherokee*, 33.

2. Galphin to Pinckney, November 3, 1750, DRIA, 1:4–5; Memorial of Robert Bunning and Others, November 22, 1751, DRIA, 1:148; Glen to the Upper Creek Nation, DRIA, 1:210; *London Evening Post*, December 1, 1750; Beamer to Glen, April 26, 1752, DRIA, 1:256; Talk from Skiogusto Kehowee and the Good Warrior Estuttowe to Glen, April 15, 1752, DRIA, 1:247.

3. *London Evening Post*, December 1, 1750; Deposition of John Elliot, May 25, 1752, DRIA, 1:249; Talk of the Head Men of Ioree, April 17, 1752, DRIA, 1:254; Beamer to Glen, November 2, 1752, DRIA, 1:357.

4. Talk of the Raven and Others, August 9, 1751, DRIA, 1:118–19; Beamer to Glen, November 2, 1752, DRIA, 1:357; Proceedings of the Council Concerning Indian Affairs, DRIA, 1:448–49; Alden, *John Stuart and the Southern Colonial Frontier*, 20; Captain Fairchild to Glen, September 29, 1751, DRIA, 1:131; Burwell to Glen, October 26, 1751, DRIA, 1:159–60; Bunning to Glen, February 22, 1752, DRIA, 1:219; Patrick Brown to Glen, April 25, 1752, DRIA, 1:246–47; Grant to Governor Glen, May 3, 1752, DRIA, 1:261–62. These 50 to 60 Cherokees at Aurora provided an easy target for hostile northern Indians. A report in April 1752 indicated that Northward Indians killed fourteen of these villagers, causing them to "break up their new Settlement and return to their respective Towns again."

5. Beamer to Glen, June 1, 1752, *DRIA*, 1:267; Jacobs, ed., *Appalachian Indian Frontier*, 53.

6. Talk of the Over Hill Cherokees, April 9, 1751, *DRIA*, 1:64; Sludders to Pinckney, November 11, 1750, *DRIA*, 1:3; Sludders to Glen, November 11, 1750, *DRIA*, 1:5; Affidavit of Timothy Millin, July 19, 1751, *DRIA*, 1:35–36; Talk of the Raven, May 14, 1751, *DRIA*, 1:74–76; Talk from the Raven of Highwassee to Glen, March 31, 1752, *DRIA*, 1:243; Talk from Jud's Friend to Glen, March 31, 1752, *DRIA*, 1:244; Galphin to Glen, April 20, 1752, *DRIA*, 1:254–55; Proceedings of the Council Concerning Indian Affairs, *DRIA*, 1:399; Corkran, *The Carolina Indian Frontier*, 44–45.

7. Jacobs, ed., *Appalachian Indian Frontier*, 62; Crell to Glen, April 6, 1751, *DRIA*, 1:8; Tasattee of Hywassee to Glen, November 28, 1752, *DRIA*, 1:363.

8. Governor of South Carolina to Governor of Pennsylvania, July 7, 1750, Letters from James Logan et al.; Klinck and Talman, eds., *Journal of Major John Norton*, 46–47, 83, 198; Talk of Two Cherokee Messengers, *DRIA*, 1:493–94; Glen to the Cherokee Head Men, April 30, 1754, *DRIA*, 1:492–93; Glen to the Cherokee Head Men, June 13, 1754, *DRIA*, 1:521.

9. Gage to Johnson, August, 27, 1769, *SWJP*, 7:140–41; Journal of John Stuart, October 8–17, 1768, CO 5/70/76; Francis to Glen, May 14, 1751, *DRIA*, 1:63; Glen to Clinton, May 24, 1751, *DRIA*, 1:85; King and Headmen of the Catawbas to Glen, October 15, 1754, *DRIA*, 2:14. The Onis River is most likely the Delaware or Susquehanna River in Pennsylvania. "Onas" was a title given to the governor of Pennsylvania by Native Americans in the region. *Pennsylvania Gazette*, Philadelphia, April 4, 1792.

10. Hatley, *The Dividing Paths*, 94–95, 224; Reid, *A Law of Blood*, 8; Proceedings of the Council Concerning Indian Affairs, *DRIA*, 1:399–400, 443; Old Hopp to Demere, October 26, 1756, *DRIA*, 2:235. "Nuntuways" could refer more specifically to the Nottoway Indians, an Iroquoian-speaking group located chiefly in Virginia at midcentury.

11. March 29, 1747/48, SCCJ; *Echo or Edinburgh Weekly Journal*, October 21, 1730; April 16, 1748, SCCJ; Talk of Governor Glen to the Cherokees Concerning their Treaty, November 26, 1751, *DRIA*, 1:193.

12. March 29, 1747/48, SCCJ; April 16, 1748, SCCJ.

13. *Echo or Edinburgh Weekly Journal*, October 21, 1730; April 16, 1748, SCCJ; Moore, *Columbia and Richland County*, 14–15.

14. April 16, 1748, SCCJ; April 21, 1748, SCCJ; April 27, 1748, SCCJ; Jacobs, ed., *Appalachian Indian Frontier*, 48, 52–53.

15. *London Evening Post*, December 1, 1750. The two Creeks killed by the Shawnees were actually adopted Chickasaws. Adair, *American Indians*, 278; Talk of the Cherokee Indians to Glen, November 5, 1751, *DRIA*, 1:178–80.

16. Clark to Glen, March 26, 1751, *DRIA*, 1:7; Affidavit of Alexander Rattray, May 24, 1751, *DRIA*, 1:62; Alexander Gordon to . . . in the Creek Nation, August, 1, 1751, *DRIA*, 1:133; Talk of the Cherokee Indians to Glen, November 5, 1751, *DRIA*, 1:180; Stevens to Clinton, December 3, 1751, *DRIA*, 1:205; Glen to the Upper Creek Nation, March 20, 1752, *DRIA*, 1:207; Jacobs, ed. *Appalachian Indian Frontier*, 54.

17. Glen to the Six Nations, n.d., *DRIA*, 1:166; Glen to Clinton, n.d., *DRIA*, 1:214; Talk of Governor Glen to the Cherokees Concerning their Treaty, November 26, 1751, *DRIA*, 1:190. Indian "Nations," such as the Cherokees or Creeks, differed from Settlement Indians, Glen noted, because of "their being numerous and having Lands of their own." Glen, *A Description of South Carolina*, 60. Edmond Atkin wrote during the Seven Years' War that Settlement Indians "cannot in the whole exceed four hundred Men." Jacobs, ed., *Appalachian Indian Frontier*, 44–45.

18. Deposition of Stephen Creagh, March 22, 1750, *DRIA*, 1:13; Glen to the Catawba King, n.d., *DRIA*, 1:373; Proceedings of the Council Concerning Indian Affairs, *DRIA*, 1:388; Adair, *American Indians*, 344; Burnaby, *Burnaby's Travels through North America*, 41–42, 190–91. For a concise and thoughtful discussion on Native American identity, including feared identity, see Fogelson, "Perspectives on Native American Identity." Fogelson's discussion on the several components of identity was adapted from his earlier work with Anthony Wallace. See Wallace and Fogelson, "The Identity Struggle." For a discussion on South Carolina's Settlement Indians and blurred identities, see Merrell, *The Indians' New World*, 106–109.

19. Bull to Glen, 1751, *DRIA*, 1:35; Talk of the Head Men of Chotee and Tanacy, August 9, 1751, *DRIA*, 1:100; Talk of the Raven and Others, August 9, 1751, *DRIA*, 1:119; Grant to Glen, March 5, 1752, *DRIA*, 1:224; Squirrel King to the Head Men of Keowee, March 30, 1752, *DRIA*, 1:252; Proceedings of the Council Concerning Indian Affairs, *DRIA*, 1:432; Glen to Hamilton, October 3, 1753, *DRIA*, 1:463; Adair, *American Indians*, 346–47; Journal of John Evans, *DRIA*, 2:86; Jacobs, ed., *Appalachian Indian Frontier*, 45–46. For more on the Savannah River Chickasaws, see Cashin, *Guardians of the Valley*.

20. LeJau to Captain Thompson and Others, May 4, 1751, *DRIA*, 1:17; Glen to Hamilton, October 3, 1753, *DRIA*, 1:463; Oglethorpe, *A New and Accurate Account of the Provinces of South-Carolina and Georgia*, 28–29; Jacobs, ed., *Appalachian Indian Frontier*, 44–45.

21. Jacobs, ed., *Appalachian Indian Frontier*, 53; The White People of the Lower Towns to——, January 18, 1750, *DRIA*, 1:10; Petition of William Anderson, May 10, 1751, *DRIA*, 1:18–19; Francis to Glen, May 14, 1751, *DRIA*, 1:63; Affidavit of Mary Gould, May 8, 1751, *DRIA*, 1:126–27; Glen's Talk to the Cherokees, November 13, 1751, *DRIA*, 1:157; A Proclamation by Governor Glen, *DRIA*, 1:372; Glen to the Catawba King, n.d., *DRIA*, 1:373; Glen to Hamilton, October 3, 1753, *DRIA*, 1:463.

22. Orders to Ensign Gray, *DRIA*, 1:17–18; Gibson to Glen, July 22, 1751, *DRIA*, 1:32–33; Francis to Glen, July 24, 1751, *DRIA*, 1:31; Glen to the Ranger Commander, n.d., *DRIA*, 1:42–43; Affidavit of Alexander Rattray, May 24, 1751, *DRIA*, 1:61–62; Gordon to Thomson, August 8, 1751, *DRIA*, 1:132–33.

23. *Pennsylvania Gazette*, July 26, 1753; Governor Glen's Talk to the Cherokees, November 13, 1751, *DRIA*, 1:158–59.

24. Graham to Glen, June 15, 1751, *DRIA*, 1:81; Proceedings of the Council Concerning Indian Affairs, *DRIA*, 1:390, 395, 399; Grant to Glen, April 29, 1755, *DRIA*, 2:51.

25. *Pennsylvania Gazette*, July 26, 1753; Talk of Governor Glen to the Cherokees Concerning Their Treaty, November 26, 1751, *DRIA*, 1:194; Proceedings of the Council Concerning Indian Affairs, *DRIA*, 1:395, 403, 444, 453; Richard Smith and John Hatton to Glen, n.d., *DRIA*, 1:488.

26. Germany to McGillvery, July 15, 1753, *DRIA*, 1:379; Proceedings of the Council Concerning Indian Affairs, *DRIA*, 1:399; Talk of Two Cherokee Messengers, n.d., *DRIA*, 1:494.

27. Grant to Glen, February 8, 1753, *DRIA*, 1:367; Malatchi to Glen, May 7, 1754, *DRIA*, 1:508; Information of George Johnston, *DRIA*, 2:10–12; Journal of an Indian Trader, *DRIA*, 2:62. Although peace seemed to be confirmed by 1754, scholars generally attribute the following year as the official end to the Cherokee-Creek War. In 1755, a great battle was allegedly fought between the Cherokees and Creeks, with the former people decidedly defeating Creek warriors and forcing them to move their settlements out of north Georgia. The Battle of Taliwa, as it is known, has been uncritically accepted as fact by scholars of southeastern Indians. However, there is some reason to suspect the authenticity of the only account that mentions this epic battle. As James Mooney noted, "All our information concerning it" comes from James Wafford, "who heard the story when a boy, about the year 1815, from an old trader named Brian Ward, who had witnessed the battle sixty years before." While it is a possibility the Battle of Taliwa occurred, its absence in the documentary evidence raises serious doubts. Mooney, *Myths of the Cherokee*, 38, 384–85; Brown, *Old Frontiers*, 26; Hatley, *The Dividing Paths*, 93. Hatley mistakenly attributes 1751 as the date of the alleged engagement.

28. Richard Smith and John Hatton to Glen, n.d., *DRIA*, 1:488; Warriors of Highwassee and Tommothy to Glen, April 15, 1754, *DRIA*, 1:505–506; Malatchi to Glen, May 7, 1754, *DRIA*, 1:507; Journal of an Indian Trader, *DRIA*, 2:70; Glen to the Cherokee Headmen, June 13, 1754, *DRIA*, 1:521.

29. Cherokee Head Men to Glen, September 21, 1754, *DRIA*, 2:8; The Tuckesaws to Glen, October 10, 1754, *DRIA*, 2:13–14; Grant to Glen, July 22, 1754, *DRIA*, 2:15–19; Paper Signed by Captain Rayd. Demere, August 3, 1756, *DRIA*, 2:158.

30. Proceedings of the Council Concerning Indian Affairs, *DRIA*, 1:422–23, 432; Old Hop's Talk to Stuart and Wall, November 15, 1756, *DRIA*, 2:246–47. The historian Ian Steele gives deserved attention to this consequential incident in "Shawnee Origins of the Seven Years' War."

31. Tistoe of Keowee and Wolf to McIntosh, July 29, 1758, enclosed within McIntosh to Lyttelton, August 1, 1758, WLP; Proceedings of the Council Concerning Indian Affairs, *DRIA*, 1:425; Commanding Officer of Fort Prince George to Glen, n.d., *DRIA*, 1:516; Grant to Glen, July 22, 1754, *DRIA*, 2:19; Old Hop's Talk to Stuart and Wall, November 15, 1756, *DRIA*, 2:246–47.

32. Grant to Glen, July 22, 1754, *DRIA*, 2:15–19.

33. Speech of Captain Raymond Demere to the Chiefs of the Five Lower Cherockee Towns, June 20, 1756, *DRIA*, 2:122; Shaw to Lyttelton, 1757, WLP; Smith, "Distribution of Eighteenth-Century Cherokee Settlements," 48–49. A British officer in

1757 listed the following warrior populations for the different regions: Lower (160), Middle (610*), Out (280), Valley (390), Overhills (560). Beamer to Demere, July 28, 1756, *DRIA*, 2:151; List of Towns in the Cherokee Nation, February 21, 1757, *DRIA*, 2:412–13.

*The officer estimated Ellijay could raise 400 warriors. This is most likely a misprint. I therefore used Beamer's estimates of the Ellijay warrior population (100) for these totals.

34. Stuart to Board of Trade, CO 323/17/240.

Chapter 4. "the disaffected people of Great Tellico"

1. Alden, *John Stuart and the Southern Colonial Frontier*, 61; Outerbridge to Lyttelton, October 22, 1756, *DRIA*, 2:211; Demere to Lyttelton, October 13, 1756, *DRIA*, 2:214; Demere to Lyttelton, April 1, 1757, *DRIA*, 2:358; Kerlerec to the French Ministry, December 13, 1756, *SWJP*, 9:569–73; Kerlerec to France, Minister of the Marine, December 12, 1756, WLP.

2. Demere to Lyttelton, November 7, 1756, *DRIA*, 2:240; Demere to Lyttelton, November 18, 1756, *DRIA*, 2:249; Kerlerec to the French Ministry, December 13, 1756, *SWJP*, 9:569–73.

3. Grant to Glen, August 20, 1755, *DRIA*, 2:75; Reid, *A Law of Blood*, 26–27.

4. Dobbs to Lyttelton, July 19, 1757, WLP; *JCIT*, 123–25, 188; "Journal of Sir Alexander Cuming," 122–23, 130; Demere to Lyttelton, November 18, 1756, *DRIA*, 2:249–50; Mooney, *Myths of the Cherokee*, 36–37; Corkran, *The Carolina Indian Frontier*, 33. Even the French recognized the centrality of Tellico to their Cherokee affairs. In 1736 Christian Priber, supposed by the British to be a German Jesuit in the French interest, ingratiated himself among the Overhill Cherokees and proposed a grand political scheme whereby a newly formed Cherokee confederacy would have its capital at Great Tellico.

5. "Journal of Colonel George Chicken's Mission," 111–12; "Journal of Antoine Bonnefoy," 245; Demere to Lyttelton, October 16, 1756, *DRIA*, 2:225; Old Hop's Talk to Captain Stuart and Lieutenant Wall, November 15, 1756, *DRIA*, 2:247; List of Towns in the Cherokee Nation, February 21, 1757, *DRIA*, 2:412–13. For changing Cherokee defensive strategies, which includes fortification, see Lee, "Fortify, Fight, or Flee." Another example of towns "joining each other" was Tomatly and Connechitoiga in 1760; Journal, 1760, reel 31, JGBP.

6. "Journal of Antoine Bonnefoy's Captivity," 251; Lewis to Demere, September 11, 1756, *DRIA*, 2:202–204.

7. Lewis to Demere, September 11, 1756, *DRIA*, 2: 202–204; Proceedings of the Council concerning Indian Affairs, *DRIA*, 1:446–48.

8. Bull to Board of Trade, November 18, 1760, CO 5/7/264; A List of the Licensed Creek Traders, *DRIA*, 1:128; Bull to Amherst, November 18, 1760, British Public Record Office, War Office, 34/35/182; McGilvray to Glen, n.d., *DRIA*, 2:40; Demere to Lyttelton, October 13, 1756, *DRIA*, 2:219; Demere to Lyttelton, October 16, 1756, *DRIA*,

2:225; Old Hop's Talk to Captain Stuart and Lieutenant Wall, November 15, 1756, *DRIA*, 2:246; Demere to Lyttelton, November 28, 1756, *DRIA*, 2:260; "Account of the Chevalier De Lantagnac," 182; *Représentations* from Lantagnac to Kerlerec, October 1, 1755, Kerlerec to Minister, July 26, 1762, Anderson and Lewis, *Guide to Cherokee Documents in Foreign Archives*, 63, 68.

9. "Account of the Chevalier De Lantagnac," 177–78.

10. Lewis to Demere, September 11, 1756, *DRIA*, 2:203; Demere to Lyttelton, June 15, 1756, *DRIA*, 2:122; Demere to Lyttelton, August 10, 1757, *DRIA*, 2:397–98; Demere to Lyttelton, July 30, 1757, *DRIA*, 2:392. For more on Indian captivity and slavery, see Snyder, *Slavery in Indian Country*.

11. Lewis to Demere, September 11, 1756, *DRIA*, 2:203; Demere to Lyttelton, October 13, 1756, *DRIA*, 2:214; Corkran, *The Carolina Indian Frontier*, 36–37. Tom Hatley mistakenly attributes the Emperor of Tellico's query to Old Hop; Hatley, *The Dividing Paths*, 94.

12. Beamer to Glen, September 22, 1754, *DRIA*, 2:8–9; Demere to Lyttelton, January 15, 1757, *DRIA*, 2:315; Talk of the Mankiller of Great Tellico to Demere, January 15, 1757, *DRIA*, 2:320; Corkran, *The Carolina Indian Frontier*, 27–28. For more on the pluralism of Cherokee diplomacy, see Hatley, *The Dividing Paths*, chapter 8.

13. The Old Warrior of Tomotley to Demere, November 9, 1756, *DRIA*, 2:245; Kerlerec to the French Ministry, December 13, 1756, *SWJP*, 9:569–73.

14. Kerlerec to the French Ministry, December 13, 1756, *SWJP*, 9:569–73; Preliminary Articles of Peace between Kerlerec and the Cherokees, December 13, 1756, *SWJP*, 9:574–580; Abstract of a Talk between the Governor of New Orleans and the Cherokee and Shawanese Indians, December 4, 1756, *DRIA*, 2:368–69.

15. Talk of Oxinaa to Demere, April 8, 1757, *DRIA*, 2:411–12; Demere to Lyttelton, October 16, 1756, *DRIA*, 2:225; Old Hop's Talk to Demere, November 16, 1756, *DRIA*, 2:247–48; Cherokee Head Men to the Governor of Virginia, December 21, 1756, *DRIA*, 2:278; Alden, *John Stuart and the Southern Colonial Frontier*, 62–64.

16. Demere to Lyttelton, December 11, 1756, *DRIA*, 2:267–68; Paul Demere to Lyttelton, October 11, 1757, WLP.

17. Demere to Lyttelton, December 23, 1756, *DRIA*, 2:282; Demere to Lyttelton, January 12, 1757, *DRIA*, 2:311–12; Dobbs to Lyttelton, July 19, 1757, WLP.

18. Demere to Lyttelton, January 6, 1757, *DRIA*, 2:309–10; Demere to Lyttelton, January 12, 1757, *DRIA*, 2:312.

19. Demere to Lyttelton, January 13, 1757, *DRIA*, 2:314; Corkran, *The Carolina Indian Frontier*, 36–37, 42.

20. Intelligence from Captain Rayd. Demere, November 8, 1756, *DRIA*, 2:247–48; McGillivray to Lyttelton, July 15, 1758, WLP.

21. Demere to Old Hop and the Little Carpenter, October 3, 1756, *DRIA*, 2:222–23; Intelligence from Demere, November 8, 1756, *DRIA*, 2:243–44; Old Hop's Talk to Captain Stuart and Lieutenant Wall, November 15, 1756, *DRIA*, 2:246–47; Intelligence from Indian Nancy to Demere, December 12, 1756, *DRIA*, 2:269; Intelligence from Nancy Butler, December 20, 1756, *DRIA*, 2:275–76; Demere to Lyttelton, January 2, 1757, *DRIA*, 2:302–304; Demere to Lyttelton, March 26, 1757, *DRIA*, 2:349–50.

22. Demere to Lyttelton, March 26, 1757, *DRIA*, 2:349; Demere to Lyttelton, December 23, 1756, *DRIA*, 2:283; Demere to Lyttelton, January 2, 1757, *DRIA*, 2:302–303.

23. Report of Lieutenant Wall to Demere, January 13, 1757, *DRIA*, 2:321–22.

24. Demere to Lyttelton, January 15, 1757, *DRIA*, 2:315; Report of Lieutenant Wall to Demere, January 13, 1757, *DRIA*, 2:324; Stuart to Lyttelton, July 11, 1757, WLP.

25. Report of Lieutenant Wall to Demere, January 13, 1757, *DRIA*, 2:321–23.

26. Adair, *American Indians*, 429–30; Demere to Lyttelton, January 6, 1757, *DRIA*, 2:308–309; Intelligence from Nancy Butler to Demere, December 20, 1756, *DRIA*, 2:276; Demere to Lyttelton, December 23, 1756, *DRIA*, 2:281; Demere to Lyttelton, January 12, 1757, *DRIA*, 2:312; Demere to Lyttelton, August 26, 1757, *DRIA*, 2:404.

27. Ostenaco [Judge's Friend], Willanawaw to Lyttelton, March 2, 1759, WLP; Demere to Lyttelton, November 7, 1756, *DRIA*, 2:240; Pepper to Lyttelton, November 18, 1756, *DRIA*, 2:255.

28. Talk of the Blind Slave Catcher of Chatuga, January 2, 1757, *DRIA*, 2:305–306; Alden, *John Stuart and the Southern Colonial Frontier*, 12, 53; Oliphant, *Peace and War*, 32–34.

29. Talk of the Blind Slave Catcher of Chatuga, January 2, 1757, *DRIA*, 2:305–306.

30. Demere to Lyttelton, June 10, 1757, *DRIA*, 2:381; Demere to Lyttelton, June 13, 1757, *DRIA*, 2:384–85; Adamson to Lyttelton, June 13, 1757, *DRIA*, 2:386; Stuart to Lyttelton, June 12, 1757, WLP.

31. Demere to Lyttelton, June 10, 1757, *DRIA*, 2:381–83; Demere to Lyttelton, July 9, 1757, WLP.

32. Demere to Lyttelton, June 10, 1757, *DRIA*, 2:382–83; Demere to Lyttelton, June 13, 1757, *DRIA*, 2:384; Adamson to Lyttelton, June 13, 1757, *DRIA*, 2:386; Demere to Lyttelton, July 30, 1757, *DRIA*, 2:394; Demere to Lyttelton, August 26, 1757, *DRIA*, 2:404; Demere to Lyttelton, June 26, July 4, 1757, WLP.

33. The Swallow Warriour to Demere, September 15, 1756, *DRIA*, 2:197; Demere to Lyttelton, August 10, 1757, *DRIA*, 2:400; Paul Demere to Lyttelton, August 18, 1757, *DRIA*, 2:402; Demere to Lyttelton, August 26, 1757, *DRIA*, 2:404–405; Demere to Lyttelton, July 23, 1757, WLP; Paul Demere to Lyttelton, August 31, 1757, WLP.

34. Paul Demere to Lyttelton, August 18, 1757, *DRIA*, 2:402–403.

35. Peters to Johnson, February 2, 1756, *SWJP*, 2:427–28; Dinwiddie to Lyttelton, November 20, 1756, WLP; Corkran, *The Carolina Indian Frontier*, 48–52; Oliphant, *Peace and War*, 21–22; Hatley, *The Dividing Paths*, 95.

36. Dinwiddie to Lyttelton, November 20, 1756, WLP; Dobbs to Lyttelton, April 10, 1757, WLP; Atkin to Lyttelton, April 30, May 25, August 13, 1757, WLP; Dinwiddie to Lyttelton, May 26, July 22, 1757, WLP; Lewis to Demere, September 11, 1756, *DRIA*, 2:204; Boggs to Lyttelton, February 21, 1757, *DRIA*, 2:343; Oliphant, *Peace and War*, 38–39; Alden, *John Stuart and the Southern Colonial Frontier*, 67; Corkran, *The Carolina Indian Frontier*, 51; Demere to Lyttelton, September 12, 1756, *DRIA*, 2:200–201.

37. Stuart to Lyttelton, July 23, 1757, WLP; Dobbs to Lyttelton, July 19, 1757, WLP; Demere to Lyttelton, July 20, July 4, 1757, WLP; Demere to Lyttelton, February

15, 1757, *DRIA*, 2:339; Benn to Demere, March 25, 1757, *DRIA*, 2:351; Corkran, *The Carolina Indian Frontier*, 52.

38. Paul Demere to Lyttelton, October 11, 1757, WLP.

39. Lyttelton to Paul Demere, October 28, 1757, Lyttelton Letterbooks; Paul Demere to Lyttelton, March 7, 1758, *DRIA*, 2:440; Lyttelton to Paul Demere, December 15, 1757, Lyttelton Letterbooks; Paul Demere to Lyttelton, February 20, 1758, WLP.

40. Paul Demere to Lyttelton, December 30, 1757, *DRIA*, 2:428–29.

Chapter 5. "in a discontented mood"

1. Burd to Denny, April 3, 1758, *SWJP*, 2:811; *Pennsylvania Gazette*, Philadelphia, April 20, May 4, May 18, 1758; Forbes to Abercrombie, April 20, 1758, Forbes to Pitt, May 19, 1758, James, ed., *Writings of General John Forbes*, 65, 91–92; Cherokees to Six Nations, June 27, 1758, *SWJP*, 2:859–62.

2. Gallay, *Indian Slave Trade*, 283–84; Hatley, *The Dividing Paths*, 23–28; "Journal of Colonel George Chicken's Mission," 128; Talk of the Headmen of Tenassee to Glen, August 9, 1751, *DRIA*, 1:64; *JCIT*, 299–300; *Echo or Edinburgh Weekly Journal*, October 21, 1730; The Answer of the Indian Chiefs to the Foregoing Articles, as it was delivered by Ketagustah, September 9, 1730, Williams, ed., *Early Travels in the Tennessee Country*, 142–43.

3. *JCIT*, 216, 306; "Journal of Colonel George Chicken's Mission," 137; *Echo or Edinburgh Weekly Journal*, October 21, 1730; Journals of His Majesty's Council in South Carolina, August 10, 1726, CO 5/429; Conley, *The Cherokee Nation*, 25–37; Reid, *A Better Kind of Hatchet*, 91, 104.

4. *A Treaty Held with the Catawba and Cherokee Indians*, 9–23.

5. Ibid., 9–23, 25; *Journal of the House of Burgesses*, 2–3; Hatley, *The Dividing Paths*, 94.

6. Demere to Lyttelton, July 23, 1757, WLP; Washington to Stanwix, June 28, 1757, GW; Washington to Forbes, June 19, 1758, GW.

7. Forbes to Abercrombie, April 22, 1758, Forbes to Loudoun, April 23, 1758, Forbes to Bouquet, June 16, 1758, James, ed., *Writings of General John Forbes*, 68–69, 70–71, 115; Washington to Dinwiddie, October 5, 1757, GW; Washington to Forbes, June 19, 1758, GW.

8. Glen to Dinwiddie, June 1, 1754, *DRIA*, 1:526; Johnson to Denny, June 22, 1757, *SWJP*, 2:716–17.

9. Paul Demere to Lyttelton, July 30, 1758, WLP; Fauquier to Amherst, March 17, 1759, Reese, ed., *The Official Papers of Francis Fauquier*, 1:186–87.

10. President and Council, April 30, 1758, Tinling, ed., *The Correspondence of the Three William Byrds*, 2:648; Byrd to Lyttelton, May 1, 1758, WLP.

11. Washington to Dinwiddie, June 12, 1757, GW.

12. Atkin to Lyttelton, May 25, August 1, 1757, WLP. A Pennsylvania officer criticized Virginia for pursuing "their old Method of making great promises performing

nothing by it," while Washington lamented "the present management of Indian affairs." General Forbes added prophetically, "I foresee an immensity of trouble to manage the Indians." Trent to Croghan, March 19, 1758, *SWJP*, 2:784; Washington to Dinwiddie, October 5, 1757, GW; Forbes to Abercrombie, May 4, 1758, James, ed., *Writings of General John Forbes*, 85–86; Atkin to Lyttelton, October 15, November 24, 1758, WLP.

13. Forbes to Abercrombie, May 1758, Forbes to Pitt, May 1, 1758, Forbes to Pitt, May 19, 1758, Forbes to Bouquet, June 10, 1758, Forbes to Pitt, June 17, 1758, Forbes to Abercrombie, July 18, 1758, James, ed., *Writings of General John Forbes*, 74–75, 77–78, 91–92, 112, 117–18, 151; Washington to Forbes, June 19, 1758, GW. Lieutenant Governor Fauquier of Virginia was not surprised about this Cherokee defection. He informed George Washington several months later that he "never entertain'd any high Opinion of the Friendship of any Indians, nor form'd any great Expectations from their Service." Fauquier to Washington, July 20, 1758, Reese, ed., *The Official Papers of Francis Fauquier*, 1:53. For more on the importance of gift-giving to the Anglo-Cherokee alliance, see Dowd, "'Insidious Friends': Gift Giving and the Cherokee-British Alliance in the Seven Years' War."

14. As reported by Denny to Washington, March 25, 1758, *SWJP*, 2:297–99.

15. Proceedings of Council of Officers, March 1758, *SWJP*, 2:803; Johnson to Abercromby, April 28, 1758, *SWJP*, 2:828–29.

16. Demere to Lyttelton, April 2, 1757, *DRIA*, 2:360; Paul Demere to Lyttelton, June 24, 1758, WLP; Mackintosh to Lyttelton, June 5, 1758, *DRIA*, 2:462; Depositions Concerning Indian Disturbances in Virginia, June 1, 1758, *DRIA*, 2:469.

17. Warriors of Estertoe to Lyttelton, March 20, 1758, *DRIA*, 2:449–50; Mackintosh to Lyttelton, March 21, 1758, *DRIA*, 2:451; Little Carpenter to Lyttelton, June 3, 1758, *DRIA*, 2:463; Oliphant, *Peace and War*, 41–43, 53–54, 63–64.

18. Beamer to Lyttelton, September 16, 1758, WLP; Turner to Lyttelton, July 2, 1758, *DRIA*, 2:472–73; Thomas Beamer to Atkin, September 1758, enclosed within Atkin to Lyttelton, October 15, 1758, WLP; Ohatchie and Young Warrior of Estatoe to McIntosh, enclosed within McIntosh to Lyttelton, September 18, 1758, WLP. For more on the offspring of Anglo-Indian unions, particularly within Creek Country, see Frank, *Creeks and Southerners*.

19. Little Carpenter to Lyttelton, June 3, 1758, *DRIA*, 2:463; Paul Demere to Lyttelton, July 30, 1758, WLP; Ohatchie and Young Warrior of Estatoe to McIntosh, enclosed within McIntosh to Lyttelton, September 18, 1758, WLP; Paul Demere to Lyttelton, July 30, October 15, 1758, WLP; Adair, *American Indians*, 246–49.

20. Ohatchie and Young Warrior of Estatoe to McIntosh, enclosed within McIntosh to Lyttelton, September 18, 1758, WLP; Paul Demere to Lyttelton, September 30, 1758, WLP.

21. Forbes to Abercrombie, October 16, 1758, Forbes at camp near Loyal Hanna, November 19, 1758, James, ed., *Writings of General John Forbes*, 233, 256–57; Forbes to Lyttelton, November 26, 1758, WLP; Oglethorpe to Wyly, enclosed within Wyly to Lyttelton, February 9, 1759, WLP; Washington to Fauquier, November 28, 1758,

Reese, ed., *The Official Papers of Francis Fauquier*, 1:115–16; Little Carpenter to Lyttelton, March 20, 1759, enclosed within McIntosh to Lyttelton, March 21, 1759, WLP; Fauquier to Lyttelton, February 27, 1759, WLP.

22. McIntosh to Lyttelton, September 18, 1758, WLP; Lyttelton to the Lower and Middle Cherokee Headmen and Warriours, September 26, 1758, *DRIA*, 2:481; Lyttelton to the Head-men & Warriors of the Middle and Lower Settlements, September, 1758, Lyttelton Letterbooks.

23. Atkin to Lyttelton, November 4, 1758, WLP; Outerbridge to Lyttelton, July 2, 1759, WLP; Lyttelton to Atkin, October 29, 1758, Lyttelton Letterbooks; Beamer to Lyttelton, October 20, 1758, WLP; Ellis to Lyttelton, November 5, 1758, WLP; Talk of Wawhatchee and Young Warrior of Estatoe, October 16, 1758, enclosed within McIntosh to Lyttelton, October 21, 1758, WLP; Journal of the Council of South Carolina, November 8–16, 1758, Reese, ed., *The Official Papers of Francis Fauquier*, 1:120–27; McIntosh to Lyttelton, December 21, 1758, WLP. The commanding officer at Fort Augusta seconded these views: "It was only for fear of the resentments of the Creeks that made them, the Cherokees, be slow in their measures and so long hesitate about taking full satisfaction for the many Injurys they have received from the English." Outerbridge to Lyttelton, September 11, 1759, WLP.

24. McIntosh to Lyttelton, September 18, 1758, WLP; Journal of the Council of South Carolina, November 8–16, Reese, ed., *The Official Papers of Francis Fauquier*, 1:120–27; Atkin to Lyttelton, November 4, 1758, WLP; Fauquier to Lyttelton, September 5, 1759, WLP; Paul Demere to Lyttelton, September 30, 1758, WLP; Cherokees, Black Dog, Long Dog address to McIntosh, October 15, 1758, WLP.

25. Reid, *A Law of Blood*, 155–56; Oliphant, *Peace and War*, 6.

26. Sharpe to Cherokee Indians, 1756, George Washington Papers at the Library of Congress, 1741–1799: Series 4, General Correspondence, 1697–1799; Atkin to Thomas Beamer, September 27, 1758, enclosed within Atkin to Lyttelton, October 15, 1758, WLP; *Pennsylvania Gazette*, November 13, 1760; Journal of the Council of South Carolina, November 8–16, 1758, Reese, ed., *The Official Papers of Francis Fauquier*, 1:120–27; Lyttelton to Demere, July 5, 1758, Lyttelton Letterbooks.

27. Francis to Lyttelton, August 29, 1759, WLP; Alexander to Lyttelton, May 4, 1759, WLP; Lyttelton to Fauquier, June 7, 1759, Reese, ed., *The Official Papers of Francis Fauquier*, 1:218; *Pennsylvania Gazette*, June 28, 1759; Entick, *The General History of the Late War*, 7; Wyly to Lyttelton, May 5, 1759, WLP; Coytmore to Lyttelton, May 8, 1759, WLP; Adair, *American Indians*, 246–47.

28. Bogges to Lyttelton, April 10, 1759, WLP; Paul Demere to Lyttelton, May 12, 1759, *DRIA*, 2:488; Oliphant, *Peace and War*, 72–73.

29. Ellis to Lyttelton, August 27, September 14, 1759, WLP; Outerbridge to Lyttelton, July 2, 1759, WLP; McIntosh to Lyttelton, March 31, 1759, WLP; Coytmore to Lyttelton, June 11, 1759, WLP; Paul Demere to Lyttelton, March 26, May 2, August 28, 1759, WLP; Coytmore to Lyttelton, July 23, 1759, WLP.

30. Hewat, *An Historical Account of the Rise and Progress of the Colonies of South Carolina and Georgia*, 1:216; Oliphant, *Peace and War*, 66; Coytmore to Lyttelton,

May 8, May 17, 1759, WLP; [Cherokee] Lower Towns to Lyttelton, May 11, 1759, *DRIA*, 2:491–92; Tistoe to Lyttelton, May 13, 1759, *DRIA*, 2:492; Thirteen Cherokee Towns to Lyttelton, May 16, 1759, *DRIA*, 2:494; Entick, *The General History of the Late War*, 5–11.

31. Coytmore to Lyttelton, July 23, August 23, 1759, WLP; Lyttelton to Little Carpenter, December 19, 1759, WLP; Paul Demere to Stuart and Coytmore, September 13, 1759, enclosed within Coytmore to Lyttelton, October 28, 1759, WLP; *Pennsylvania Gazette*, November 22, 1759; Paul Demere to Lyttelton, October 1, 1759, WLP.

32. Byrd to Fauquier, August 15, 1759, Fauquier to Board of Trade, August 30, 1759, in Reese, ed., *The Official Papers of Francis Fauquier*, 1:234–35, 242; Paul Demere to Lyttelton, August 28, 1759, WLP; Stuart to Lyttelton, September 26, 1759, WLP.

Chapter 6. "every Town wept for some"

1. Demere to Lyttelton, August 29, 1756, *DRIA*, 2:172; Brown, *Old Frontiers*, 110; Journal of March and Operations under Grant, 1761, reel 32, JGBP.

2. Jacobs, *Appalachian Indian Frontier*, 49; Adair, *American Indians*, 251.

3. Journal of March and Operations under Grant, reel 32, JGBP; Reid, *A Law of Blood*, 12–13; Reid, *A Better Kind of Hatchet*, 2.

4. Hatley notes that the death of Old Hop and other notable leaders during the war, combined with changing geopolitical circumstances, allowed Attakullakulla to emerge as a principal Cherokee leader in the war's aftermath. Hatley, *The Dividing Paths*, 159–60.

5. Hewat, *An Historical Account*, 1:216. Records indicated that the Oconastota-led delegation included headmen from the Overhill Towns of Chota, Great Tellico, Chatuga, and Toqua, from the Valley Towns of Hiwassee and Little Tellico, and from the Lower Towns of Keowee, Estatoe, and Sugar Town. A List of the Cherokees in Charlestown, October 19, 1759, WLP; *Pennsylvania Gazette*, Philadelphia, November 22, 1759; Mooney, *Myths of the Cherokee*, 42; Oliphant, *Peace and War*, 97–102; Brown, *Old Frontiers*, 91, 93.

6. South Carolina Assembly to Lyttelton, October 11, 1759, WLP; Lyttelton to Assembly, October 12, October 13, 1759, WLP; Savage to Lyttelton, November 13, 1759, WLP; Declaration of War against the Cherokees, 1759, WLP.

7. *Pennsylvania Gazette*, December 13, 1759, February 28, 1760; Proceedings of the Council Concerning Indian Affairs, *DRIA*, 1:453; Paul Demere to Lyttelton, January 26, 1760, WLP; Adair, *American Indians*, 249–50; Stuart to Lyttelton, October 6, 1759, WLP; John Stuart to Allan Stuart, May 15, 1760, reel 31, JGBP; Hatley, *The Dividing Paths*, 121–23; Oliphant, *Peace and War*, 101–5. Adair believed English traders called the headman Round O "on account of a blue impression he bore in that form." The Stecoe headman's trading name may also have had some connection to a location in present-day Colleton County, South Carolina. An early South Carolina law described "the road from Pon pon to the round O, and from thence to Red Bank, on Edisto

river, be hereafter deemed a public road." The name of the community continues to this day. *The Public Laws of the State of South-Carolina*, 390.

8. Proceedings of the Council Concerning Indian Affairs, *DRIA*, 1:453; Coytmore to Lyttelton, June 11, 1759, WLP; *Pennsylvania Gazette*, January 28, 1762.

9. Coytmore to Lyttelton, October 16, November 11, 1759, WLP; Stuart to Lyttelton, October 13, 1759, WLP; *Pennsylvania Gazette*, November 22, December 13, 1759.

10. Saunt, "'The English has now a Mind to make Slaves of them all';" Adair, *American Indians*, 246, 250; Pepper to Lyttelton, December 21, 1756, *DRIA*, 2:298; Pepper to Lyttelton, May 7, 1757, *DRIA*, 2:371; Demere to Lyttelton, August 21, 1756, *DRIA*, 2:118; Harrison to Shrubshoal, June 6, 1756, *DRIA*, 2:164; Abstract of a Talk between the Governor of New Orleans and the Cherokee and Shawanese Indians, *DRIA*, 2:368; Brown, *Old Frontiers*, 89–91.

11. Lyttelton to Atkin, June 10, 1758, Lyttelton Letterbooks; McGillivray to Lyttelton, April 25, 1759, WLP; Outerbridge to Lyttelton, April 25, May 17, June 12, July 2, 1759, WLP; *Pennsylvania Gazette*, January 24, 1760.

12. Coytmore to Lyttelton, November 11, November 14, December 3, 1759, WLP; *Pennsylvania Gazette*, January 24, January 31, February 14, 1760; Lyttelton to Little Carpenter, December 19, 1759, WLP; Adair, *American Indians*, 346; A talk from the Young Warrior of Estatoe to Mr. McIntosh, April 8, 1761, Stuart to Amherst, March 15, 1763, Mays, ed., *Amherst Papers*, 240, 374; Miln to Lyttelton, February 24, 1760, *DRIA*, 2:498; Hatley, *The Dividing Paths*, 122–24; Oliphant, *Peace and War*, 109.

13. Coytmore to Lyttelton, January 7, February 7, 1760, WLP; *Pennsylvania Gazette*, February 28, 1760.

14. Stuart to Lyttelton, January 29, 1760, WLP; Coytmore to Lyttelton, January 7, February 7, 1760, WLP.

15. Coytmore to Lyttelton, December 3, December 6, 1759, WLP; *Pennsylvania Gazette*, February 14, September 4, 1760; Coytmore to Lyttelton, January 7, February 7, 1760, WLP; Dowd, *War under Heaven*, 190.

16. Coytmore to Lyttelton, February 7, 1760, WLP; Miln to Lyttelton, February 24, 1760, *DRIA*, 2:498; John Stuart to Allan Stuart, May 15, 1760, reel 31, JGBP; Paul Demere to Lyttelton, January 26, 1760, WLP.

17. Miln to Lyttelton, February 24, 1760, *DRIA*, 2:498–500.

18. Entick, *The General History of the Late War*, 17; Adair, *American Indians*, 249–50; Hewat, *An Historical Account*, 1:228; Atkin to Lyttelton, February 13, 1760, WLP.

19. Adair, *American Indians*, 134, 248; *Pennsylvania Gazette*, April 3, April 10, May 1, May 22, 1760; Outerbridge to Lyttelton, February 7, 1760, WLP; Alexander Milne, John Bell to Lyttelton, February 8–24, 1760, WLP; Atkin to Lyttelton, February 16, 1760, WLP; Proclamation, March 1760, Amherst to Fauquier, March 17, 1760, Reese, ed., *The Official Papers of Francis Fauquier*, 1:326, 335; Amherst to Montgomery, March 6, 1760, Mays, ed., *Amherst Papers*, 83.

20. Montgomery to Amherst, June 4, 1760, Mays, ed., *Amherst Papers*, 122; *Pennsylvania Gazette*, July 3, 1760; Oliphant, *Peace and War*, 123–25.

21. Demere to Lyttelton, October 26, 1756, *DRIA*, 2:229; Return of the Killed and Wounded of the Detachment of Royal, and First Highland Battalion commanded by the Hon. Col. Archibald Montgomery, Montgomery to Amherst, July 2, 1760, Mays, ed., *Amherst Papers*, 127, 130; Oliphant, *Peace and War*, 130–32.

22. Montgomery was not wholly unaware of the expedition's limitations, noting that it was impossible for his body of troops to either "extirpate them" or "proceed over the mountains" to the other Cherokee regions. *Pennsylvania Gazette*, September 4, 1760; Montgomery to Amherst, June 4, July 2, 1760, Mays, ed., *Amherst Papers*, 123, 128; Gadsden, *Some Observations on the Two Campaigns against the Cherokee Indians*, 37–39; Oliphant, *Peace and War*, 130–32.

23. *Pennsylvania Gazette*, September 4, September 25, 1760; Croghan to Johnson, July 25, 1761, *SWJP*, 10:316; Byrd to Abercromby, September 16, 1760, Tinling, ed., *The Correspondence of the Three William Byrds*, 2:703–705; Hewat, *An Historical Account*, 1:216, 234–44.

24. Paul Demere to Lyttelton, January 26, 1760, WLP; Coytmore to Lyttelton, February 7, 1760, WLP; *Pennsylvania Gazette*, June 19, 1760.

25. *Pennsylvania Gazette*, May 22, May 29, July 24, 1760.

26. *Pennsylvania Gazette*, May 22, July 3, July 24, August 7, December 18, 1760; Gadsden, *Some Observations*, 58; Perdue, *Cherokee Women*, 74, 80, 100–101. Kathryn Braund, in her study of the Creeks, recognizes the "potent political force" of women. Braund, *Deerskins & Duffels*, 23. Threats of whipping women and cutting their hair came from Saluy of the Lower Towns whose men besieged Fort Prince George, but they correlate to those methods employed by Overhill headmen.

27. Perdue, *Cherokee Women*, 74; *Pennsylvania Gazette*, July 24, September 4, 1760.

28. *The Annual Register, or a View of the History, Politicks, and Literature, for the year 1760*, 219; *Pennsylvania Gazette*, September 25, October 30, November 13, 1760; Byrd to Abercromby, September 16, 1760, Tinling, ed., *The Correspondence of the Three William Byrds*, 2:703–705; Oliphant, *Peace and War*, 137.

29. Byrd to Abercromby, September 16, 1760, Governor and Council, September 19, 1760, Tinling, ed., *The Correspondence of the Three William Byrds*, 2:703–705, 705–706; *Pennsylvania Gazette*, November 13, 1760, February 19, May 14, 1761; Mortimer, *A New History of England*, 3:701; Hewat, *An Historical Account*, 1:236, 243; Bull to Amherst, October 19, 24, 29, 1760, reel 31, JGBP.

30. Hewat, *An Historical Account*, 1:236; Byrd to Abercromby, September 16, 1760, Tinling, ed., *The Correspondence of the Three William Byrds*, 2:703–705; *Pennsylvania Gazette*, September 25, October 30, 1760.

31. *Pennsylvania Gazette*, September 4, November 13, December 4, December 18, 1760, February 19, 1761.

32. Letter from Lachland Mackintosh, April 26, 1761, reel 32, JGBP; Bull to Amherst, October 19, October 24, October 29, 1760, reel 31, JGBP; *Pennsylvania Gazette*,

September 4, November 13, December 4, December 18, 1760, February 19, 1761; Governor and Council, September 19, 1760, Tinling, ed., *The Correspondence of the Three William Byrds*, 2:705–706.

33. Fauquier to Byrd, February 16, 1761, Amherst to Byrd, March 24, 1761, Tinling, ed., *The Correspondence of the Three William Byrds*, 2:712, 723; Fauquier to Bullitt, February 16, 1761, Address from the Burgesses; March 12, 1761, Reese, ed., *The Official Papers of Francis Fauquier*, 2:474, 487; *Pennsylvania Gazette*, September 4, 1760.

34. Hewat, *An Historical Account*, 1:246; Hatley, *The Dividing Paths*, 138–40; *Pennsylvania Gazette*, August 6, 1761; French, "Journal of an Expedition to South Carolina," 288–92; Governor and Council, June 23, 1761, Tinling, ed, *The Correspondence of the Three William Byrds*, 2:736–37. Gadsden, *Some Observations*, 41. The anthropologist Russell Thornton conjectures that the Cherokees had 5,000 warriors in 1757, but the smallpox epidemic drastically reduced this figure to 2,000 men in 1760. Such estimates are as speculative as contemporary reports, which Thornton recognizes. Ensign Jonathan Boggs, for instance, apprised the number of warriors to be near 2,300 in 1757. Trader James Adair found the Cherokees had 2,300 warriors at the conclusion of the Anglo-Cherokee War, while Superintendent John Stuart believed the Cherokees to have 2,700 gunmen in 1764. Thus, it appears that a reasonable estimate for the number of fighting men throughout Cherokee country in 1760–61 falls somewhere between 2,000 and 2,700 warriors. Thornton, *A Population History*, 31; List of Towns in the Cherokee Nation, February 21, 1757, DRIA, 2:412–13; Adair, *American Indians*, 227; Stuart to Board of Trade, March 9, 1764, CO 323/17/240.

35. Oliphant asserts Neowi and Canuga were built by Lower Town refugees, but James Grant found they consisted of both Lower and Middle Cherokees, noting "one of them [had been] settled by the People who formerly lived at Etchoe the other by some of the Inhabitants of the lower Towns." Journal of March and Operations under Grant, reel 32, JGBP. The Middle Towns destroyed were, according to Grant, Tasee, Nequassee, Neowi, Canuka, Watauga, Joree, Cowee, Ussanah, Cowechee, Burning Town, Estatoe, and Ellijay. From Lt. Col. Grant, July 10, 1761, Byrd to Amherst, August 1, 1761, Attakullakulla's Talk to Grant, August 29, 1761, Mays, ed., *Amherst Papers*, 280, 285, 294; French, "Journal of an Expedition to South Carolina," 284–88; Laurens to Etwein, July 11, 1761, Hamer and Rogers, eds., *Laurens Papers*, 3:75; John Moultrie, July 10, 1761, Moultrie Family Papers; Oliphant, *Peace and War*, 162.

36. Laurens to Etwein, July 11, 1761, Hamer and Rogers, eds., *The Papers of Henry Laurens*, 3:75; *Pennsylvania Gazette*, September 4, October 30, 1760; Hatley, *The Dividing Paths*, 280n1.

37. Gadsden, *Some Observations*, 58; Hewat, *An Historical Account*, 1:253; *Pennsylvania Gazette*, October 29, 1761, January 28, 1762. Bull had earlier replaced Lyttelton, who assumed his new post as the governor of Jamaica.

38. Fauquier to Byrd, July 1, 1761, Tinling, ed., *The Correspondence of the Three William Byrds*, 2:740; Fauquier to St. Clair, June 6, 1758, Fauquier to Lyttelton, October 13, 1758, Fauquier to the Board of Trade, January 5, 1759, Reese, ed., *The Official Papers of Francis Fauquier*, 1:16, 89–91, 146; "The First Remonstrance from South

Carolina against the Stamp Act [MSS of Christopher Gadsden], Charles Town, September 4, 1764," Gibbes, ed., *Documentary History of the American Revolution*, 14; Price to Stuart, June 13, 1765, CO 323/23/216.

39. Williams, ed., *Lieutenant Henry Timberlake's Memoirs*, 63–66; Fauquier to Earl of Egremont, May 1, 1762, Reese, ed., *The Official Papers of Francis Fauquier*, 2:730.

40. Journal of March and Operations under Grant, reel 32, JGBP; *Pennsylvania Gazette*, October 30, 1760, August 6, 1761.

41. Williams, ed., *Lieutenant Henry Timberlake's Memoirs*, 95; A Talk from Tistoe, & the Wolfe to Capt. Mackintosh, November 1, 1761, reel 32, JGBP; Talk from Saluy to Boone, January 26, 1764, CO 323/17/172.

42. Journal, 1761, reel 32, JGBP; Journal of March and Operations under Grant, reel 32, JGBP; List of Towns in the Cherokee Nation, DRIA, 2:412–13; Stuart to Board of Trade, March 9, 1764, CO 323/17/240; Klinck and Talman, eds., *Journal of Major John Norton*, 62.

Chapter 7. "now all our Talks are about Lands"

1. Hatley, *The Dividing Paths*, 161.
2. Stuart to Board of Trade, CO 323/17/240; Thornton, *A Population History*, 31.
3. Journal of John Stuart regarding Cherokee and Creek land cessions and boundary line, October 8–17, 1768, CO 5/70/76.
4. Copy of the Report of the General Meeting of the Principal Chiefs and Warriors of the Cherokee Nation with John Stuart, October 18–20, 1770, CO 5/72/22.
5. Boone to the Directors, June 21, 1762, DRIA, 2:563; Stuart to Board of Trade, March 9, 1764, CO 323/17/240.
6. Act to Regulate the Cherokee Trade, DRIA, 2:557–58; Calloway, *The Scratch of a Pen*, 102; *Journal of the Congress of the Four Southern Governors*, 19.
7. *Journal of the Congress of the Four Southern Governors*, 31–32; Stuart to Board of Trade, March 9, 1764, CO 323/17/240.
8. Report on the Colony, January 30, 1763, Reese, ed., *The Official Papers of Francis Fauquier*, 2:1017; *Georgia Gazette*, Savannah, April, 14, 1763; *Journal of the Congress of the Four Southern Governors*, 28–29, 35–36.
9. Fauquier to the Earl of Egremont, November 10, 1763, Reese, ed., *The Official Papers of Francis Fauquier*, 2:1044–45; Braund, *Deerskins & Duffels*, 100; DRIA, 2:xxxvi.
10. *Journal of the Congress of the Four Southern Governors*, 19, 22; Copy of talk from Little Carpenter, January 19, 1764, CO 323/17/174; Stuart to Board of Trade, December 1, 1763, CO 323/17/160.
11. *Pennsylvania Gazette*, Philadelphia, February 2, 1764; Declaration from Arthur Cuddie (Cherokee trader), December 1763, CO 323/17/180; Copy of Affidavit from Arthur Coodey, December 28, 1763, CO 5/648/284; Proceedings and Minutes of the Governor and Council from January 4, 1763 to December 2, 1766, Candler, ed., *The Colonial Records of the State of Georgia*, 9:115; Copy of talk from Togulkee (Young

Twin), January 8, 1764, CO 323/17/186; Talk from Stuart to Saluy, January 14, 1764, CO 323/17/193; Talk from Stuart to Head Beloved Men and Principal Warriors of Chote, January 14–16, 1764, CO 323/17/195.

12. Gage to Johnson, February 3, 1764, *SWJP*, 4:315–16; Talk from Coweta Headmen to Stuart, February 6, 1764, CO 323/17/281; Copy of talk from Togulkee, January 8, 1764, CO 323/17/186; Talk from Saluy to Boone, January 26, 1764, CO 323/17/172; *Pennsylvania Gazette*, May 3, 1764.

13. Talk from Saluy to Boone, January 26, 1764, CO 323/17/172; Extract of letter from Ensign George Price, April 22, 1764, CO 323/18/19; *Pennsylvania Gazette*, May 3, 1764.

14. Copy of talks from Great Warrior and Kittagusta, February 18, 1764, CO 323/18/17.

15. Stuart to Board of Trade, December 1, 1763, CO 323/17/160; Stuart to Board of Trade, April 19, 1764, CO 323/17/170; *Georgia Gazette*, November 3, 10, 1763; Stuart to Board of Trade, December 1, 1763, CO 323/17/160. A small contingent of Creeks did join the Cherokees during the British invasions of Cherokee country in 1760–61.

16. Copy of Affidavit from Arthur Coodey, December 28, 1763, CO 5/648/284; *Pennsylvania Gazette*, February 2, May 3, 1764; Declaration of Arthur Cuddie, December 1763, CO 323/17/180; Talk from Saluy to Boone, January 26, 1764, CO 323/17/172; Copy of talks from Great Warrior and Kittagusta, February 18, 1764, CO 323/18/17; Stuart to Board of Trade, March 23, 1764, CO 323/18/1.

17. Proceedings and Minutes of the Governor and Council, Candler, ed., *The Colonial Records of the State of Georgia*, 9:116; White, *The Middle Ground*; Anderson, *Crucible of War*; Dowd, *A Spirited Resistance* and *War under Heaven*; Hinderaker, *Elusive Empires*; Indian Intelligence, September 28, 1762, Croghan to Amherst, October 5, 1762, Johnson to Amherst, July 24, 1763, *SWJP*, 10:534, 543, 754–55.

18. Hatley, *The Dividing Paths*, 158–59; Cameron to Stuart, June 29, July 2, 1765, CO 323/23/226; Blair to Colden, October 22, 1763, *SWJP*, 10:909.

19. *Georgia Gazette*, June 23, 1763, June 28, September 20, August 16, 1764, June 13, April 11, October 5, 25, 1765; Copy of talks from Great Warrior and Kittagusta, February 18, 1764, CO 323/18/17; Van Schaack to Johnson, April 1764, *SWJP*, 4:395; Price to Stuart, August 5, 1765, CO 323/23/236; Talk from Great Warrior to Stuart, January 19, 1764, CO 323/17/176; Cameron to Stuart, February 3, 1765, CO 323/23/234.

20. Cameron to Stuart, June 29 and July 2, 1765, CO 323/23/226; Stuart to d'Abbadie, January 16, 1765, CO 323/23/161; *Pennsylvania Gazette*, April 25, 1765.

21. *Journal of the House of Burgesses, October 30–June 1, 1765*, 123; *Pennsylvania Gazette*, June 6, 1765; *Georgia Gazette*, July 4, 1765; Journal of John Stuart, October 8–17, 1768, CO 5/70/76.

22. Cameron to Stuart, June 12, 1765, CO 323/23/222; *Pennsylvania Gazette*, June 13, September 5, October 24, 1765; *Georgia Gazette*, July 10, July 19, August 7, 1765; Hatley, *The Dividing Paths*, 183–84. Evidence suggests that some members of the Cherokee party attacked near Staunton killed two people in Virginia just days after

the initial incident. Nevertheless, clan members under obligation to revenge their lost kinsmen did not immediately retaliate.

23. *Pennsylvania Gazette*, August 14, October 9, 1766, March 5, 1767; *Georgia Gazette*, July 16, 1766; Stuart to Board of Trade, July 10, 1766, CO 5/67/45; Letter from Ensign Price, January 21, 1767, CO 5/68/99; Talk from Kittagusta and head men of Cherokee nation, February 5, 1767, CO 5/68/100; Talk from Lower Cherokees, March 16, 1767, CO 5/68/106; Talk from Overhill Cherokees to Stuart, March 5, 1767, CO 5/68/102; Stuart to Fauquier, April 11, 1767, CO 5/68/121; Stuart to Gage, July 21, 1767, *SWJP*, 12:337-39. Tom Hatley misdated and therefore misinterpreted this quote from Saluy, believing instead Saluy referenced the Cherokee-Creek War. Hatley, *The Dividing Paths*, 281, n12.

24. Journal of John Stuart, October 8-17, 1768, CO 5/70/76; Copy of Talk from Cherokee Headmen and Warriors, October 20, 1765, CO 323/23/298; Talk led by Kittagusta, May 8, 1766, CO 5/67/5; Cameron to Stuart, May 10, 1766, CO 323/23/289; *Georgia Gazette*, March 14, 1765, September 24, 1766, January 1, 1767; Gage to Johnson, February 3, 1766, *SWJP*, 5:31; Talk from Upper Cherokees to Stuart, August 22, 1766, CO 5/67/244; Letter from John Stuart, April 1, 1767, CO 5/68/87; Talk from Cherokee Chiefs to Stuart, September 22, 1766, CO 5/67/240; *Pennsylvania Gazette*, October 9, 1766, May 14, 1767.

25. Fauquier to Johnson, July 22, 1765, *SWJP*, 11:863; Johnson to Stuart, September 17, 1765, *SWJP*, 4:848-49; Johnson to Stuart, September 17, 1765, CO 5/67/9; Copy of letter from Governor Johnson, May 19, 1766, CO 5/67/23; Stuart to Bull, June 1, 1766, CO 5/67/13; Talk from John Stuart to Prince of Chota, February 1, 1766, CO 323/23/300; Stuart to Cherokees, February 1, 1766, CO 5/67/1; Gage to Johnson, April 5, 1767, *SWJP*, 12:295.

26. *Pennsylvania Gazette*, December 17, 1767; Johnson to Gage, March 16, 1768, *SWJP*, 12:470-71; *Georgia Gazette*, May 18, June 22, 1768; Journal of Indian Affairs, March 1-3, 1768, *SWJP*, 12:456-58; Johnson to Stuart, May 17, 1768, *SWJP*, 6:224-25.

27. *Journal of the Congress of the Four Southern Governors*, 31-32, 35-36; *Georgia Gazette*, April 21, 1763; Hatley, *The Dividing Paths*, 167; Stuart to Board of Trade, March 9, 1764, CO 323/17/240.

28. Stuart to Pownall, August 24, 1765, CO 323/23/176; Talk from Oconastota, Willinawa, Ottassittie, Kittagusta, and others to Bull, July 11, 1765, CO 323/23/243; Price to Stuart, July 19, 1765, CO 323/23/230; Price to Stuart, August 9 and 12, 1765, CO 323/23/232; Copy of talk from Cherokee Headmen and Warriors, October 25, 1765, CO 323/23/298.

29. Cession of Lands by Cherokees to the Province of South Carolina, October 19, 1765, CO 323/23/275; Certificate from Alexander Cameron, May 10, 1766, CO 323/23/277.

30. Talk from Kittagusta to Cameron, May 8, 1766, CO 323/23/302; Talk led by Kittagusta, May 8, 1766, CO 5/67/5; Talk from Cherokee to Stuart, September 22, 1766, CO 5/67/240; Tryon to Stuart, April 9, 1765, CO 323/23/279; Stuart to Tryon, February 5, 1766, CO 323/23/278; Talk from Upper Cherokees to Stuart, August 22, 1766, CO

5/67/244; *Pennsylvania Gazette*, July 30, 1767; Stuart to Board of Trade, December 2, 1766, CO 323/24/65, Part I; Fauquier to Stuart, September 17, 1767, CO 5/70/140; Blair to Stuart, March 12, 1768, CO 5/70/144; Journal of John Stuart, October 8–17, 1768, CO 5/70/76; Copy of treaty with the Cherokees, October 14, 1768, CO 5/70/95.

31. *Pennsylvania Gazette*, November 24, 1768; Johnson Hall minutes of conference with Six Nations and Delawares, May 2–6, 1765, CO 5/69/102; Board of Trade to Earl of Shelburne, December 23, 1767, CO 5/68/220; Journal of John Stuart, October 8–17, 1768, CO 5/70/76; Johnson to Stuart, September 25, 1768, *SWJP*, 6:407.

32. Proceedings at a Treaty held by William Johnson with Six Nations, October and November, 1768, CO 5/69/314; Stuart to Hillsborough, February 12, 1769, CO 5/70/124; *Pennsylvania Gazette*, November 24, 1768.

33. Hillsborough to Johnson, January 4, 1769, CO 5/70/1; Colonel Lewis and Dr. Walker to Stuart, January 10, 1769, CO 5/70/167; Johnson to Franklin, August 23, 1769, *SWJP*, 7:119; Johnson to Gage, August 30, 1769, *SWJP*, 7:151; Hillsborough to Stuart, May 13, 1769, CO 5/70/203; Hillsborough to Johnson, May 13, 1769, CO 5/70/206; Botetourt to Stuart, December 20, 1768, CO 5/70/162; Holton, "The Ohio Indians and the Coming of the American Revolution in Virginia."

34. Hillsborough to Johnson, December 9, 1769, CO 5/70/331; Botetourt to Stuart, December 18, 1769, CO 5/71/54, Part I; Stuart to Hillsborough, February 12, 1769, CO 5/70/124; Stuart to Head Beloved Man of Chota, January 19, 1769, CO 5/70/171; Stuart to Hillsborough, February 12, 1769, CO 5/70/124; Talk from Oconastota to Stuart, March 29, 1769, CO 5/70/246; Stuart to Hillsborough, July 25, 1769, CO 5/70/243; Letter from John Stuart on the Congress with the Cherokees, April 10–12, 1770, CO 5/71/107, Part I; Copy of the Report of the General Meeting of the Principal Chiefs and Warriors of the Cherokee Nation with John Stuart, October 18–20, 1770, CO 5/72/22; Treaty ceding Cherokee land to Virginia, October 18, 1770, CO 5/72/29.

35. Memorial from the Principal Traders to the Creek and Cherokee Nations to Governor Wright, 1771, CO 5/661/213; Speech from Judd's Friend to Scotchie, March 7, 1771, CO 5/661/194; Talk from Headmen and Warriors of the Cherokee to Stuart, July 29, 1769, CO 5/70/295. Tom Hatley contends that the Carolina-Cherokee trade steadily decreased also because of a lessened Cherokee demand for European goods as well as falling prices for leather in Europe. Hatley, *The Dividing Paths*, 163–66.

36. Memorial of the Principal Traders, 1771, CO 5/661/213; Copy of talk from Little Carpenter, January 19, 1764, CO 323/17/174; Copy of the Report of the General Meeting, October 18–20, 1770, CO 5/72/22; Letter from John Stuart, April 10–12, 1770, CO 5/71/107, Part I; Stuart to Pownall, August 24, 1765, CO 323/23/176.

37. Letter from John Stuart on the congress with the Cherokees, April 10–12, 1770, CO 5/71/107, Part I; Cameron to Stuart, January 23, 1771, CO 5/72/215; Watts to Stuart, May 17, 1770, CO 5/71/33, Part II; Cameron to Stuart, June 27, 1770, 5/71/31, Part II; Copy of the minutes of the Council of Virginia, August 17, 1770, CO 5/72/35; Hatley, *The Dividing Paths*, 205–208.

38. Stuart to Hillsborough, November 28, 1770, CO 5/72/20; James Spalding et al. (Indian traders) to Habersham, April 16, 1772, CO 5/661/121; Copy of treaty with

Cherokees and Creeks, June 14, 1773, CO 5/662/51; *Pennsylvania Gazette*, June 30, 1773; Stuart to Hillsborough, November 28, 1770, CO 5/72/20.

39. Dowd, *A Spirited Resistance*, 26–27; Piker, *Okfuskee*, 52–63. Piker argues against Mortar's direct involvement in the Creek killing of traders in 1760. His discussion instead addresses the ways in which historians have viewed Mortar's connection to the incident as well as his own reinterpretation of the event within the context of clan and town at Okfuskee. Stuart to Board of Trade, December 1, 1763, CO 323/17/160; Declaration from Arthur Cuddie, December 1763, CO 323/17/180; *Pennsylvania Gazette*, February 2, 1764; Journal of Proceedings of John Stuart, November 1-December 1, 1764, CO 323/23/91.

40. *Pennsylvania Gazette*, June 20, 1765; Cameron to Stuart, May 10, 1766, CO 323/23/289; Talk from Cherokees to the Mortar and Creeks, November 8, 1773, CO 5/57/19; Stuart to Board of Trade, March 9, 1764, CO 323/17/240; Cameron to Stuart, March 19, 1771, CO 5/72/219; Cameron to Stuart, February 3, 1765, 323/23/234; Cameron to Stuart, June 6, 1765, CO 323/23/220; Stuart to Tryon, May 28, 1765, CO 323/23/281; Stuart to Johnson, June 1, 1766, *SWJP*, 12:98–99; Letter from John Stuart, August 8, 1766, CO 5/67/102; Stuart to Pownall, August 24, 1765, CO 323/23/176. Stuart related that a beloved man was chosen to maintain peace between two peoples and "on all occasions interests himself in the affairs of his constituents." Thus, just as Mortar had been selected a beloved man of Chota, the Mortar and other headmen would appoint a Cherokee beloved man to reside among their towns.

41. Tasattee of Hywassee to Governor Glen, November 28, 1752, *DRIA*, 1:363; Dowd, *A Spirited Resistance*, 42.

42. Stuart to Chester, August 30, 1771, CO 5/72/350; Stuart to Hillsborough, April 27, 1771, CO 5/72/210; *Georgia Gazette*, September 27, 1769; Johnson to Gage, December 8, 1769, Gage to Johnson, December 25, 1769, *SWJP*, 7:294–95, 319.

43. Stuart to Botetourt, January 13, 1770, CO 5/71/61, Part I; Talk from Creeks to Charles Stuart, September, 1770, CO 5/72/99; Gage to Stuart, October 16, 1770, CO 5/72/41; Letter from John Stuart, April 10–12, 1770, CO 5/71/107, Part I; Stuart to Dartmouth, June 21, 1773, CO 5/74/146; McKee to Croghan, February 20, 1770, Croghan to Johnson, March 10, 1770, Journal of Daniel Claus, 1770, *SWJP*, 7:404–405, 652–53, 954–57.

44. Hillsborough to Johnson, October 3, 1770, CO 5/71/63, Part II; Information Concerning an Indian Conspiracy, March 7, 1771, *SWJP*, 8:6–8.

45. Stuart to Dartmouth, June 21, 1773, CO 5/74/146; Cameron to Stuart, March 4, 1771, CO 5/72/217; Cameron to Stuart, June 3, 1774, CO 5/75/174; Talk from Headmen of Lower Towns to Headmen of the Overhill Towns, February 12, 1771, CO 5/72/221.

46. Earl of Dartmouth to Johnson, December 1, 1773, CO 5/74/179.

Chapter 8. "half war half peace"

1. Calloway, *The American Revolution in Indian Country*, 26, 44, 201; O'Donnell, *The Cherokees of North Carolina in the American Revolution*, 21; Hatley, *The Dividing*

Paths, 223; Dowd, *A Spirited Resistance*, 54; Conley, *The Cherokee Nation*, 65–66; Brown, *Old Frontiers*, 163; Raulston and Livingood, *Sequatchie*, 35; Pate, "The Chickamauga," iii, 81. Jon Parmenter rightly faults historians for characterizing the Chickamauga withdrawal as a secessionist movement, noting that such views misrepresent Dragging Canoe and his faction. Parmenter takes issue with this perspective, in part, because it minimizes the long-held Cherokee right and obligation to withdraw politically if competing policies could not be reconciled. He does not connect his critique to Cherokee regionalism, however. Parmenter, "Dragging Canoe," 124.

2. Thornton, *A Population History*, 41; Hatley, *The Dividing Paths*, 185, 206; Cashin, "From Creeks to Crackers," 69–75.

3. Stuart to Hillsborough, January 3, 1769, CO 5/70/105; Talk from Oconostota to Stuart, March 29, 1769, CO 5/70/246.

4. *Georgia Gazette*, Savannah, November 30, 1768; Cameron to Stuart, March 1, 1774, CO 5/75/79; Cameron to Stuart, June 3, 1774, CO 5/75/174.

5. Dowd, *A Spirited Resistance*, 46.

6. Cameron to Stuart, July 9, 1776, CO 5/77/167; Henry Stuart to John Stuart, August 25, 1776, CO 5/77/169; *Pennsylvania Gazette*, Philadelphia, August 14, 1776; Dowd, *A Spirited Resistance*, 47–49.

7. Henry Stuart, brother to John Stuart, noted that the Chilhowee headman had strong connections to the Six Nations, as he had resided among the Mohawks where his "Wife had Constantly lived in Sir William Johnsons House." Henry Stuart to John Stuart, August 25, 1776, CO 5/77/169; Stuart to Cameron, May 23, 1776, CO 5/77/153; Thornton, *A Population History*, 41; O'Donnell, *The Cherokees of North Carolina in the American Revolution*, 6–8; Brown, *Old Frontiers*, 13–14; Mooney, *Myths of the Cherokee*, 46.

8. Rae to Thomas, May 3, 1776, CO 5/77/137; Cameron to Stuart, May 7, 1776, CO 5/77/139; *Pennsylvania Ledger*, Philadelphia, July 20, 1776; O'Donnell, *The Cherokees of North Carolina in the American Revolution*, 11–12.

9. *Remembrancer*, 1776, 180–81; Jacob Sommerhall to Stuart, November 10, 1768, CO 5/70/107. Not every report about the Stuarts and Cameron proved veracious, but their private correspondence reflected a strenuous effort to engage "the Indians firmly in his Majesty's interest." While undoubtedly influential, too much can be made of the role played by these British Indian agents in instigating Cherokee hostility. Other evidence points toward the influence of American Tories in Cherokee country, the cross-tribal delegation at Chota, the militarization of the frontier by anti-Indian settlers, land encroachments, access to trade, an appreciation of British power, and the political break between Britain and America, which provided militant Cherokees the means to attack backcountry settlers without producing a war with Britain. Narrative of William Grant, November 24, 1777, CO 5/78/182; Stuart to Germain, August 23, 1776, CO 5/77/126; Henry Stuart to John Stuart, August 25, 1776, CO 5/77/169; Hamer, "John Stuart's Indian Policy during the Early Months of the American Revolution"; "Correspondence of Henry Stuart and Alexander Cameron with the Wataugans."

10. Hoffman and Tate, eds., *An Uncivil War*; Hatley, *The Dividing Paths*, 191–203; Ramsay, *History of the Revolution of South-Carolina*, 156–57; Dowd, *A Spirited Resistance*, 53.

11. *Remembrancer*, 1776, 274; *Pennsylvania Packet*, Philadelphia, January 17, 1777.

12. Cameron to Stuart, September 23, 1776, CO 5/78/45; Narrative of William Grant, November 24, 1777, CO 5/78/182; *Pennsylvania Evening Post*, Philadelphia, November 12, 1776; Stuart to Germain, November 24, 1776, CO 5/78/72. Christian's army also included one battalion of North Carolinians.

13. Stuart to Germain, January 23, 1777, CO 5/78/76; Copy of minutes of West Florida Council, September 4, 1776, CO 5/593/9; Stuart to Germain, June 14, 1777, CO 5/78/143; Cameron to Stuart, September 23, 1776, CO 5/78/45; Taitt to Tonyn, May 23, 1777, CO 5/557/299.

14. Cameron to Stuart, September 23, 1776, CO 5/78/45; "Arthur Fairies' Journal," 26; Henry Stuart to John Stuart, August 25, 1776, CO 5/77/169.

15. Braund, *Duffels & Deerskins*, 165; Lower Creeks to Stuart, March 23, 1776, CO 5/77/130; Stuart to Germain, August 23, 1776, CO 5/77/126.

16. Taitt to Tonyn, May 23, 1777, CO 5/557/299; Taitt to Brown, May 23, 1777, CO 5/557/305; Cameron to Stuart, September 23, 1776, CO 5/78/45; Henry Stuart to John Stuart, August 25, 1776, CO 5/77/169; Stuart to Germain, June 14, 1777, CO 5/78/143; *Remembrancer*, 1777, 343; O'Donnell, *The Cherokees of North Carolina in the American Revolution*, 21–22; Hatley, *The Dividing Paths*, 219–20.

17. O'Donnell, *The Cherokees of North Carolina in the American Revolution*, 21–22. Some Lower Cherokees had long resided along these rivers, which Edmond Atkin labeled "the Western lower Cherokee Towns," but the war witnessed the bulk of the Lower Cherokee population shifting to this north Georgia region. Jacobs, ed., *Appalachian Indian Frontier*, 54.

18. *Pennsylvania Evening Post*, Philadelphia, November 12, 1776; Talk from William Christian to the Raven, January 19, 1777, CO 5/78/147; Charles Stuart to John Stuart, April 8, 1777, CO 5/78/128; Colbert to Taitt, June 1, 1777, CO 5/557/337; Stuart to Germain, June 14, 1777, CO 5/78/143. Dragging Canoe emerged as the central force behind the war faction and the Overhill exodus. Christian believed the Cherokee leader had "begun the war" by instigating attacks against backcountry settlers. During their initial campaign, the Virginians did not "destroy the Towns that were willing to be at peace," but instead selectively burnt "three towns under the influence of . . . Dragon Canoe, who was the principal cause of the war." His position as the most influential war leader was further evinced by a false report of his death in 1778. The purported event was of such significance, read the account, it likely "will unite the [Cherokee] nation in the interest of America." Talk from William Christian to the Raven, January 19, 1777, CO 5/78/147; *Pennsylvania Evening Post*, December 19, 1776; *Pennsylvania Packet*, December 12, 1778.

19. ASP, 451; Calloway, *The American Revolution in Indian Country*, 200–201; Brown, *Old Frontiers*, 163; McLoughlin, *Cherokee Renascence*, 20.

20. *Pennsylvania Gazette*, October 27, 1779; *Pennsylvania Packet*, June 4, 1779; *New England Chronicle*, March 1, 1781; Mooney, *Myths of the Cherokee*, 57–60; Ramsay, *History of the Revolution of South-Carolina*, 1:273–75; Cashin, *Colonial Augusta*, 123; Extract of a letter from Colo[nel] E. Clarke, November 5, 1781, Keith Read, Hargrett Rare Book and Manuscript Library, University of Georgia Libraries, presented in the Digital Library of Georgia; Calloway, *The American Revolution in Indian Country*, 206; Pate, "The Chickamauga," 123–25.

21. Dowd, *A Spirited Resistance*, 55; Cornish to Shelby, May 21, 1779, Chiefs of Chuccamogga to Shelby, May 22, 1779, Thomas Jefferson Papers; *Pennsylvania Gazette*, February 28, 1781; *ASP*, 264, 431–32.

22. Mooney, *Myths of the Cherokee*, 61–65; *Pennsylvania Packet*, August 9, 1787; *Independent Journal*, New York City, August 19, 1787; *ASP*, 28; *Vermont Journal*, Windsor, April 27, 1789.

23. *Pennsylvania Packet*, October 30, 1788, August 25, 1789; *ASP*, 28, 46–47, 56; *Newport Herald*, Newport, R.I., October 2, 1788; King and Olinger, "Oconastota," 222; Mooney, *Myths of the Cherokee*, 71; "Bro. Schneider's Journey to the Cherokee Country," 256; Conley, *The Cherokee Nation*, 74.

24. Calloway, *The American Revolution in Indian Country*, 201–202.

25. *New-York Packet*, January 27, 1789; *Freeman's Journal*, Philadelphia, October 5, 1785; *ASP*, 28, 46–48, 56; *Pennsylvania Packet*, October 30, 1788; Pate, "The Chickamauga," 186; Dowd, *A Spirited Resistance*, 96–99. Duane King mistakenly identifies Hanging Maw as one of the Cherokee elders killed in the attack on Old Tassel. King and Olinger, "Oconastota," 222.

26. *ASP*, 326, 329, 331–32, 437–39, 443–45, 469–70.

27. *ASP*, 255, 263, 265, 288–91.

28. *ASP* 204–205, 291, 293, 327, 329, 331, 449–50; *Pennsylvania Gazette*, January 9, 1793, August 13, 1794; *New-York Packet*, January 27, 1789. Watts and Noon-day may have been cousins, since Watts specifically mentioned that Noon-day's "own two brothers was very cross" after his death at the hands of the Americans.

29. *Mail; or, Claypoole's Daily Advertiser*, Philadelphia, November 1, 1792; *ASP*, 277, 431–32; *Independent Gazetteer*, Philadelphia, November 24, 1792.

30. *Mail; or, Claypoole's Daily Advertiser*, November 1, 1792; *ASP*, 294, 431–32; *Gazette of the United States*, Philadelphia, November 7, 1792.

31. Pate, "The Chickamauga," 250; *Mail; or, Claypoole's Daily Advertiser*, Philadelphia, November 1, 1792; *South Carolina Gazette*, July 10, 1792; *ASP*, 265.

32. *ASP*, 276–77, 293.

33. *Mail; or, Claypoole's Daily Advertiser*, November 1, 1792; *Pennsylvania Packet*, August 9, 1787; *Pennsylvania Gazette*, June 26, 1793. Knoxville was about twenty-five miles from Chota. *Dunlap's American Daily Advertiser*, Philadelphia, March 30, 1792.

34. *ASP*, 264, 267; *Mail; or, Claypoole's Daily Advertiser*, November 1, 1792; *Pennsylvania Packet*, June 4, 1779, October 30, 1788; *New Jersey Gazette*, Trenton, December

4, 1782; *Virginia Journal and Alexandria Advertiser*, March 18, 1784; *Pennsylvania Gazette*, August 30, 1786, November 14, 1792; "Bro. Schneider's Journey to the Cherokee Country," 256–57.

35. Nagel, *American Indian Ethnic Renewal*, 11, 20; Calloway, *The American Revolution in Indian Country*, 201.

36. *Mail; or, Claypoole's Daily Advertiser*, November 1, 1792; *ASP*, 317–18; *Philadelphia Gazette and Universal Daily Advertiser*, December 3, 1794.

37. *ASP*, 261, 295, 363, 429, 436, 452, 455; *Independent Gazetteer*, Philadelphia, July 20, 1793. For recent accounts of the disconnect between the federal government and border citizens, see Barksdale, *The Lost State of Franklin*, and Nichols, *Red Gentlemen and White Savages*.

38. *ASP*, 459–60, 466, 469–70, 530–31, 632; *General Advertiser*, July 22, 1793; *Pennsylvania Gazette*, December 24, 1793.

39. Conley, *The Cherokee Nation*, 74–76; Pate, "The Chickamauga," 155–56; *Treaty with the Cherokee, 1785; Treaty with the Cherokee, 1791; Pennsylvania Gazette*, June 22, 1791.

40. *ASP*, 267–69, 271.

41. *ASP*, 536–38.

42. *ASP*, 534–36; Mooney, *Myths of the Cherokee*, 79.

43. *ASP*, 282, 293, 633–34; *Philadelphia Gazette and Universal Daily Advertiser*, August 23, 1794.

44. *ASP*, 275–76; *Pennsylvania Packet*, August 25, 1789.

45. *ASP*, 316–17, 536–38, 542; *North-Carolina Journal*, May 29, 1793; *Norwich Packet*, Norwich, Conn., October 2, 1794.

46. *ASP*, 446, 450–51.

47. McLoughlin, *Cherokee Renascence*, 29.

48. Raulston and Livingood, *Sequatchie*, 57; Hatley, *The Dividing Paths*, 228.

49. McLoughlin, *Cherokee Renascence*, 58–60.

Epilogue

1. "Brethren Steiner and DeSchweinitz," 459, 474; McLoughlin, *Cherokee Renascence*, 58–59; McLoughlin, "Thomas Jefferson," 564.

2. Perlman, *The Myth of Marginality*, 125; McLoughlin, "Cherokee Anomie, 1794–1810," 453, 459, 474; Perdue, *Cherokee Women*, 9.

3. African slaves never became a significant percentage of the Cherokee population. In 1809, there were less than six hundred slaves in Cherokee country. Few Cherokees owned slaves, either, since they were usually concentrated in the hands of a small number of elites. About 7 percent of Cherokees held slaves by the 1830s, but as Perdue notes, "those who did dominated Cherokee economic and political life," thus making slaves and slave owning more significant than the numbers allow. Thornton, *A Population History*, 53; Perdue, *Cherokee Women*, 105–107, 126, 144–45; Hatley, "The Three Lives of Keowee," 246; "Brethren Steiner and DeSchweinitz," 472, 479–80.

4. *Treaty with the Cherokee, 1785*; *Treaty with the Cherokee, 1791.*
5. McLoughlin, "Thomas Jefferson," 552; Perdue, *Cherokee Women*, 107.
6. Fauquier to Lyttelton, September 5, 1759, WLP; *ASP*, 532–33; *Freeman's Journal*, Philadelphia, March 21, 1792; Perdue, *Cherokee Women*, 99.
7. *ASP*, 46–47, 52–53; "Brethren Steiner and DeSchweinitz," 460; McLoughlin, *Cherokee Renascence*, 29; Perdue, *Cherokee Women*, 158.
8. McLoughlin, *Cherokee Renascence*, 110; Perdue, *Cherokee Women*, 135, 142; McLoughlin, "Thomas Jefferson," 547.
9. McLoughlin, "Cherokee Anomie," 454, 474; Hatley, *The Dividing Paths*, 227; Thornton, *A Population History*, 40; Grove and Orr to Steele, December 12, 1794, Wagstaff, ed., *The Papers of John Steele*, 129.

Bibliography

Primary

"Account of the Chevalier De Lantagnac." In *Early Travels in the Tennessee Country*, ed. Samuel Cole Williams, 177–86. Johnson City: Watauga Press, 1928.

Adair, James. *The History of the American Indians: particularly those nations adjoining to the Mississippi East and West Florida, Georgia, South and North Carolina, and Virginia*. London: Printed for E. and C. Dilly, 1775.

American State Papers: Indian Affairs. Vol. 1. Washington, D.C.: Gales and Seaton, 1832.

The Annual Register, or a View of the History, Politicks, and Literature, for the Year 1760. London: Printed for J. Dodsley, 1775.

"Arthur Fairies' Journal of Expedition against the Cherokee Indians from July 18th, to October 11th, 1776." Transcribed and annotated by Will Graves. *Southern Campaigns of the American Revolution* 2 (October 2005): 20–34.

Bartram, William. *Travels through North & South Carolina, Georgia, East & West Florida, the Cherokee Country, the Extensive Territories of the Muscogulges, or Creek Confederacy, and the Country of the Chactaws; Containing an Account of the Soil and Natural Productions of Those Regions, Together with Observations on the Manners of the Indians*. Philadelphia: James and Johnson, 1791.

"Bro. Schneider's Journey to the Cherokee Country." In *Early Travels in the Tennessee Country, 1540–1800*, ed. Samuel Cole Williams, 245–65. Johnson City: Watauga Press, 1928.

Burnaby's Travels through North America. Reprinted from the third edition of 1798, with introduction and notes by Rufus Rockwell Wilson. New York: A. Wessels, 1904.

Candler, Allen D., et al., eds. *The Colonial Records of the State of Georgia*. 26 vols. Atlanta: Franklin-Turner, 1904–16.

"Correspondence of Henry Stuart and Alexander Cameron with the Wataugans." Ed. Philip M. Hamer. *Mississippi Valley Historical Review* 17 (December 1930): 451–59.

Entick, John. *The General History of the Late War: Containing It's Rise, Progress, and Event, in Europe, Asia, Africa, and America*. London: Printed for Edward Dilly and John Millan, 1763–64.

"A Faithful Relation of My Westoe Voyage, by Henry Woodward." In *Narratives of Early Carolina, 1650–1708*, ed. Salley Alexander, 127–34. New York: Charles Scribner's Sons, 1911.

"The First Remonstrance from South Carolina against the Stamp Act [MSS of Christopher Gadsden], Charles Town, September 4, 1764." In *Documentary History of the American Revolution*, ed. Robert Wilson Gibbes. New York: D. Appleton, 1855.

French, Christopher. "Journal of an Expedition to South Carolina." *Journal of Cherokee Studies* 2 (Summer 1977): 275–301.

Gadsden, Christopher. *Some Observations on the Two Campaigns against the Cherokee Indians, in 1760 and 1761. In a Second Letter from Philopatrios*. Charles-Town: Peter Timothy, 1762.

Glen, James. *A Description of South Carolina; Containing, Many Curious and Interesting Particulars Relating to the Civil, Natural and Commercial History of That Colony*. London: Printed for R. and J. Dodsley, 1761.

Hamer, Phillip M. and George C. Rogers Jr., eds. *The Papers of Henry Laurens*. Vol. 3: January 1, 1759–August 31, 1763. Columbia: University of South Carolina Press, 1972.

Hewat, Alexander. *An Historical Account of the Rise and Progress of the Colonies of South Carolina and Georgia. In two volumes*. Vol. 1. London: Printed for Alexander Donaldson, 1779.

Jacobs, Wilbur R., ed. *The Appalachian Indian Frontier: The Edmond Atkin Report and Plan of 1755*. Lincoln: University of Nebraska Press, 1967.

James, Alfred P., ed. *Writings of General John Forbes: Relating to His Service in North American*. Menasha: Collegiate Press, 1938.

"Journal of Antoine Bonnefoy's Captivity among the Cherokee Indians, 1741–42." In *Travels in the American Colonies*, ed. Newton Mereness, 239–55. New York: Macmillan, 1916.

"Journal of Colonel George Chicken's Mission from Charleston, S.C., to the Cherokees, 1725." In *Travels in the American Colonies*, ed. Newton Mereness, 95–174. New York: Macmillan, 1916.

Journal of the Congress of the Four Southern Governors, and the Superintendent of that District, with the Five Nations of Indians, at Augusta, 1763. Charles-town, S.C.: Peter Timothy, 1764.

Journal of the House of Burgesses. Williamsburg: W. Hunter, 1756.

Journal of the House of Burgesses, October 30–June 1, 1765. Williamsburg: Joseph Royle, 1765.

"Journal of Sir Alexander Cuming (1730)." In *Early Travels in the Tennessee Country, 1540–1800*, ed. Samuel Cole Williams, 115–46. Johnson City: Watauga Press, 1928.

King, Duane, ed. *The Memoirs of Lt. Henry Timberlake: The Story of a Soldier, Adventurer, and Emissary to the Cherokees, 1756–1765*. Chapel Hill: University of North Carolina Press, 2007.

Klinck, Carl F. and James J. Talman, eds. *The Journal of Major John Norton*. Toronto: Champlain Society, 1970.

Lewis, Theodore H., ed. "The Narrative of the Expedition of Hernando de Soto by the Gentleman of Elvas." In *Original Narratives of Early American History: Spanish Ex-*

plorers in the Southern United States, 1528–1543, ed. J. Franklin Jameson, 127–272. New York: Charles Scribner's Sons, 1907.

Mays, Edith, ed. *Amherst Papers, 1756–1763: The Southern Sector: Dispatches from South Carolina, Virginia and His Majesty's Superintendents of Indian Affairs.* Bowie: Heritage Books, 1999.

McDowell, William L., Jr., ed. *Journals of the Commissioners of the Indian Trade, September 20, 1710–August 29, 1718.* Columbia: South Carolina Department of Archives and History, 1955.

———, ed. *Documents Relating to Indian Affairs, May 21, 1750–August 7, 1754.* Columbia: South Carolina Department of Archives and History, 1958.

———, ed. *Documents Relating to Indian Affairs, 1754–1765.* Columbia: South Carolina Department of Archives and History, 1970.

Mortimer, Thomas. *A New History of England, from the Earliest Accounts of Britain, to the Ratification of the Peace of Versailles, 1763.* 3 vols. London: Printed for J. Wilson and J. Fell, 1764–66.

Oglethorpe, James E. *A New and Accurate Account of the Provinces of South-Carolina and Georgia.* London: Printed for J. Worrall, 1732.

The Public Laws of the State of South-Carolina, from Its First Establishment as a British Province Down to the Year 1790. Philadelphia: R. Aitken & Son, 1790.

Ramsay, David. *The History of the Revolution of South-Carolina, from a British Province to an Independent State.* Vol. 1. Trenton: Printed by Isaac Collins, 1785.

Reese, George, ed. *The Official Papers of Francis Fauquier Lieutenant Governor of Virginia 1758–1768.* 2 vols. Charlottesville: University Press of Virginia, 1980–81.

"Report of the Journey of the Brethren Abraham Steiner and Frederick C. DeSchweinitz to the Cherokees and the Cumberland Settlements (1799)." In *Early Travels in the Tennessee Country, 1540–1800,* ed. Samuel Cole Williams, 445–525. Johnson City: Watauga Press, 1928.

Salley, A. S., ed. *Journal of Colonel John Herbert, Commissioner of Indian Affairs for the Province of South Carolina, October 17, 1727, to March 19, 1727/8.* Columbia: Historical Commission of South Carolina, 1936.

Sullivan, James, et al., eds. *The Papers of Sir William Johnson,* 14 vols. Albany: University of the State of New York, 1921–65.

Tinling, Marion, ed. *The Correspondence of the Three William Byrds of Westover, Virginia, 1684–1776.* Vol. 2. Charlottesville: University Press of Virginia, 1977.

A Treaty Held with the Catawba and Cherokee Indians, at the Catawba-Town and Broad-River, in the months of February and March 1756. Williamsburg: W. Hunter, 1756.

Treaty with the Cherokee, 1785. In *Indian Affairs: Laws and Treaties,* vol. 2, ed. Charles J. Kappler. Washington, D.C.: Government Printing Office, 1904.

Treaty with the Cherokee, 1791. In *Indian Affairs: Laws and Treaties,* vol. 2, ed. Charles J. Kappler. Washington, D.C.: Government Printing Office. 1904.

Vorsey, Louis De, Jr., ed. *De Brahm's Report of the General Survey in the Southern District of North America.* Columbia: University of South Carolina Press, 1971.

Wagstaff, H. M., ed. *The Papers of John Steele.* Raleigh: Edwards and Broughton Printing, 1924.

Williams, Samuel Cole, ed. *Early Travels in the Tennessee Country, 1540–1800*. Johnson City: Watauga Press, 1928.

———, ed. *Lieutenant Henry Timberlake's Memoirs, 1756–1765*. Marietta: Continental Book, 1948.

Secondary

Alden, John Richard. *John Stuart and the Southern Colonial Frontier: A Study of Indian Relations, War, Trade, and Land Problems in the Southern Wilderness, 1754–1775*. Ann Arbor: University of Michigan Press, 1944.

Anderson, Fred. *Crucible of War: The Seven Years' War and the Fate of Empire in British North America, 1754–1766*. New York: Vintage Books, 2000.

Anderson, William L., and James A. Lewis. *Guide to Cherokee Documents in Foreign Archives*. Metuchen: Scarecrow Press, 1983.

Barksdale, Kevin T. *The Lost State of Franklin: America's First Secession*. Lexington: University Press of Kentucky, 2009.

Bohaker, Heidi. "Nindoodemag: The Significance of Algonquian Kinship Networks in the Eastern Great Lakes Region, 1600–1701." *William and Mary Quarterly* 63 (January 2006): 23–52.

Bolstad, Paul V., and Ted L. Gragson. "Resource Abundance Constraints on the Early Post-Contact Cherokee Population." *Journal of Archaeological Science* 35 (2008): 563–76.

Booker, Karen M., Charles M. Hudson, and Robert L. Rankin. "Place-Name Identification and Multilingualism in the Sixteenth-Century Southeast." *Ethnohistory* 39 (Autumn 1992): 399–451.

Braund, Kathryn E. Holland. *Deerskins & Duffels: Creek Indian Trade with Anglo-America, 1685–1815*. Lincoln: University of Nebraska Press, 1993.

Brown, John P. *Old Frontiers: The Story of the Cherokee Indians from the Earliest Times to the Date of Their Removal to the West, 1838*. Kingsport: Southern Publishers, 1938.

Calloway, Colin G. *The American Revolution in Indian Country: Crisis and Diversity in Native American Communities*. Cambridge: Cambridge University Press, 1995.

———. *The Scratch of a Pen: 1763 and the Transformation of America*. New York: Oxford University Press, 2006.

Cashin, Edward. *Colonial Augusta: "Key of the Indian Countrey."* Macon: Mercer University Press, 1986.

———. "From Creeks to Crackers." In *An Uncivil War: The Southern Backcountry during the American Revolution*, ed. Ronald Hoffman and Thade Tate, 69–75. Charlottesville: University Press of Virginia, 1985.

———. *Guardians of the Valley: Chickasaws in Colonial South Carolina and Georgia*. Columbia: University of South Carolina Press, 2009.

Conley, Robert J. *The Cherokee Nation: A History*. Albuquerque: University of New Mexico Press, 2005.

Corkran, David H. *The Carolina Indian Frontier*. Columbia: University of South Carolina Press, 1970.

DeMallie, Raymond J. "Kinship: The Foundation for Native American Society." In *Studying Native America: Problems and Prospects*, ed. Russell Thornton, 306–56. Madison: University of Wisconsin Press, 1998.

Dickens, Roy S., Jr. "The Origins and Development of Cherokee Culture." In *The Cherokee Indian Nation: A Troubled History*, ed. Duane King, 3–32. Knoxville: University of Tennessee Press, 1979.

Dowd, Gregory Evans. *A Spirited Resistance: The North American Indian Struggle for Unity, 1745–1815*. Baltimore: Johns Hopkins University Press, 1992.

———. *War under Heaven: Pontiac, the Indian Nations and the British Empire*. Baltimore: Johns Hopkins University Press, 2002.

———. "'Insidious Friends': Gift Giving and the Cherokee-British Alliance in the Seven Years' War." In *Contact Points: American Frontiers from the Mohawk Valley to the Mississippi, 1750–1830*, ed. Andrew R. L. Cayton and Fredrika J. Teute, 114–50. Chapel Hill: University of North Carolina Press, 1998.

———. "The Panic of 1751: The Significance of Rumors on the South Carolina–Cherokee Frontier." *William and Mary Quarterly* 53, no. 3 (July 1996): 527–60.

Fogelson, Raymond D. "The Cherokee Ball Game: A Study in Southeastern Ethnology." PhD diss., University of Pennsylvania, 1962.

———. "The Cherokee Ballgame Cycle: An Ethnographer's View." *Ethnomusicology* 15 (September 1971): 327–38.

———. "Perspectives on Native American Identity." In *Studying Native America: Problems and Prospects*, ed. Russell Thornton, 40–59. Madison: University of Wisconsin Press, 1998.

———. "Report on a Summer's Field Work among the Cherokee." 1960. American Philosophical Society. Phillips Fund for Native American Research Collection.

Frank, Andrew K. *Creeks and Southerners: Biculturalism on the Early American Frontier*. Lincoln: University of Nebraska Press, 2005.

Gallay, Alan. *The Indian Slave Trade: The Rise of the English Empire in the American South, 1670–1717*. New Haven: Yale University Press, 2002.

Gearing, Fred. *Priests and Warriors: Social Structures for Cherokee Politics in the Eighteenth Century*. American Anthropological Association, Memoir 93. Menasha: American Anthropological Association, 1962.

Gragson, Ted L., and Paul V. Bolstad. "A Local Analysis of Early-Eighteenth-Century Cherokee Settlement." *Social Science History* 31 (Fall 2007): 435–68.

Greer, Allan. "Comparisons: New France." In *A Companion to Colonial America*, ed. Daniel Vickers, 469–88. Malden: Blackwell, 2006.

Hally, David J. "The Nature of Mississippian Regional Systems." In *Light on the Path: The Anthropology and History of the Southeastern Indians*, ed. Thomas J. Pluckhahn and Robbie Ethridge, 26–42. Tuscaloosa: University of Alabama Press, 2006.

Hamer, Philip M. "John Stuart's Indian Policy during the Early Months of the American Revolution." *Mississippi Valley Historical Review* 17 (December 1930): 351–66.

Harmon, Michael. "Eighteenth-Century Lower Cherokee Adaptation and Use of European Material Culture." MA thesis, University of South Carolina, 1986.

Hatley, Tom. *The Dividing Paths: Cherokees and South Carolinians through the Revolutionary Era*. New York: Oxford University Press, 1995.

———. "The Three Lives of Keowee: Loss and Recovery in Eighteenth-Century Cherokee Villages." In *American Encounters: Natives and Newcomers from European Contact to Indian Removal, 1500–1850*, ed. Peter Mancall and James Merrell, 241–60. New York: Routledge, 2000.

Herndon, Marcia. "The Cherokee Ballgame Cycle: An Ethnomusicologist's View." *Ethnomusicology* 15 (September 1971): 339–52.

Hinderaker, Eric. *Elusive Empires: Constructing Colonialism in the Ohio Valley, 1673–1800*. Cambridge: Cambridge University Press, 1997.

Hoffman, Ronald, and Thade Tate, eds. *An Uncivil War: The Southern Backcountry during the American Revolution*. Charlottesville: University Press of Virginia, 1985.

Hoig, Stanley. *The Cherokees and Their Chiefs: In the Wake of Empire*. Fayetteville: University of Arkansas Press, 1998.

Holton, Woody. "The Ohio Indians and the Coming of the American Revolution in Virginia." *Journal of Southern History* 60 (August 1994): 453–78.

Horr, David Agee. *Cherokee and Creek Indians*. New York: Garland, 1974.

Hudson, Charles. *The Southeastern Indians*. Knoxville: University of Tennessee Press, 1976.

King, Duane, ed. *The Cherokee Indian Nation: A Troubled History*. Knoxville: University of Tennessee Press, 1979.

King, Duane, and Danny E. Olinger. "Oconastota." *American Antiquity* 37 (April 1972): 222–28.

Lee, Wayne E. "Fortify, Fight, or Flee: Tuscarora and Cherokee Defensive Warfare and Military Culture Adaptation." *Journal of Military History* 68 (July 2004): 713–70.

McLoughlin, William G. *Cherokee Renascence in the New Republic*. Princeton: Princeton University Press, 1986.

———. "Cherokee Anomie, 1794–1810: New Roles for Red Men, Red Women, and Black Slaves." *American Encounters: Natives and Newcomers from European Contact to Indian Removal, 1500–1850*, ed. Peter Mancall and James Merrell, 452–76. New York: Routledge, 2000.

———. "Thomas Jefferson and the Beginning of Cherokee Nationalism." *William and Mary Quarterly* 32 (October 1975): 547–80.

Merrell, James. *The Indians' New World: Catawbas and Their Neighbors from European Contact through the Era of Removal*. Chapel Hill: University of North Carolina Press, 1989.

Montgomery, Michael B., and Joseph S. Hall. *Dictionary of Smoky Mountain English*. Knoxville: University of Tennessee Press, 2004.

Mooney, James. *Historical Sketch of the Cherokee*. Chicago: Aldine, 1975.

———. *Myths of the Cherokee*. New York: New York University Press, 1970.

———. "The Cherokee Ball Play." *American Anthropologist* 3 (April 1890): 105–32.

———. "The Sacred Formula of the Cherokees." *James Mooney's History, Myths, and Sacred Formulas of the Cherokees*. Asheville: Bright Mountain Books, 1992.

Moore, John Hammond. *Columbia and Richland County: A South Carolina Community, 1740–1990*. Columbia: University of South Carolina Press, 1992.

Nagel, Joane. *American Indian Ethnic Renewal: Red Power and the Resurgence of Identity and Culture*. New York: Oxford University Press, 1997.

Nichols, David Andrew. *Red Gentlemen and White Savages: Indians, Federalists, and the Search for Order on the American Frontier*. Charlottesville: University of Virginia Press, 2008.

O'Donnell, James H., III. *The Cherokees of North Carolina in the American Revolution*. Raleigh: Department of Cultural Resources, Division of Archives and History, 1976.

Oliphant, John. *Peace and War on the Anglo-Cherokee Frontier, 1756–1763*. Baton Rouge: Louisiana State University Press, 2001.

Parmenter, Jon W. "Dragging Canoe (Tsi'yu-gûnsi'ni): Chickamauga Cherokee Patriot." *The Human Tradition in Revolutionary America*, ed. Ian K. Steele and Nancy Rhoden, 117–37. Wilmington: Scholarly Resources Press, 2000.

Pate, James. "The Chickamauga: A Forgotten Segment of Indian Resistance on the Southern Frontier." PhD diss., Mississippi State University, 1969.

Perdue, Theda. *Cherokee Women: Gender and Culture Change, 1700–1835*. Lincoln: University of Nebraska Press, 1998.

———. "Cherokee Planters: The Development of Plantation Slavery before Removal." *The Cherokee Indian Nation: A Troubled History*, ed. Duane King, 110–28. Knoxville: University of Tennessee Press, 1979.

———. "Race and Culture: Writing the Ethnohistory of the Early South." *Ethnohistory* 51 (Fall 2004): 701–24.

Perlman, Janice E. *The Myth of Marginality: Urban Poverty and Politics in Rio de Janeiro*. Berkeley: University of California Press, 1976.

Persico, V. Richard, Jr. "Early Nineteenth-Century Cherokee Political Organization." In *The Cherokee Indian Nation: A Troubled History*, ed. Duane King, 92–109. Knoxville: University of Tennessee Press, 1979.

Piker, Joshua. *Okfuskee: A Creek Indian Town in Colonial America*. Cambridge: Harvard University Press, 2004.

Raulston, J. Leonard, and James W. Livingood. *Sequatchie: A Story of the Southern Cumberlands*. Knoxville: University of Tennessee Press, 1974.

Reid, John P. *A Better Kind of Hatchet: Law, Trade, and Diplomacy in the Cherokee Nation during the Early Years of European Contact*. University Park: Pennsylvania State University Press, 1976.

———. *A Law of Blood: The Primitive Law of the Cherokee Nation*. New York: New York University Press, 1970.

Saunt, Claudio. "'The English has now a Mind to make Slaves of them all': Creeks, Seminoles, and the Problem of Slavery." *American Indian Quarterly* 22 (Winter–Spring 1998): 157–80.

Saunt, Claudio, Barbara Krauthamer, Tiya Miles, Celia E. Naylor, and Circe Sturm. "Rethinking Race and Culture in the Early South." *Ethnohistory* 53 (Spring 2006): 399–406.

Shoemaker, Nancy. "An Alliance between Men: Gender Metaphors in Eighteenth-Century American Indian Diplomacy East of the Mississippi." *Ethnohistory* 46 (Spring 1999): 239–64.
Smith, Betty Anderson. "Distribution of Eighteenth-Century Cherokee Settlements." In *The Cherokee Indian Nation: A Troubled History*, ed. Duane King, 46–60. Knoxville: University of Tennessee Press, 1979.
Snyder, Christina. *Slavery in Indian Country: The Changing Face of Captivity in Early America*. Cambridge: Harvard University Press, 2010.
Starkey, Marion L. *The Cherokee Nation*. North Dighton: J. G. Press, 1973.
Steele, Ian. "Shawnee Origins of the Seven Years' War." *Ethnohistory* 53 (2006): 657–87.
Thornton, Russell. *The Cherokees: A Population History*. Lincoln: University of Nebraska Press, 1990.
Vennum, Thomas, Jr. *American Indian Lacrosse: The Little Brother of War*. Washington, D.C.: Smithsonian Institution Press, 1994.
Wallace, Anthony F. C., and Raymond D. Fogelson. "The Identity Struggle." In *Intensive Family Therapy: Theoretical and Practical Aspects*, ed. Ivan Boszomenyi-Nagy and James L. Framo, 365–406. New York: Harper and Row, 1965.
White, Richard. *The Middle Ground: Indians, Empires, and Republics in the Great Lakes Region, 1650–1815*. Cambridge: Cambridge University Press, 1991.
———. "Using the Past: History and Native American Studies." *Studying Native America: Problems and Prospects*, ed. Russell Thornton. Madison: University of Wisconsin Press, 1998.
Woodward, Grace Steele. *The Cherokees*. Norman: University of Oklahoma Press, 1963.
Zogry, Michael J. *Anetso, the Cherokee Ball Game: At the Center of Ceremony and Identity*. Chapel Hill: University of North Carolina Press, 2010.
Zuckerman, Michael. "Regionalism." In *A Companion to Colonial America*, ed. Daniel Vickers, 311–33. Malden: Blackwell, 2006.

Periodicals

Dunlap's American Daily Advertiser. Philadelphia.
Echo or Edinburgh Weekly Journal. Edinburgh, Scotland.
Freeman's Journal; or, The North-American Intelligencer. Philadelphia.
Gazetteer and London Daily Advertiser. London.
Gazette of the United States. Philadelphia.
General Evening Post. London.
Georgia Gazette. Savannah.
Independent Gazetteer. Philadelphia.
Independent Journal. New York City.
London Evening Post. London.
London Magazine, or, Gentleman's Monthly Intelligencer, for the Year 1755. London.
Mail; or, Claypoole's Daily Advertiser. Philadelphia.
New Jersey Gazette. Trenton, N.J.
Newport Herald. Newport, R.I.
New-York Packet. New York City.

North-Carolina Journal. Halifax, N.C.
Norwich Packet. Norwich, Conn.
Pennsylvania Evening Post. Philadelphia.
Pennsylvania Gazette. Philadelphia.
Pennsylvania Ledger: or the Virginia, Maryland, Pennsylvania, & New-Jersey Weekly Advertiser. Philadelphia.
Pennsylvania Packet. Philadelphia.
Philadelphia Gazette and Universal Daily Advertiser. Philadelphia.
Remembrancer, or Impartial Repository of Public Events. London: Printed for J. Almon, 1775–84.
South-Carolina Gazette. Charleston.
Vermont Journal, and the Universal Advertiser. Windsor, Vt.
Virginia Journal and Alexandria Advertiser. Alexandria, Va.

Collections

British Public Record Office. Colonial Office. Microfilm at Hunter Library, Western Carolina University, Cullowhee, N.C.
British Public Record Office, War Office. Microfilm at Hunter Library, Western Carolina University, Cullowhee, N.C.
Extract of a letter from Colo[nel] E. Clarke, November 5, 1781. Athens: Digital Library of Georgia, 2001.
George Washington Papers at the Library of Congress, 1741–99. Series 2 Letterbooks.
Hicks, Charles. "Manners, Customs, &c., of Cherokees in 1818." Speck Cherokee Collection, American Philosophical Society.
James Grant of Ballindalloch Papers. National Archives of Scotland, Edinburgh. Microfilm at the David Library of the American Revolution, Washington Crossing, Pa.
Journals of His Majesty's Council in South Carolina. British Public Record Office, Colonial Office. South Carolina Department of Archives and History, Columbia.
Journals of the South Carolina Upper House of Assembly. British Public Record Office. South Carolina Department of Archives and History, Columbia.
Letters from James Logan, Richard Peters, Conrad Weiser, Levin Gale, Thomas Lee, James Hamilton, George Thomas, G. Clinton, etc. [1726–56]. American Philosophical Society.
Moultrie Family Papers. South Carolina Historical Society, Charleston, S.C.
South Carolina Council Journals. Microfilm at South Carolina Department of Archives and History, Columbia, S.C.
Speck, Frank. Juan Pardo's Letter (1566). Frank G. Speck Papers, American Philosophical Society.
Speck, Frank G. Papers. American Philosophical Society.
———. Speck Cherokee Collection. American Philosophical Society.
Thomas Jefferson Papers, Series 1: General Correspondence, 1651–1827.
William Henry Lyttelton Letterbooks. William L. Clements Library, University of Michigan.
William Henry Lyttelton Papers. William L. Clements Library, University of Michigan.

Index

Adair, James, comments by, about: agriculture, 15; clans, 29, 188n37; the council house, 14; methods of social control, 86; regionalism, 18, 186n18; town autonomy, 11; warfare, 57, 65, 102, 106, 111, 114–15, 118, 183n2; the warrior population, 205n34

Amherst, Jeffery, 119–20, 126

Atkin, Edmond, 99–100, 104

—comments by, about: British colonists, 106; the council house, 14; the deerskin trade, 50, 53; Lower Cherokee refugees, 60; regionalism, 22, 212n17; Settlement Indians, 65–67, 194n17; traveling in Cherokee country, 21; warfare, 57, 61; warrior demands for goods, 99

Attakullakulla (Little Carpenter): and the Anglo-Cherokee War, 112, 115–16, 118, 120–26, 141; authority of, 12, 129, 202n4; and the crisis in Virginia, 96, 102–3, 108; and the deerskin trade, 13, 131–34; and diplomacy, 139–40, 149; and the preeminence of Chota, 28, 83; and the Tellico Affair, 89, 91–92; and the Treaty of 1730, 48; and the Treaty of Lochaber, 131; as a warrior, 12, 137–38; and women, 112, 121–22

Augusta, Congress of (1763), 132–36, 141

Ball play, 2, 16, 52, 156

Beamer, James: and Thomas Beamer, 102, 104; and the Cherokee-Creek War, 59–60; and Creek attacks against Little Estatoe, 124; and concerns about the French, 78; and the deerskin trade, 50, 187n23; as an interpreter for the Lower Cherokees, 23, 63; and the Lower Cherokee warrior population, 74; and Northward Indians, 63–64

Bedford County (Virginia), 102, 105–6, 113

Beloved towns, 24–27. *See also* Chota; Kituhwa; Nequassee; Noyowee; Tellico; Tenasee; Tugaloo

Bloody Fellow, 172–73

Blount, William, 166–68, 171–74

Braddock's Defeat, 75, 90, 97

Byrd, William, 50, 109, 120, 124, 126–27

Caesar, 38

Cameron, Alexander, 137, 150, 158

Canuga (and Neowi), 125, 128

Captives/captivity: and the Anglo-Cherokee War, 114, 119, 123–24; and the Cherokee-Creek War, 69; and French captives, 78, 99; and the imprisonment of Shawnee warriors in Charlestown, 71–72; and Northward Indians, 58, 138;

Catawbas: and the Congress of Augusta, 132; decline of, 181; and language, 29; and Lower Cherokee refugees, 60; and Northward Indians, 58, 66–67, 70, 97; and Settlement Indians, 66; and smallpox, 115, 117

Chatooga River, 41, 74
Chattahoochee River, 41, 74, 153, 161, 175
Chatuga, 76–77, 80, 82, 84, 86–88, 122
Chickamauga Towns (Lower, Five Lower Towns): and connections to the Upper Towns, 166–70, 172–74, 178, 181; and regional formation, 8–9, 19, 153, 155, 162–63, 176; and war with the United States, 165, 167–69, 172, 175. *See also* Lookout Mountain Town; Nickajack; Running Water; Willstown
Chickamauga Towns, headmen. *See* Bloody Fellow; Dragging Canoe; Watts, John
Chickasaws: and the Anglo-Cherokee War, 129; and the Cherokee-Creek War, 44–46, 190n22, 193n15; and the Congress of Augusta, 132; and language, 29; and the Savannah Chickasaws, 66, 115; and threats against Cherokees, 67
Chicken, George, 18, 33, 40–43, 46–48
Chilhowee, 1–2, 39, 122, 138, 140, 157, 162, 165
Choatehee of Tellico, 47–48
Chota: and the Anglo-Cherokee War, 121–22, 124; ascendancy of, 58, 76, 83; as a beloved town, 24, 27; challenges to, 90–91, 191n29; decline of, 155, 164, 179; and the French, 75, 81; and Mortar of Okchai, 147, 210n40; as a national council seat, 27–28; and Northward Indians, 65, 72; and pan-Indianism, 150, 156–57; and its proximity to Knoxville, 213n33; and the Tellico Affair, 75, 81–85, 87, 91; and its townhouse, 14; and the Virginia fort, 96
Clan revenge: and its challenge to the authority of headmen, 89, 122–23, 135, 180; and the Cherokee-Creek War, 60; description of, 2, 29; and liability for Cherokee security, 44, 180–81; and Virginia, 102, 104–6, 139, 207–8n22
Clans: and Cherokee headmen, 10, 51–52; and Cherokee identity, 3–5, 28–29;

and localism, 15–16; obligations of, 185–86n14, 188n37; and Tellico, 77
Congarees, 37–38, 68, 113–14, 189n4
Conjuror of Tugaloo (Charity Hagey), 34, 37, 41, 189n5
Coosa River, 107, 153, 161–63, 166, 168, 171, 174–77
Cowee, 1–2, 38–39, 139
Coweta, 44–45, 65, 68–70, 134–35, 156, 160
Coyatee, 165, 171–72
Coytmore, Richard, 109, 113, 115–18, 121
Creeks: and the American Revolution, 159–60, 171, 174–75; and the Battle of Taliwa, 195n27; and borderlands with Cherokees, 8, 22, 37, 39, 41, 146, 161; Cherokee hostility toward, 27, 40, 134, 136–37; and language, 29; and Northward Indians, 7, 57–58, 61, 64–65, 68–70; and peace talks concerning Cherokees, 43–44, 70–71, 107; and warfare with Cherokees, 6, 32–33, 39–40, 42, 58, 61, 104, 201n23. *See also* Creeks, Lower; Creeks, Upper
Creeks, Lower: Cherokee hostility toward, 43, 45, 57, 65; and the Long Cane murders, 134–35; and Northward Indians, 68–69; and peace talks concerning Cherokees, 43–45, 69; and the Tugaloo Incident, 44; and warfare with Cherokees, 57–61. *See also* Coweta; Cussita; Malatchi
Creeks, Upper: and Chickamaugas, 171, 174; and peace talks concerning Cherokees, 45–46, 61, 70; and Shawnees, 86–88; and the Tugaloo Incident, 135; and warfare with Cherokees, 57, 61, 65. *See also* Little Okfuskee; Mortar of Okchai; Okfuskee
Cuming, Alexander, 33, 47–49, 77
Cussita, 43, 60, 134

Daugherty, Cornelius, 50
Demere, Paul, 89, 91–92, 107–8, 123
Demere, Raymond, 79–89, 97, 110

Dowd, Gregory Evans, 53, 156, 158, 174
Dragging Canoe: and assertion of identity, 170; and Cherokee militancy, 157, 159, 161; 212n18; and Cherokee resettlement, 8, 129, 152, 162–63, 211n1; death of, 166

Ellijay, 40–42, 190n12
Emperor of Tellico (Moytoy of Tellico), 13, 47–50, 77, 191n29
Estatoe: and the Anglo-Cherokee War, 119; and James Beamer, 50, 64; and the Cherokee-Creek War, 59, 61, 70; and the crisis in Virginia, 101–2, 104; endurance of, 11; and the Long Cane murders, 135; and Northward Indians, 64; and Old Estatoe, 40, 107
Etchoe, 119–20, 125
Etchoe Pass, 119–20, 125
Etowah, 172

Fauquier, Francis, 124–25, 127, 133, 139–40, 142, 200n13
Fitch, Tobias, 43–45
Fogelson, Raymond, 12, 31, 52
Forbes' Campaign, 94, 97, 100, 103, 200n12
Fort Duquesne, 75, 90, 97–98, 100, 103
Fort Loudoun, 80, 87–89, 97, 108–10, 112, 115, 120–23
Fort Pitt, 140–41, 149
Fort Prince George: attacks against, 123–24; and the Congress of Augusta, 132–33; establishment of, 96; and the hostage crisis, 13, 24, 114–18, 120; and its importance to the Lower Cherokees, 74
France/French: agents of, 75, 78; Cherokee attacks against, 94–97, 137; at Fort Toulouse, 7, 75, 78–81, 83–84, 86; as a potential Cherokee trading ally, 7, 34, 39, 49, 55–56, 72. *See also* Fort Duquesne; French John; de Kerlerec, Louis Billouart; L'antignac, Anthony; Northward Indians; Tellico French John, 79–81, 88

Georgia, 49, 55–56, 131, 146, 155, 158, 161–62
Gifts/gift-giving: and Cherokee regionalism, 37–38; and the crisis in Virginia, 7, 90, 93–94, 98–100; and the deerskin trade, 37, 51, 189n5; and the French, 81, 124; and the Spanish entradas, 11; and the Tellico Affair, 83–85, 87, 92
Glen, James: concerns about the French, 78; concerns about Virginia, 98–99; and correspondence with Cherokee headmen, 14, 30, 46, 52–53, 59, 61; and the imprisonment of Shawnee warriors, 71, 87; and Northward Indians, 61–63, 65, 68, 70–71; and the Panic of 1751, 53–55; and Settlement Indians, 66–67
Grant, James, 110, 119, 125–26
Great Island (Mialoquo), 129, 162
Green Corn Ceremony, 15–16, 26–27, 42–43, 91–92

Hanging Maw, 166, 171–75, 213n25
Hatley, Tom, 195n27, 197n11, 208n23; and Cherokee localism, 4, 10, 17, 130; and Cherokee warfare, 137; and the deerskin trade, 209n35; and the rise of Attakullakulla, 202n4; and the Treaty of 1730, 48
Herbert, John, 33, 45–46, 48
Hiwassee, 72, 159, 166
Hiwassee River, 17, 19, 162, 176–77
Horse stealing, 101, 155–56, 165, 167, 171, 174–75
Hudson, Charles, 5, 16–17, 29, 39
Hunting grounds: and Creek attacks, 134; and peace with the Creeks, 61, 70; and the regional demarcation of, 128; and threats to, 8, 60, 138, 141–46, 157, 181. *See also* Treaty/treaties

Iroquois (Six Nations): and hostility toward Creeks, 65; and pan-Indianism, 149–50; and relations with Cherokees, 62, 65, 131, 137, 140, 143–44, 148; and territorial claims, 143–45, 148. *See also* Northward Indians

Johnson, William, 98, 140, 143–44, 149

Kenoteta, 79–80, 82, 84, 86–87, 147
Keowee: and the Anglo-Cherokee War, 110–11, 113–15, 117–19; and the Cherokee-Creek War, 59, 69; and George Chicken's visit, 42; and the deerskin trade, 50, 190n14; and Fort Prince George, 13, 74; and national councils, 28; and Northward Indians, 64–65; and the Panic of 1751, 53–54; and its preeminence among the Lower Towns, 41, 56, 74; and its proximity to Tenasee and Charlestown, 21; warrior population of, 74
Keowee River, 40–41, 59, 73–74, 119
de Kerlerec, Louis Billouart, 75–76, 79–81
King Crow, 12–13, 34, 41–43, 47
Kinship, 2–6, 25, 28–29, 51–52, 113, 153, 166
Kituhwa, 11, 24, 26, 53, 111, 125, 129

L'antignac, Anthony, 78, 80, 124
Little Chota, 38, 135
Little Okfuskee, 61
Little Tellico, 27, 43, 72
Little Tennessee River, 18–19, 159, 176
Little Turkey, 162, 165, 168–69
Long Cane: murders at, 134–38, 147
Long Warrior of Tenasee, 45, 191n29
Lookout Mountain Town, 163, 172
Lower Towns: and the American Revolution, 19, 157–62; and the Anglo-Cherokee War, 7, 119–20, 123–26, 128–29, 205n35; and the Cherokee-Creek War, 6, 39–40, 42–43, 57–60, 69; and the crisis in Virginia, 24, 27, 93–94, 101–5, 107–8, 112–14, 202n5; and the deerskin trade, 34, 37–38, 50, 52–53, 131–33, 146; and diplomacy following the Anglo-Cherokee War, 130–31, 134, 140; and land cessions, 131, 141–43, 161; and language, 22; location of, 19; and the murder of Edward Carrol, 63; and Northward Indians, 63–65; and the Panic of 1751, 53–55; population of, 74, 130, 195–96n33; and regional categorization of, 18, 22, 38, 186nn18, 19, 187n21, 212n17; and regional hunting grounds, 145–46; and relations with Creeks, 107, 135–36; and shifts in regional power, 40–41, 56, 58, 72–74, 130, 161, 176; and the Tellico Affair, 7, 76–77, 90–91. *See also* Estatoe; Keowee; Little Chota; Nacoochee; Qualatchie; Seneca; Sugar Town; Toxaway; Tugaloo
Lower Towns, headmen. *See* Conjuror of Tugaloo; King Crow; Old Breakerface; Old Warrior of Estatoe; Raven of Toxaway; Raven of Tugaloo; Saluy; Tistoe of Keowee; Wawhatchee of Keowee
Lyttelton, William Henry: and the crisis in Virginia, 95, 99, 104–6, 108–9, 112; and the decision for war, 113; and detaining Cherokee headmen, 113–14; and the Fort Prince George hostage crisis, 24, 115–19; and the Tellico Affair, 92

Malatchi, 68–70
Mankiller of Nequasee, 116, 125
Mankiller of Tellico, 79–80, 82–87, 89–92, 107, 147. *See also* Tellico
McLoughlin, William, 178–80
Middle Towns: and the American Revolution, 155, 157–59, 161–64, 168, 172, 176; and the Anglo-Cherokee War, 7, 110, 113–14, 116–20, 123, 125–26, 128–30, 205n35; and the Cherokee-Creek War, 40–41, 43, 45, 59; and the crisis in Virginia, 24–27, 94, 102–5, 108; and distance from Fort Prince George, 133; and language, 22; location

of, 19; population of, 74, 195–96n33; and regionalism, 18, 38, 190n11; and relationship to Chota, 27; and the Tellico Affair, 7, 76–77, 90–91, 93. *See also* Canuga; Cowee; Etchoe; Nequassee; Watauga

Middle Towns, headmen: of Cowee, 1; of Joree, 59, 70; of Watauga, 114. *See also* Caesar; Mankiller of Nequasee

Montgomery, Archibald, 119–22, 124, 125, 128, 204n22

Mortar of Okchai, 106–7, 147–48, 210nn39, 40

Moytoy of Hiwassee, 136

Moytoy of Settico, 95, 106–9

Nacoochee, 18, 42

Nequassee, 11, 24, 45, 47–49, 110

Nickajack, 163, 171, 173

North Carolina, 106–7, 142, 146, 161

Northward Indians: description of, 62; and hostility toward Creeks, 61, 64–65; and pan-Indianism, 149, 156, 165; and relations with Cherokees, 7, 57–58, 62–72, 109, 130–31, 136–37, 140, 145, 192n4; and Settlement Indians, 65–67; and South Carolina, 67–68. *See also* Iroquois; Shawnees

Noyowee, 25, 72, 187n27

Oconastota (Great Warrior of Chota): and the Anglo-Cherokee War, 108, 112, 114–15, 118, 121–23, 127, 202n5; and concerns about the Creeks, 134–36; and diplomacy, 140, 150; and land cessions, 143–44, 146; and Mortar of Okchai, 107, 147; and the preeminence of Chota, 28, 83; and relationships between towns, 25; and the Virginians, 155; and warfare, 138

Okfuskee, 43, 45–46, 69, 134–35

Old Breakerface, 47

Old Hop (Beloved Man of Chota): authority of, 12–13; and the crisis in Virginia, 102; death of, 202n4; and Northward Indians, 69–72; and the preeminence of Chota, 28; and the Tellico Affair, 79–83, 87–88, 91–92

Old Tassel, 165–67

Old Warrior of Estatoe, 24, 141

Ostenaco (Judd's Friend): brother of, 113; and the preeminence of Chota, 27–28, 83; peace efforts of, 139, 142; and the Tellico Affair, 89; and Henry Timberlake, 127; and warfare, 61, 138, 145

Out Towns: and the American Revolution, 159; and the Anglo-Cherokee War, 7, 125–26, 129; and the Cherokee-Creek War, 59; and the crisis in Virginia, 102; and distance from Fort Prince George, 133; location of, 19, 21; and the Northward Indians, 71; and the Panic of 1751, 53–55; and population of, 74, 195–96n33; as a regional power, 111–12, 129; and the Tellico Affair, 76, 88. *See also* Kituhwa; Stecoe

Out Towns, headmen: of Kituhwa, 129; of Stecoe, 113–14; of Tuckasegee, 54, 71. *See also* Round O of Stecoe; Warrior of Stecoe

Overhill Towns: and the American Revolution, 8, 152–53, 155, 157, 159, 161–65, 168, 172–73, 176; and the Anglo-Cherokee War, 24, 112, 115–18, 120–27; ascendancy of, 7, 28, 34, 56, 58, 76; and the Cherokee-Creek War, 39–41, 43, 45–46, 59–62; and the crisis in Virginia, 94–96, 101–9; and the deerskin trade, 53, 60, 132–33; and diplomacy following the Anglo-Cherokee War, 130–32, 134; and land cessions, 141–43, 145–46, 157, 161; and language, 22; location of, 19; and Northward Indians, 62, 65, 69–72, 140; and the Panic of 1751, 53–55; and population of, 74, 195–96n33; and regionalism, 2, 18–19, 21, 38, 186nn18, 19, 186–87n21, 190n11; and the Tellico Affair, 7, 75–93, 196n4.

Overhill Towns—*continued*
 See also Chatuga; Chilhowee; Chota; Great Island; Settico; Tellico; Tenasee; Toqua; Toskegee
Overhill Towns, headmen. See Attakullakulla; Choatehee of Tellico; Emperor of Tellico; Kenoteta; Long Warrior of Tenasee; Mankiller of Tellico; Moytoy of Settico; Oconastota; Old Hop; Ostenaco; Prince of Chota; Smallpox Conjuror of Settico; Willanawaw

Panic of 1751, 53–56
Pan-Indianism, 128, 140, 144, 147–51, 156–57, 173
Perdue, Theda, 4–5, 28, 122, 179, 214n3
Piker, Joshua, 4, 184n7, 210n39
Pontiac's Uprising, 8, 117, 128, 131, 137–38, 147–48
Prince of Chota (Kittagusta), 28, 83, 140, 142

Qualatchie, 74, 102, 119
Quanasee, 38, 50, 117

Raven of Hiwassee, 23–24, 54–55, 61, 63, 70
Raven of Toxaway, 52–53, 101
Raven of Tugaloo, 52, 140
Reid, John Phillip, 18, 29, 37, 40, 62, 105, 111, 188n36
Round O of Stecoe, 27, 111, 113–18, 129, 202n7
Running Water, 163, 171, 173

Saluy (Young Warrior of Estatoe): and the Anglo-Cherokee War, 115–16, 128; and clan revenge, 139; and the Congress of Augusta, 133; as headman of Tugaloo and Estatoe, 52; and land cessions, 141–42, 146; and the Long Cane murders, 135–36; and Mortar of Okchai, 147; and warfare, 138
Savannah Town, 37–38, 189n4

Seneca, 11, 159, 162
Settico, 26, 39, 106–8, 122, 127, 147, 162, 165
"Settlement" Indians, 57, 65–67, 194n17
Sevier, John, 162, 164–67, 171, 174
Shawnees: and Peter Chartier, 86–88; and hostility toward South Carolina, 68, 71–72; and language, 29; and pan-Indianism, 148–50, 156, 174; and relations with Cherokees, 1, 22, 60, 62, 65–66, 69, 71, 100, 141, 182; and the Tellico Affair, 75, 86–91. See also Northward Indians
Smallpox, 115, 117, 126, 129, 136, 205n34
Smallpox Conjuror of Settico, 13, 87–88
South Carolina: and the American Revolution, 158–61, 166; and the Anglo-Cherokee War, 112–14, 118, 123–24, 127; and the Cherokee-Creek War, 39, 42–46, 61; and Cherokee land cessions, 141–42, 145–46; and the deerskin trade, 6–8, 33–34, 37–38, 40–41, 49, 60, 92, 95–96, 131–34; and the Indian slave trade, 32, 34; and Northward Indians, 67–68
Stecoe, 53, 125, 129
Stuart, Henry, 157–58, 160, 211nn7, 9
Stuart, John, 123, 139–40, 143–47, 158–60, 211n9
—comments by, about: the authority of headmen and warriors, 12, 14, 23, 210n40; Cherokee-Creek relations, 136; Cherokee land ownership, 15, 140; Cherokee views of backcountry settlers, 155; the deerskin trade, 32, 51, 133; the Long Cane murders, 135; the national council, 28; pan-Indianism, 149–50; Round O of Stecoe, 113; settlement patterns, 21; the warrior population, 205n34
Sugar Town, 74, 116, 119, 142

Tellico: and the American Revolution, 162, 179; and the Anglo-Cherokee War, 122, 202n5; as a beloved town, 24; and the Cherokee-Creek War, 45; and the crisis in Virginia, 108; and the deerskin trade, 38; and the Tellico Affair, 7, 75–96, 107, 196n4

Tenasee, 21, 24, 38–39, 41, 53, 121, 191n29

Tennessee River, 143, 152–53, 161–63, 175, 177

Tistoe of Keowee: and the Anglo-Cherokee War, 115, 128; and brother of Attakullakulla, 188n37; and the crisis in Virginia, 108; and the deerskin trade, 50; and diplomacy, 140; and land cessions, 141–42; and Oconastota, 150; as a regional leader, 24, 26

Tomatly, 25, 64, 72, 88, 117, 121, 196n5

Toqua, 11, 108, 121, 157, 162, 179

Toskegee, 39, 110

Toxaway, 40, 59, 74, 102, 119

Trade: and the American Revolution, 160–61; Cherokee demand for, 12–13, 32–33, 60; and the crisis in Virginia, 7, 96–99, 109; decline of, 8, 130–31, 145–46, 209n35; and embargos (including threats of), 54–55, 64, 104, 112, 132; and the factory system, 37–39, 49–50, 77; and hunting, 67, 138, 145, 189n2; and the Indian slave trade, 32, 34; local and regional tensions over, 6, 33–34, 37–39, 50–51, 56; and packhorsemen, 37, 49, 55, 63; and pan-Indianism, 8, 131, 137–38, 156; and the Tellico Affair, 75–93; and treaties, 34, 49, 95–96, 132–34; widens intertown connections, 6, 33, 52–53, 56, 112, 150. *See also* France; South Carolina; Virginia

Traders: and the Cherokee-Creek War, 59–61, 70–71; and debt, 99, 138, 145–46; influence of, 50–51; and information concerning the French, 78–79; limits to influence of, 64, 150; and the Long Cane murders, 134, 136; murder of, 39, 53, 139, 147, 210n39; and the public monopoly, 132–34; and the Tellico Affair, 80, 82, 85, 92–93; and understanding of Cherokee regionalism, 18, 38. *See also* Adair, James; Beamer, James; Daugherty, Cornelius

Treaty/treaties: of 1730, 34, 48–49, 55, 63–64, 95–96; of DeWitt's Corner (1777), 161; of Easton (1758), 100; of Fort Prince George (1759), 115–16, 121; of Fort Stanwix (1768), 148–49; of Hard Labor (1768), 142–45; of Holston (1791), 168, 172; of Hopewell (1785), 164, 168, 172, 179–80; of Lochabar (1770), 145; of Long Island (1777), 161; of Sycamore Shoals (1775), 157

Tuckasegee River, 21, 26, 111, 113, 129, 159

Tugaloo: as a beloved town, 24, 26; and the death of Edward Carrol, 63–64; decline of, 41, 59, 74; and the deerskin trade, 37–38, 40–41, 56, 189n5, 190n14; endurance of, 11; and the Long Cane murders, 135; and the Tugaloo Incident, 39–41, 44, 61, 95, 135

Tugaloo River, 40–42, 59, 74

Turkey's Town (New Seneca), 162, 166

Upper Towns (Revolutionary Era): peace efforts of, 168–69, 172–75; and regional formation, 155, 162, 176, 178; and war with the United States, 165–68, 171, 173. *See also* Coyatee; Etowah; Lower Towns; Middle Towns; Out Towns; Overhill Towns; Turkey's Town; Ustanali; Valley Towns

Upper Towns, headmen (Revolutionary Era). *See* Hanging Maw; Little Turkey; Old Tassel; Watts, John

Ustanali (Estanaula), 155, 164, 166, 172, 176

Valley Towns: and the American Revolution, 155, 157, 159–64, 168, 172, 176; and the Anglo-Cherokee War, 112, 117, 123, 125–26; and George Chicken's visit, 40–41, 43; and the crisis in Virginia, 94, 102; and distance from Fort Prince George, 133; and language, 22; location

Valley Towns: —*continued*
of, 19, 21; and Mortar of Okchai, 107, 147; and Northward Indians, 71–72; as part of the Upper Towns, 18, 38, 186n19, 190n11; population of, 74, 195–96n33; and the Tellico Affair, 76, 91; and warfare against the Creeks, 45, 61. *See also* Ellijay; Hiwassee; Little Tellico; Noyowee; Quanasee; Tomatly

Valley Towns, headmen. *See* Moytoy of Hiwassee; Raven of Hiwassee

Virginia/Virginians: and the American Revolution, 158–62, 180, 212n18; and the Anglo-Cherokee War, 109–10, 124, 127; Cherokee hostility toward, 7, 94, 98, 101–6, 108, 138–40, 147, 155–57, 170, 207–8n22; and a Cherokee trading alliance, 8, 39, 55, 60, 83, 90, 93, 95–96, 98, 103, 109, 127, 133, 146, 160; Creek views of, 155–56; and expansion, 131, 142–46, 155; and the recruitment of Cherokee warriors, 50, 90–91, 93–94, 98–100, 199–200nn12, 13. *See also* Byrd, William; Fauquier, Francis

Wall, Robert, 84–86

Wampum (beads/belts): and pan-Indianism, 150, 156–57; and the Tellico Affair, 82, 91; as tokens of peace, 70, 112, 116, 126, 139, 173; and war, 72, 114, 156–57; and Western Indians, 149

Warrior of Stecoe, 117–18, 129

Washington, George, 90, 97–99, 200n12

Watauga, 38–39

Watts, John (Young Tassel), 166–67, 173–74, 213n28

Wawhatchee of Keowee, 23–24, 107

Western Indians: as Cherokee enemies, 8, 71, 130–31, 136–38, 140, 145, 148–49; Cherokee peace efforts with, 140, 149, 156–57; description of, 62, 148

Whig Indian War (1776), 158–62

Willanawaw, 23, 83, 138

Willstown, 155, 166, 176

Women, 15–16, 25, 51; intelligence from, 81, 107, 116, 160; political activity of, 75, 84–85, 112, 121–22, 204n26; as victims of violence, 1, 59, 63, 66, 96, 114–15, 160

Yamasee War, 32, 34, 37, 39–40, 48, 95